MICHENER'S ELOQUENT REPORT ON THE HUNGARIANS' GALLANT REBELLION

"Nobody had ever heard of the little Austrian town of Andau before thousands of young Hungarians reached it across a rickety little footbridge. They had fought the Russians and survived.

"James Michener had seen other refugees, on Pacific Islands and in Korea. But he had never witnessed anything like this. Here were no old folks plodding dully away from disaster but young people, often very young, the flower of one of the most heroic nations in old Europe, with glory in their hearts for what they had managed to do.

"Out of this sweet and bitter crusade, with its incredible courage and equally unfathomable heartbreak, Michener has made his book, a sob in his throat and surges of passion bidding his pulse beat quickly. . . . Standing by the bridge at Andau, he has bared a section of his own soul."

NEW YORK HERALD TRIBUNE
BOOK REVIEW

B 106

BANTAM PATHFINDER EDITIONS

Bantam Pathfinder Editions provide the best in fiction and nonfiction in a wide variety of subject areas. They include novels by classic and contemporary writers; vivid, accurate histories and biographies; authoritative works in the sciences; collections of short stories, plays and poetry.

Bantam Pathfinder Editions are carefully selected and approved. They are durably bound, printed on specially selected high-quality paper, and presented in a new and handsome format.

THE BRIDGE
AT ANDAU
BY JAMES A. MICHENER

BANTAM BOOKS

BANTAM PATHFINDER EDITIONS
NEW YORK / TORONTO / LONDON

*This low-priced Bantam Book
has been completely reset in a type face
designed for easy reading, and was printed
from new plates. It contains the complete
text of the original hard-cover edition.*
NOT ONE WORD HAS BEEN OMITTED.

🐓

RLI: $\dfrac{\text{VLM 8}}{\text{IL 8.12}}$

THE BRIDGE AT ANDAU

*A Bantam Book / published by arrangement with
Random House, Inc.*

PRINTING HISTORY

*Random House edition published March 1957
2nd printing........April 1957
Condensation published in* READER'S DIGEST *March 1957
Christian Herald Family Bookshelf edition published June 1957
Catholic Digest Book Club edition published July 1957
Bantam edition published September 1957*

2nd printing ... October 1957	4th printing .. November 1957
3rd printing ... October 1957	5th printing ... February 1958
6th printing.....November 1961	

Bantam Pathfinder edition published February 1963

8th printing .. February 1963	11th printing .. February 1965
9th printing .. February 1964	12th printing . September 1965
10th printing . November 1964	13th printing ...... June 1966

*Bantam Books are published by Bantam Books, Inc., a subsidiary
of Grosset & Dunlap, Inc. Its trade-mark, consisting of the words
"Bantam Books" and the portrayal of a bantam, is registered in the
United States Patent Office and in other countries. Marca Registrada.
Bantam Books, Inc., 271 Madison Avenue, New York, N. Y. 10016.*

PRINTED IN THE UNITED STATES OF AMERICA

TO ALBERT ERSKINE

Contents

Foreword

At dawn, on November 4, 1956, Russian communism showed its true character to the world. With a ferocity and barbarism unmatched in recent history, it moved its brutal tanks against a defenseless population seeking escape from the terrors of communism, and destroyed it.

A city whose only offense was that it sought a decent life was shot to pieces. Dedicated Hungarian communists who had deviated slightly from the true Russian line were shot down ruthlessly and hunted from house to house. Even workers, on whom communism is supposed to be built, were rounded up like animals and shipped in sealed boxcars to the USSR. A satellite country which had dared to question Russian domination was annihilated.

After what the Russians did to Hungary, after their destruction of a magnificent city, and after their treatment of fellow communists, the world need no longer have even the slimmest doubt as to what Russia's intentions are. Hungary has laid bare the great Russian lie.

In Hungary, Russia demonstrated that her program is simple. Infiltrate a target nation (as she did in Bulgaria and Rumania, for example); get immediate control of the police force (as she did in Czechoslovakia); initiate a terror which removes all intellectual and labor leadership (as she did in Latvia and Estonia); deport to Siberia troublesome people (as she did in Lithuania and Poland); and then destroy the nation completely if the least sign of independence shows itself. This final step in the Russian plan is what took place in Hungary.

From this point on it is difficult to imagine native-born communists in Italy or France . . . or America . . . trusting blindly that if they join the Russian orbit their fate will be any different. At the first invitation from some dissident communist group inside the nation, Russian tanks will ride in, destroy the capital city, terrorize the population, and deport to slave-labor camps in Central Asia most of the local communist leaders who organized the communist regime in the first place.

In this book I propose to tell the story of a terror so complete as to be deadening to the senses. I shall have to relate the details of a planned bestiality that is revolting to the human mind, but I do so in order to remind myself and free men everywhere that there is no hope for any nation or group that allows itself to be swept into the orbit of international communism. There can be only one outcome: terror and the loss of every freedom.

I propose also to tell the story of how thousands of Hungarians, satiated with terror, fled their homeland and sought refuge elsewhere. It is from their mass flight into Austria that this book takes its title, for it was at the insignificant bridge at Andau that many of them escaped to freedom.

That Budapest was destroyed by Russian tanks is tragic; but a greater tragedy had already occurred: the destruction of human decency. In the pages that follow, the people of Hungary—many of them communists—will relate what Russian communism really means.

Author's note to second and subsequent printings.

A second printing of this book provides an opportunity to amend certain sections, for although few errors were found in the first edition, even those should be corrected.

On page 64 I originally wrote that Hungarian names could be given in either order—Imre Nagy or Nagy Imre—and my notebooks were filled with examples proving that while talking with me, at least, Hungarians used the two forms indiscriminately. But I was wrong when I concluded that they followed the same practice at home. Several reviewers pointed out that in Hungary names are always given in what Americans would term reverse order: Nagy Imre. Why did my notes prove otherwise? Because the refugees, wanting to help me, tried at first to give their names in western order, reverting to the natural Hungarian style as they became involved in the depressing narratives they were sharing with me.

More importantly, it is now possible to extend my remarks concerning America's role in the Hungarian revolution and her subsequent acceptance of its refugees. Four separate developments warrant comment.

First, I left the Hungarian border just as Vice-President Nixon departed for Washington with plans to speed up American acceptance of refugees. I was therefore not in a position to report upon the good his mission was to accomplish.

Second, protests like that of the *New York Times* concerning conditions during the first days at Camp Kilmer achieved their purpose, and the camp was quickly transformed into the warm, decent operation it should have been in the first place.

Third, while I was writing my report, new studies of Radio Free Europe's role were completed and its function in the revolution was further clarified.

Fourth, and most important of all, it was only after I had completed my manuscript that America seriously considered, debated and adopted the Eisenhower Doctrine, which in effect warns that insofar as one section of the world is concerned, no new Hungary will be tolerated. This statement of American determination fills some of the policy hiatus I spoke of and forms, I believe, one of the major outcomes of the Hungarian revolution.

Several critics regretted that some of the characters through whom I told the story of the great Hungarian uprising were composites. They correctly pointed out that this dampened the force of the narrative. I agree. But it was not I who chose to use composites. It was my Hungarian narrators, who said simply, "If the secret police identify me in any way, they will kill my mother and father." A writer thinks twice before betraying an identity in such circumstances, even though by using masked composites he does somewhat diminish the impact of his story.

Finally, one critic spoke harshly of my faith that the seeds of the Hungarian revolution will mature in other soil. He pointed out that so far this has not happened. He is correct. And it may not happen within a year, or three years, or even before both my critic and I are dead.

But I will stand by my statement. Somewhere within the Soviet hegemony the seeds of this Hungarian revolution will mature and grow into a profound struggle for human freedom.

In the long sweep of man's history, three months are simply not enough time in which to detect significant movements.

Therefore I not only repeat what I said originally; I wish to intensify it. I am absolutely convinced that the yearning for freedom which motivated Hungarians will operate elsewhere within the Soviet orbit with results that we cannot now foresee. It would be inconceivable for me to conclude otherwise.

1 Young Josef Toth

On Tuesday evening, October 23, 1956—a day which the world will be slow to forget—a boy of eighteen interrupted his work on the early-evening shift and entered the foreman's office in the locomotive factory on Kobanyai Street in the Hungarian capital of Budapest.

"You must attend more meetings of the communist study group," his foreman warned him abruptly.

Because the boy was young, he was tempted to argue back, but something in the foreman's cold stare warned him and he accepted the reprimand. Outside the office he thought, "I work ten hours a day and don't get enough food. Why should I have to attend communist meetings after work?"

He was a handsome youth, blond, straight, gray-eyed, and with a skin that was spotted for the time being but which seemed to be clearing up as he approached manhood. He wore cheap corduroy pants, a very cheap windbreaker with a zipper that rarely worked, and heavy, warm shoes. In his locker he had a stiff overcoat that was not warm, and a cap. Apart from one very thin Sunday suit, at his father's, those were all the clothes he owned, although he had worked for nearly four years. Bad food, trolley fare, and a little money to help his father accounted for all his wages, which were pitifully low.

Josef Toth had no mother. She had died two years before, mysteriously, and her death had been not only a family tragedy, but an economic hardship as well. It had happened this way. His mother was a big, jovial, talkative woman who could never resist a joke, and one of the reasons why her son Josef had such a ready smile was his long acquaintance with this warm-hearted woman.

1

But one day she had said, sitting in a casual group which had been having supper in her home, "Everywhere you look you see the Russian flag. I long for the old Hungarian flag."

Someone in the group that night, some trusted friend, had sought temporary advantage in Budapest's bitter struggle for food by reporting Mrs. Toth to the AVH (Allam Vedelmi Hatosag, State Protecting Organization), who were generally known as the AVO (Allam Vedelmi Osztag, State Protecting Special Group), which had originally been a highly selected group within the AVH. Next day, a small truck called at the Toth home and two AVO agents hauled Mrs. Toth away.

Nobody saw her for six months, and when she returned home the terror of her situation became apparent. She smiled and assured her family that nothing had happened to her while she was in the hands of the AVO. Resolutely she met all queries with one reply, "Nothing happened," but when she fell sick from the exhaustion, starvation and torture she had suffered in prison, and when it became apparent that she was certainly going to die, she let drop a few hints—not enough to imperil the safety of her family, should there happen to be another unsuspected spy in its midst, but enough to give her son Josef some idea of what had happened.

Once she said to him, "I had to stand on one foot for hours every day." That was all she told him, but the look of terror on her face was unforgettable. Soon she was dead. Young Josef tried standing on one foot for fifteen minutes, and he was not plump the way his mother had been before she entered prison. Even so, the pain quickly became unbearable and he could not imagine how his mother could have stood that way for hours.

Now, as he left the foreman's office, he kept his thoughts to himself, for no one knew who the AVO men in the factory were. They were there, of that he was sure, for a man down the line from him had said, some time ago, "This damned wrench. It must be a Russian wrench."

For this the man had been spirited away, badly beaten and sent back to work. Josef also knew of a man in his mother's village, outside of Budapest, who had fallen behind in his taxes. Unfortunately he mentioned, to friends, that he had a brother in America and the AVO heard of this and gave the villager six weeks to get the money from America, and when he failed, he was dragged off and nobody ever saw him again. The strange thing was that there was no speculation as to what had happened to the taxpayer, because even a logical guess, if reported to the AVO, might cause a man to be horribly beaten, so it was better just to keep one's mouth shut.

Even doing a job well wasn't always a safeguard from the AVO, because a man at the locomotive works who had been to college before the communists took over Hungary had had the bad luck to translate a technical article from an English magazine about locomotive engines and he had translated the title as it was written, "New Technological Developments Behind the Iron Curtain." The AVO took him away and held him for three weeks, doing nobody knew what to him, for he never talked. The AVO pointed out that the man had made a most severe ideological mistake, because everyone knew there was no such thing as an iron curtain, and to foolishly pick up a capitalist slander like that meant that a man was probably corrupted inside his brain, and the way to cure that was to turn him over to the AVO for three weeks. But nobody except the translator knew exactly what the cure consisted of, because if anyone even so much as mentioned it, he would probably disappear altogether.

Fear of the AVO kept young Josef Toth attentive to his talk, his actions and his beliefs. Since he had never known a world where the AVO did not operate, he fell easily into line. He knew that most of the locomotives built at his plant went direct to Russia or were traded to countries like Egypt, but he never mentioned this to anyone, not even to the man who painted the addresses on the locomotives, because he might turn out to be an AVO man.

So after his work on the evening shift, Josef Toth went to where his coat hung, slipped into it—for Budapest was just beginning to feel the touch of winter—and started out the door of the factory, heading for the trolley car which would take him across the city to where his father lived. "Tomorrow I'll go to the communist study group," he resolved, keeping his bitter resentment to himself, because he felt that perhaps the foreman was the AVO man in his gang.

But as he stepped into the brisk night air he was swept up by a group of young people who shouted simply, "If you are a Hungarian, join us."

He had no idea what these young men—they were all under twenty-five—were doing, but something in the electricity of the moment caught him and he joined them. Soon he was shouting to other workers coming out of the factory, "If you are a Hungarian, join us!" And other boys, as ignorant as he, joined the crowd.

Then the fateful word, the exhilarating word, the word of hope and passion they had long awaited, was spoken. A student cried, "We are going to drive the AVO out of Hungary." This Josef Toth could understand.

In one wild surge they stormed into a police station, where the bewildered officers tried to maintain order. "Give us your guns!" some young men shouted, and to his amazement young Toth shouted in the face of a red-faced officer, "Give me your gun."

"What for?" the policeman stuttered.

Toth looked at him with no answer, and stared about him; then a student cried, "We are going to finish the AVO."

The policeman's jaw dropped and Josef grabbed his pistol, but an older boy took it for himself. Soon the entire police arsenal was confiscated, and when the young men returned to the street some of the more daring were armed.

This was fortunate for them, because at this moment a

tank manned by Hungarian troops, with two AVO men giving directions, wheeled into the narrow street and rumbled toward the very spot where Josef Toth was standing. It was an old-fashioned tank, a T-34, with noisy treads, a high turret that could revolve, and holes for a forward machine gun. Against men armed with pistols, it was a formidable thing.

As it approached the young men, everyone had a moment of terrifying indecision. The soldiers in the tank were unwilling to fire into a horde of young people. The young men were afraid to fire their puny weapons at a tank. Then perhaps the AVO man gave an order. Anyway, the tank's machine gun ripped out a volley, and several young workers fell in the street.

With a stern cry of revenge, the boys and young men hurled themselves at the tank. Those with pistols fired at the turret. Those without weapons threw rocks or clubs or bottles at the mechanical treads. Two daring boys of less than sixteen ran under the guns of the tank and tried to wedge bricks into the treads, and at last they, or others like them, succeeded, and the tank ground to a halt with its machine gun spraying bullets over the heads of the young men.

A boy standing near Josef grabbed a sub-machine gun from a wounded companion and, with unfamiliar power throbbing in his hands, began blasting at the turret of the tank. From every side the bullets splashed against the turtle-backed tank and ricocheted back into the crowd, killing some and wounding others, who would later claim they had been shot by AVO men.

Finally, as the halted tank fired ineffectively at its tormentors in the way a wounded beetle fights off attacking ants, one brave worker with a pistol leaped onto the flat-topped turret, pried open one of the escape hatches which had been undogged in hope of escape, and through this hole pumped a volley of bullets. Soon he was joined by an equally intrepid fighter with a machine gun, and after this there was no movement inside the tank.

Josef Toth, not really knowing what tremendous adventure he had embarked upon, had helped stop a tank. It lay a broken, wounded hulk in the middle of the street, and while the excited, encouraged crowd surged on to a greater adventure, some workmen who loved machines stayed behind to see if they could mend the tank for later use. They began by hauling out the dead bodies, which were thrown into the street. Young Toth had already been swept along toward the radio station when a woman from the neighborhood where the tank battle was fought studied one dead body and cried, "He was an AVO man!" The men working on the tank looked down in silent disgust, even then afraid to speak against the dead AVO man for fear some new spy might be listening.

There was to be no such restraint at the radio station.

Radio Budapest was a nerve center of the communist regime in Hungary. It was housed in a large complex of buildings on Brody Sandor Street, near the museum park. Here the daily propaganda upon which communism lives was broadcast. It was thus one of the most important buildings in Budapest, and operated under the direct supervision of the Council of Communist Ministers. More than 1,200 artists and technicians worked here, and each had to belong officially to the communist party or to one of the groups which trained young people for future membership.

As one of the most important factors in the control of Hungary, Radio Budapest was constantly guarded by eighty crack AVO men with machine guns, which the citizens of the area jokingly referred to as "Russian guitars." The nest of buildings was almost impossible to penetrate without endless written permissions and security checks. It was guarded not only by the fanatical AVO men, but also by two thick wooden doors fortified by oaken beams and studdings. The communist leaders of Hungary had long ago determined that no unruly crowd would ever storm Radio Budapest.

Nevertheless, toward dusk on October 23, young people, uneasy because of rumors that were flying about the city to the effect that an uprising of some kind had been launched by college students, began haphazardly to gather in the street in front of Radio Budapest. They saw the eighty AVO men inside dispose themselves at vantage points and open the massive doors for the entrance of large numbers of AVO reinforcements carrying fresh supplies of ammunition. The building would now be twice as difficult to capture.

At nine o'clock that night, while the crowd still hovered near the station, a group of university students arrived at the great wooden doors and demanded the right to broadcast to the people of Hungary their demand for certain changes in government policy. These young men sought a more liberal pattern of life. The AVO men laughed at them, then condescendingly proposed, "We can't let you broadcast, but we'll tell you what we'll do. We'll let you put your complaints on tape, and maybe later on we'll run the tapes over the air." The students refused to fall for this trick and tried to force their way into the building, but the AVO men swung the big doors shut.

The crowd, observing this defeat, became more menacing and, joining the students, tried to push the doors down. The AVO were well prepared for such a threat and promptly tossed scores of tear-gas bombs into the crowd, which chokingly retreated into the museum park, where there was fresher air.

But that night the mood for freedom was so great in Budapest that soon the entire crowd was again pressing at the doors, and was again driven off by tear gas. This time a new AVO weapon was brought into play, for from the corners of the roof two immense beacon lights were suddenly flashed on, so that the AVO men inside the building and their spies in the crowd could start identifying and listing the troublemakers.

A loud cry of protest rose from the crowd, and stones began to fly toward the offending beacons. This the AVO men could not tolerate. They began firing into the crowd.

"They are killing us!" women screamed.

"They are crazy dogs!" students shouted from the front ranks. "Fight them."

The unhurried AVO men, secure inside thick walls, continued firing into the crowd and many people fell, whereupon an officer in the Hungarian army made a difficult decision. He had sworn to protect Hungary—and this meant particularly the communist government—from all enemies, but these enemies attacking Radio Budapest were neither foreigners nor the capitalist dogs he had been warned against. They were his brothers and his children and the women he loved. In despair he watched such people being shot down, and then he made his choice.

Leaping onto a truck, he shouted to the murderers, "You swine! What people are you killing? Are you crazy!"

A fearful hush came over the crowd as they listened to this military man risk his life in the bright light of the beacons. "You swine!" he shouted. "Stop this shooting!"

From somewhere in the darkened building a machine gun rattled, and the army officer fell dead. He was the first soldier of communist Hungary to die fighting for freedom.

A sullen roar rose from the crowd, and those nearest the radio station began to beat senselessly on the door and on the stones of the building. Wiser leaders saw that the crowd—they were not yet revolutionists—had no hope of assaulting the station unless arms of some kind arrived.

At this moment a decisive event in the battle for Budapest—and in modern world history—took place. It was one that college students and intellectuals in their craziest dreams could not have anticipated, for up from the southern part of the city a line of trucks began to appear, and from them climbed down workmen, just average workmen in working clothes.

An observer from some country outside of Hungary would not have comprehended the astounded thrill that swept the crowd that night when these workmen appeared, for they were from Csepel, and with their arrival the lies of communism were unmasked.

"Here come the men from Csepel!" a woman shouted.

"They're bringing arms and ammunition!" cried a student.

"Look at them!"

And they were, indeed, a miracle, for they had come from nearby Csepel Island, the very heartland of the communism they were now determined to fight against. They came from the factories the communists had organized first, from the workshops where there had not been a capitalist for eleven years, from the center and the soul of communism. Once these men had been known simply as "The Reds of Csepel." Now they climbed stolidly down from their trucks and began erecting machine-gun emplacements. Without these determined men from Csepel nothing substantial could have been accomplished; with them even freedom was within reach.

Their first act epitomized their tremendous role in the revolution. They set up a heavy gun on the back of a truck, trained it on the roof, and calmly shot out the eastern beacon. With that symbolic shot the harsh glare of communism began to go out all over Budapest.

It was while the determined freedom fighters from Csepel were bringing their guns to bear upon the western beacon that young Josef Toth joined the crowd at the radio station, and if the workmen in his factory had been afraid of mentioning the word AVO, here things were much different.

"We will destroy the AVO," an excited demonstrator harangued the crowd.

The stolid men of Csepel studied their gun, fired it, and brought down the second beacon.

"Curse the AVO," shouted the crowd.

Now new proof of the terror under which Budapest had been living in communist days was provided, for from nearby Rakoczi Street an ordinary ambulance, white and with a red cross, moved slowly toward Radio Budapest. It was temporarily stopped by some students who cried, "We are glad to see you have come for the wounded." And the crowd made a path for the ambulance.

But it drove right past the rows of wounded who had been pulled aside for just such medical aid.

"Where are you going?" the students shouted. "Here are the wounded."

The lone driver replied, with some hesitation, "My orders are to pick up the wounded inside the building."

"No! No!" the people in the street cried, and Josef Toth joined the protest.

"I must go there," the driver pleaded. "Orders."

He tried to force his ambulance through the crowd, but in doing so ran over the foot of one of the fighters, who shouted in pain. This caused Toth and a group of watchers to rip open the ambulance door and drag the driver into the street. But as they did so they uncovered a cargo, not of medicine and bandages, but of guns and ammunition for the AVO.

"My God!" a woman screamed.

"Look at the grenades!" Toth shouted to the people surging up behind him.

There was a moment of horrified silence, then a hoarse whisper, "We have an AVO man."

Later that night Toth tried to explain what had happened. "A thousand hands grabbed for him. They began to tear this way and that. I heard him pleading that he was not an AVO man, but new hands grabbed at him."

Young Josef, at eighteen, had witnessed a terrible sight. "Finally," he explained quietly, "someone took a gun from the ambulance and shot him. It was better."

When the body of the AVO man had been kicked aside, young men unloaded the ambulance and passed the cache of arms out to the workers from Csepel, who, with the weapons they already had, said, "We think we can storm the building."

From the upper windows fresh volleys of AVO machine-gun fire warned the Csepel men that the job would not be easy. One Csepel man, assuming leadership, said simply, "All you without guns, go back." As the crowd retreated, he said, "Some of you men stay and build barricades, here and here." The real fight for the radio station was about to begin.

At this point a boy of sixteen, brandishing a rifle, nudged Josef Toth and gave him some startling news. "I think there used to be a tunnel into that building," the boy whispered.

"No," Toth replied. "The AVO wouldn't allow that."

"I was told by my father it was built when the Germans were here," the boy insisted. "All these buildings were connected by tunnels."

The boy stayed close to Toth, as if Josef were somehow an older man and therefore to be trusted, and together they sought out one of the Csepel men. He was twenty and his face showed the stubble of a black beard, so he seemed quite mature. "This boy says there used to be a tunnel into the radio building," Toth said, with enough disbelief in his voice to save himself embarrassment in case the Csepel man laughed.

"Let's go see," the Csepel man said, and he called three of his companions.

The six explorers, each armed, left the fighters in the street, climbed over a half-finished barricade, and entered a house well down toward Jozsef Boulevard. "Is there a tunnel in your cellar?" the Csepel man asked.

"Yes," the owner of the house said. "We built it in Hitler times."

"Where does it lead?"

"I don't know."

He led the five fighters into the cellar and pushed aside a door that had been leaned against a dark opening. "Have you a flash?" the leader asked.

The light showed that the cellar floor dropped off into a deep tunnel. The Csepel man led his companions into the tunnel and cautiously along tortuous and damp passages until he stopped and said softly, "This may lead to the radio building. You two boys go back and get two dozen men with machine guns."

Without a light, feeling the wall with their hands,

Josef Toth and his new friend picked up their way back to the house, where the owner waited apprehensively in the cellar. Inspired by a wisdom beyond his eighteen years, Toth said to the boy, "You stay here and see he doesn't move. We don't know who he is."

When he returned from the street with a score of tough Csepel men, he found the boy leaning against the wall, his gun pointed at the frightened owner of the house.

"You stay here," Toth commanded.

"What are you going to do?" the boy asked, as the Csepel men went down into the tunnel.

"There may be some fighting," Toth said. "You keep watch."

He jumped into the tunnel and followed the silent forms ahead of him. Soon his recruits reached the first four Csepel men, and the leader said, "We've been listening. I think there's AVO men in there."

The crowd fell silent and from some area beyond a flimsy door they heard voices. Possibly a group of wounded AVO had taken refuge in the cellar. The Csepel men said bluntly, "We'll go in and see."

He picked four resolute young men—they were communists from the Rakosi Metal Works—and said, "I'll rush the door. They'll be taken by surprise, and you be ready to shoot over me. I'll probably fall down."

"Why not shoot as we go in?"

"They may be prisoners thrown down here by the AVO."

"I think we'll shoot anyway," one of the four said.

The Csepel man thought a minute and said, "All right. But at first shoot a little high. That'll scare them and you can see who they are."

"We'll come in shooting," the other Csepel men replied, but they made no promises about shooting high.

Then it happened. With a rush the first Csepel man burst in the door and found fifty AVO men. The Csepel men who followed didn't shoot high. They fired with terrible vengeance and there was no battle.

The leader, who fell into the room on the door which

had been masked from the inside, allowed the shooting to go on until the remaining AVO men surrendered. Then he rounded them up and said to Toth and six of his helpers, "Take these bastards out, but don't kill them."

"What are you going to do?" one of the appointed guards asked.

"I don't know, yet," the Csepel man said, and Toth last saw him seated on a box, looking up toward the doors which separated him from the radio studios above.

Toth and his six fellow guards led the AVO men, some crying from bad wounds, back into the first cellar, where the sixteen-year-old still leaned against the wall, his rifle cocked at the owner's heart.

"We found fifty AVO men!" Toth shouted.

"They look like anybody else," the boy said.

Toth looked at them and found he was trembling furiously. This was the first time he had ever faced an AVO man, and here he was in a cellar with more than thirty of them. But they didn't look so dangerous now that six Csepel men threatened to blow them to pieces if they budged.

But when Josef Toth led the way back to the street where the fighting was going on, a different kind of AVO man—one still at large and with a machine gun on the roof of the radio building—fired a random blast and one of the bullets penetrated Toth's left leg.

It was very painful and shattering, and blood spurted out of Toth's pants. He fell to the street and the last thing he saw was some of the AVO men trying to run away in the confusion, but one of the Csepel men burped his machine gun and the AVO men pitched into the street. From the opposite direction there was a loud roar as grenades struck the heavy wooden doors leading into the radio building.

"The doors are going down!" a voice from far away shouted, and young Josef Toth fell senseless in Brody Sandor Street.

2 The Intellectuals

One aspect of the Hungarian revolution which must have caused much consternation in Soviet Russia was the fact that it was the young men whom communism had favored most who most savagely turned against it. The communist elite led the revolution against communism.

In spite of its propaganda that only communism can build a classless society, the system is actually built upon a horde of subtle class distinctions. Certain members of the party get all the rewards of society—the good apartments, the good radios, the good food, the best clothing—and it is by these constant bribes that communism builds an inner core of trusted leaders. The rest of the people can starve, for they are not of the elite, and since they lack power, they can do nothing to harm the movement.

I should like to report how two young communists, chosen by their party for top honors, reacted when faced by a choice between communism and patriotism. In the histories of these two men, the leaders of Russia will find just cause for nightmares; and young intellectuals from free countries, who sometimes think that communism might be fun as an alternative to what they already know, can see how they would probably react if a red dictatorship actually did engulf them.

Istvan Balogh got to the top because he loved books. He was the son of a laborer and therefore eligible for education beyond the high-school level, and it was a memorable day for his family when a high party official said, "We've been watching Istvan. He's got a good head. We need young men who like books. How old is he?"

"Sixteen," Istvan replied.

"To earn the right to a university education," the old

communist explained, "you must have work experience. I know a factory . . ."

"Am I old enough for a factory?" Istvan asked.

"You do seem frail," the older man said, "but without factory experience nothing is possible."

Istvan Balogh was accordingly given a job working a drill press in the Contakta electrical factory in Budapest. Although he was less strong than some of the men around him, he applied himself with extraordinary energy and month after month exceeded his quota. He became a favorite of the communist bosses and was soon appointed leader of the study group which after working hours was picking its way through Karl Marx, Lenin and Stalin.

Possibly because he began spending so much time on his books, his production fell below the quota set for him by the communist leaders, and he was hauled off by the AVO, who held him for two days to check his loyalty to the factory and the regime. Satisfied, the AVO men released him and certified him as worthy of a university education.

But in order to test him thoroughly, they kept him in the factory for five years, and never again did he allow either his production to slip or his enthusiasm for communist doctrine to flag.

At twenty-two Balogh was a thin, wiry young man with jet-black hair that he wore rather long about the ears, fanatical black eyes, and a great capacity for work. He was a highly praised official member of the communist party and was accordingly judged fit to enter law school at the University of Budapest, in Pest, the eastern half of the city. Because he had been elected by the communist party, he was given special consideration and his professors were informed that he was headed for an important post in the government.

University life was a thrilling experience for Istvan. He not only had all the books he wanted for study, but he came to know a group of excellent professors. "They taught me law, Marxism, the history of communism and military science. They were profound men."

More important, he found within the student body many alert young men whose ideas of the world were more advanced than his. He excelled them in his understanding of communism, however, and this helped him to maintain good marks, for the communist professors were highly skilled in Marxism and demanded an equal knowledge from every student who wished to become a lawyer.

Studious Istvan could not yet read Russian fluently, but when his professors warned him that he would not get a degree until he learned to do so, he applied himself to this difficult language, and because it was one of the most important subjects in his study, quickly went to the head of the class. He was on his way to becoming a leading communist lawyer when he got mixed up in a group of meetings which changed his whole life.

The meetings started simply enough on October 19, 1956, when informal bands of Buda and Pest students met to announce their solidarity with the students who were then revolting in Poland against their Russian masters. Since there had always been a friendly interest in Polish affairs, and since the riots at Poznan had led many students to think that perhaps Hungary could also throw off the Soviet yoke, these meetings were inevitable and the young law student Istvan Balogh naturally participated in them.

His behavior caught the eye of his fellow law students, and on October 21 they nominated him to be their representative at talks which were going to be conducted by students from all the schools of higher learning in Budapest. These young men were concerned with several burning problems: (1) get the Russians out of Hungary; (2) improve living conditions; (3) provide more economic goods; (4) stop the forced teaching of Russian; and (5), a point very close to their hearts, re-establish the old crest of Louis Kossuth, the leading Hungarian patriot of the revolutions of 1848, as Hungary's national emblem, in place of the universally detested hammer and sickle of Soviet Russia.

On October 22, Istvan Balogh, not yet aware that he was going to help launch a climactic revolution against communism, went across the Danube to the Technical High School in Buda, where by noon a brilliant group of communist intellectuals had gathered. They set immediately to drawing up a list of grievances, and a public meeting was announced for three o'clock that afternoon. Balogh was astonished when he got there to find hundreds of young people, including workers from Csepel, waiting to applaud the work his committee had done. He recalls, "It was the first time I realized that people were going to take seriously what we had written."

But his excitement subsided when speaker after speaker rose and made stiff, formal comments. Balogh thought, "Nothing will happen. In a way, that's a relief."

But toward evening a man who has never been identified rose from the rear of the audience and said powerfully and simply, "I would like to ask one question. Under what right are Russian troops stationed in our country?"

Immediately the meeting exploded. Students leaped to their seats and shouted, "Out with the Russians! Out with the Russians!"

Others whistled and yelled, and under this impulse the speakers became inflamed and began to deal with the sad tyranny that had been forced upon them. Istvan Balogh, caught up in the patriotism of the moment, found himself shouting from the rostrum, "Russia must leave Hungary!"

Thus inspired, the audience began asking probing questions which up to now the AVO had kept suppressed: "Why does Russia steal all our valuable uranium and give us nothing in return?" "Why cannot a man earn enough to live on?" "Why can't we read western books?"

When the flood had subsided, Istvan Balogh's committee began drawing up a series of questions it wanted the communist government to answer. The fourth item became the one that motivated all students from that moment on: "When will the Russian troops leave Hungary?"

When the protests had been codified there was a moment of quietness, during which a man in rough clothes rose from another part of the hall and said haltingly, "I don't have the good language you men have. I'm a worker from Csepel. But what I've heard tonight makes my heart beat faster. You are doing good work. Men like me are with you."

This was the encouragement Balogh needed. He made a motion which carried unanimously, that on the following day, October 23, a public meeting of sympathy would take place at the statue of General Jozsef Bem, the Polish volunteer who in 1848 had supported the Hungarian revolution against the Hapsburgs, who had called in volunteers from Russia. Then the chairman declared the meeting ended.

That night Istvan Balogh returned to his quarters in Pest in a state of great excitement. "What will happen if the AVO had spies in that meeting?" he kept asking himself. Then he tried recalling what bold and thoughtless things he had shouted from the platform. "I'm a communist," he said to himself. "Russia is our friend, and if we leave her friendship, the fascists will take over again." He concluded that his wild night was all a wretched mistake. "What we want," he said, "is merely a few changes. Say, more food and things like that."

But next day this faithful young communist was caught up in a powerful whirlpool of popular feeling. At the Jozsef Bem statue there appeared not a handful of students but more than fifty thousand patriots. The excitement of the crowd was infectious, and Istvan found himself shouting again, and meaning it, "The Russians must go!"

That evening, somewhat against his better judgment, he became part of an even larger crowd assembled at the square in front of Parliament. Here, with one of the most graceful buildings in Europe looking down from its noble position on the banks of the Danube, more than eighty thousand Hungarians had met to beg for political justice. Istvan noticed hundreds of new flags—the old communist flag with the red crest of Soviet communism ripped out.

He saw men wild with fervor for Hungarian independence and heard women shouting, "Down with our leaders! Long live freedom! We want Imre Nagy!"

Istvan heard this last cry with hope, for Imre Nagy was a faithful communist, one who had known power a long time but who almost two years ago had been deposed for being too liberal. With Imre Nagy in power, Hungary would know more freedom, but it would still remain a good communist nation.

He was astonished, therefore, when Imre Nagy appeared on the balcony of the Parliament buildings and addressed the crowd, "Dear comrades!" The crowd screamed a violent protest.

"We're not comrades! Don't use that term on us."

Accepting the rebuke, old-communist Nagy started over, "Dear friends." The crowd shouted its approval, and Istvan Balogh retreated into a kind of stupor as he heard Nagy make one concession after another. It was shocking to hear an old communist make such a surrender. "What's happening?" Balogh asked.

A chant sprang up among the people, a phrase from an old Hungarian poem, "Now or never! Now or never!" and amid this passionate rhythm Imre Nagy held up his hand for silence. Then, to the delight of the crowd he voluntarily began, in a trembling voice, the Hungarian hymn, long forbidden by communist edict: "God bless Hungary."

In exaltation the crowd began to fan out over Budapest, but as they left, an ominous word reached them: "There has been shooting at the radio station." Istvan thought that the AVO had probably had to subdue a group of rioters, but more news arrived, exciting news: "Students and workers are destroying the AVO."

In a wild rush, patriots started running toward the radio building. Others, including thin, dark-eyed Istvan Balogh, worked their way toward Budapest's largest gathering place, Stalin Square, at the southern edge of the main park in Pest. There, in the flare of torches and automobile lights, Istvan found thousands of people chanting slogans against the Russians. He was surprised that the general hatred of the common people was so openly expressed, and he began to wonder if perhaps what they were shouting to one another was not true.

"The Russians steal our uranium!" was a major chant.

"They tell the AVO to persecute us!"

"The Russians starve us."

Balogh was thinking about these things when he spied two young men climbing high toward the top of the massive metal statue of Josef Stalin. They were trailing light ropes, and when they reached the top they used these ropes to pull up a heavy cable, which they attached to the head of the statue. The crowd roared its approval, and as the two young men scrambled down, hundreds of hands started pushing against the statue, while powerful workmen pulled on the cable. Masses of people watched intently.

They were to be disappointed. The Russians had made Stalin of such thick iron that he could not be pulled down, and women began to beat upon the ugly statue with their fists, until three young workers appeared with a more effective protest. They had acetylene torches, and the crowd set up a great shout of approval as these torches cut into the back part of Stalin's knees. Now the other workers pulled mightily and the monstrous giant began to incline forward like a skater falling slowly on his face. The metal at the knees began to crack, and some young men jammed a crowbar into one joint and swung up and down.

Slowly, through the October night air, this expensive statue, which the people of Hungary had paid for, bent from its pedestal until at last, with a swift rush that was greeted with mad cheering, the dictator pitched headfirst into the public square.

Then, from far back in the memory of Hungarians who watched the dismantling of this proud statue of their oppressor, came a recollection of what this great Stalin Square had originally been. Automatically the crowd began to chant, "We want our church back! We want our church back!"

Suddenly Istvan recalled that in this square had once been a basilica. He had seen it as a boy, when his peasant mother had brought him to the park. Once there had been a church here. Now there was this fallen statue of Stalin. "We want our church back!" chanted the older people in the crowd.

What happened next amazed Istvan Balogh. The people stopped chanting for their lost church and rushed in toward the fallen idol and began spitting at it. Men and women who had suffered under the Stalin rule had a momentary revenge when they were able to defile the fallen monster.

"Roll him over, so we can spit in his face!" people shouted.

"Stop pushing, old woman. Everyone will have a chance. You must take your turn."

A workman appeared with a mallet and began banging at the metal. "We'll melt him into bullets," he said. But he was pushed away by the triumphant Hungarians, who insisted upon spitting at the fallen Soviet dictator.

"You can all come back tomorrow," a student announced, as he pushed the crowd away from Stalin's head. He had a rope, and Istvan recognized him as a fellow law student.

"What are you doing?" Istvan cried.

"We are going to give the great robber a ride," the law student replied.

When a truck backed up, the rope was lashed to it, and Istvan leaped aboard. Up Stalin Square the driver went, with ugly Josef Stalin grinding along behind. Down Stalin Street toward the center of town went the gruesome procession, with the metallic dictator—a giant of a statue, even though he had broken off at the knees—clanging along to the curses of the people.

At the main boulevard that circles Budapest, the truck turned south, and Istvan Balogh found himself cheering with intense fervor and shouting to the crowds, "We have done for the great robber."

Where the boulevard crosses Rakoczi Street this

humiliation of Josef Stalin ended, but perhaps a greater began, for a group of students had massed before the curious tier of iron balconies marking the offices of the communist propaganda newspaper, *Szabad Nep* (*Free People*). Here a major riot was in progress as young people began an assault on Budapest's major propaganda press. Their hatred of the lies they had been served so long became so intense that the building itself was torn at by bare hands.

Now Istvan Balogh, the good communist, the one chosen for preferment, joined his people wholeheartedly in their fight against the lies and oppressions of communism. Next to the *Szabad Nep* offices, which were rapidly becoming a complete ruin, were the big windows of the official salesroom for communist propaganda, the *Szabad Nep* bookstore. Here some university students, fed up forever with the trash which the store had sold them, had broken the windows, knocked in the door, and were tossing all the communist rubbish into the street.

With vigor Istvan Balogh joined the crowd, helping pitch out the hateful books and looking on approvingly as a workman from a truck poured gasoline over the pile and set it ablaze. For five hours Istvan Balogh and the other students, men dedicated to books, helped in burning the communist propaganda.

From time to time Istvan had a sickening feeling. To be burning books! But then, in the wild light of the fires he would see the ugly face of Stalin as it lay in the gutter, leering up in metallic wonderment. And he kept on pitching books onto the fire until his arms were tired.

Istvan Balogh was no hero, no flaming patriot fighting for Hungary's freedom. It was partly by accident that he defected from communism, and being a most intelligent young man, he knows that had circumstances been different his actions would have been different too. Pressing a hand over his black hair, he confesses, "If the riots had not occurred, I would still be a communist willing to support a regime whose horror I never admitted to myself. I would guide my life by my fear of the AVO, and I would accept as much of the favoritism and graft as I could get hold of." Then he drops his hands and says, "I am still amazed that in the street fighting I helped destroy Russian tanks." Listening to him, you feel that only bad luck caused the Russians to lose their prize pupil, Istvan.

But luck did not enter into the case of the young intellectual Peter Szigeti, a handsome, polished young man of twenty-seven. He studied communism from the inside, coldly, analytically, and although the system had rewarded him with fantastic wealth and power, he finally decided that it was bankrupt, cruel and a crime against Hungary.

"From the age of sixteen," he says, "I was a devoted communist. My parents were starving peasants and one day I stumbled upon the writings of Karl Marx. His ideas struck me like a whip and made everything clear. Then, in 1946, a communist talent-searching party came to our village and heard about me.

"They talked with me for a long time and were amazed that I knew more about the theory of communism than they did. They said, 'You are exactly the kind of man we want.' They arranged for me to go to school, but the teacher said I already knew enough, and I was taken right into the party as one of the youngest members.

"I made a rather great career," Peter says in excellent English. "I was trained for foreign service . . . that's the best plum of all, and from the age of eighteen I was exhibited as a prize communist youth. I served for several years on the central committee for all communist youth organizations. At the age of twenty the organization decided that I had passed the tests for foreign service, and from then on I was known as a young man who might eventually be sent overseas. I had everything I wanted."

The life of such a young man was most appealing. He was given spending money, allowed to read foreign books, kept informed of what was happening in the world, and given a large clean place in which to live. Since Szigeti was one of the first sons of peasants to accomplish so much, he had particular privileges, and it was apparent that all this would continue indefinitely, so long as he kept in the good graces of the AVO.

But when the revolution against communism came, Peter Szigeti not only joined it. He led it. How this happened is difficult to explain.

"It started, I think," he reflects, "when I first realized the tremendous gap that existed between the promises the communists made when they were trying to gain power, and what they actually did when they had it. Communist slogans always sound good when the reds are trying to take over a nation."

Szigeti, an acute young man, looks the stereotype of a communist. He has piercing eyes, eyebrows that meet far down the bridge of his nose, a wiry build, a sharp tongue, a dedication in his entire manner. Unfortunately for his career as a communist, he also has a sense of humor.

"I began in secret to make lists of the lies we told the people. First, 'Capitalism works by chance, but communism works by plan.' You would be amazed at how hit-or-miss our programs were. Whole areas would go without food because we made a wrong guess. Plan! We didn't even study the available figures.

"Second, 'Capitalism grinds down the worker, communism exalts him.' I quickly learned that the very worst thing to be in a communist state is a worker. It's better to be a dog. The worker gets nothing but big promises. I always told workers, 'You are the saints of communism.' But I noticed that it was people like me who kept hold of the goods and the food.

"Third, 'Capitalism has no soul, but communism brings to everyone a richer life.' The fact is that communism presses a man into an ever-narrowing world. It drives you into a petty, confined little Russian world. Hungary's once vital connections with all of western culture were destroyed. We had to read Russian books, see Russian plays, study Russian philosophy. The worst crime communism committed in Hungary was the confinement of our great, free, searching soul.

"I could go on for hours repeating the discoveries I made, and I used to laugh at them. But there was one"— and Szigeti's lean face grows very hard—"about which I could never laugh. We told the people of Hungary, 'You are blood brothers to the great Soviet Republic of Russia. Together we will stand against the world.' But I saw that it was not a brotherhood in which we were involved, but slavery.

"In the riots Hungarians shouted, 'Give us back our uranium. Give us back our diesel engines. Give us back our food.' These were not empty cries. These were the truth."

Peter Szigeti's hands clench as he recalls the cynical betrayal of his people, their delivery as bound slaves to the Russians. I was so impressed by his testimony that I have taken great pains to document what he said. So far as I can tell, from hundreds of interviews, the following facts are true.

"Take a workman, like one I know. He works 331 hours a month. For this he gets 1,053 forints. That's about $21 a month American money at the actual rate of 50 forints to the dollar. Now a suit of clothes costs him 980 forints. That's nearly a month's pay. Suppose we taken an American worker who gets time and a half for overtime. If he worked 331 hours a month, he'd make around $700. That means that under communism his suit of clothes would cost him about $680. I understand American workmen can buy them for about $50.

"Under communism a young couple cannot live unless each works ten hours a day. The price structure is kept so high that they can afford nothing, even with such slave hours. As a communist leader I was able to make my purchases at special stores where the reduction was sometimes seventy per cent. The working people ate little and wore less.

"But again it was the economy of the nation itself that made me first question communism. Our country was being used as an indecent experiment to strengthen Russia; I cannot recall a single decision that was ever made in terms of Hungary's good. With our productive capacity and our hard work we ought to be able to provide our people with a good living. We used to, when we knew less and worked less. But now everything goes to Russia."

It was this gloomy discovery that drove Peter Szigeti to some hard thinking . . . still in the loneliness of his own mind, for he knew no one to trust.

"I first looked at the AVO. It had numerous organizations, each checking on the other. Then a supreme AVO group checked on the setup and it was checked by the Russians. I wondered why, in a scientific world, so much suspicion was required.

"Then I looked at communism itself and I saw that it was an organization of gangsters banded together to protect themselves and to get the good things of the nation into their control. I never saw a single unselfish act by a communist.

"Finally I looked at the life of fear we led and I concluded, 'Life under communism has no hope, no future, no meaning. Yesterday, today and tomorrow are all lost!' The day I decided that, I joined the Petofi Club."

In 1848 the Hungarians revolted against their Austrian masters, and during a series of bloody engagements their spirits were kept alive by the poems of an inspired young man, Sandor Petofi. He became then, and has remained, the beacon light of Hungarian patriotism and the symbol for all who seek freedom. He led a heroic life on the battlefield and wrote a series of poems which exactly mirror the Hungarian patriot's yearning for freedom. Therefore, when a dedicated young communist like Peter Szigeti decided to join a club named after Sandor Petofi, it was a milestone in his life.

The Petofi Club in Budapest was definitely Marxist, and its members were communists, but they believed that what Hungary needed was a liberal, Hungarian communism divorced from Russian domination. Specifically, they wanted Hungarian wealth to stay in Hungary, and secondly, Soviet secret police to stay in Russia. Membership was composed of poets, playwrights, novelists, artists, actors and a few leading communist philosophers. Often the members were in their sixties; some were promising youths. They were not a daring group, but they did have access to a publication which dealt honestly with major questions. This was a literary magazine published by the Writers'

Association, but all the writers who controlled it were secretly members of the Petofi Club, and they made their journal so exciting that its 70,000 edition was snatched off the newsstands as quickly as it appeared. There were, however, mainly convinced communists in the Petofi Club, and it could not possibly be considered a reactionary group.

In the summer of 1956, when Peter Szigeti joined the club, discussions of the economic and moral ruin of Hungary under communism were drawing to a head. Holding to a philosophical rather than a revolutionary line, the Petofi men maintained an incessant pressure on the government, and as they talked they began to convince themselves that some radical change was necessary.

Says an older Petofi Club member, "In my travels through the countryside I discovered to my sorrow that I had lost the capacity of enlisting the interest of young people. They were not reactionaries. They were not fascists. But they expected me to say something powerful and honest about their problems. I began to ask myself, 'Have we older communists failed to give any kind of leadership?' Out of respect for myself as a philosopher I started to speak critically of the tragedy in which Hungary was engulfed. And the more I spoke, the more I felt the thrill of having young people drawn toward me. In this way they forced my re-education. On one memorable night at a meeting in the city of Gyor, I allowed myself to be cross-questioned for hours, and gradually I was driven into a position where I had to admit to myself—if not to the students—that our present system was bankrupt."

It was with such minds that Peter Szigeti now found himself in contact. With increasing awareness of the revolutionary position into which these quiet men were forcing him, he continued to associate with them. Ironically, they held some of their most provocative meetings in the building of the communist youth organization, with AVO men on the next floor.

By mid-October, 1956, it was apparent to all Petofi Club members that some kind of change was inescapable. Hungarian communists would have to break away from Russia, and they would have to liberalize their government so completely as to make it a liberal socialist state rather than a communist one. Peter Szigeti was one of the first to acknowledge this openly.

"I was ready for the revolution," he says. "I was even ready to launch it."

On October 23, while the university students were revising and polishing their lists of grievances, the braver spirits of the Petofi Club were producing their own demands, and to Peter Szigeti fell the task of putting them in good written form. "We proposed measures which would have liberalized Hungary and made it a decent place in which to live." The government, of course, refused to take the Petofi proposals seriously.

It was with cold satisfaction, therefore, that Szigeti heard about the riots at the radio station and at the offices of the *Szabad Nep.* "We offered them a peaceful way out. Now there'll be war."

He was therefore expecting trouble toward noon on the twenty-fifth when he joined an immense crowd that had begun shouting freedom slogans in front of the great neo-Gothic Parliament building. "The people won't leave this time without some kind of assurances from the government," he mused.

No officials appeared, so he idled the morning away studying the square. "I could see the AVO men with machine guns on the roof of Parliament. To the north more guns lined the top of the Supreme Court building, and right above where I stood the offices of the Agricultural Ministry were bristling with guns. I remember thinking, 'After the defeat the AVO men took at the radio building, they won't wait for trouble today. They'll start it.'" And although Szigeti could not see them from his position at the back of the crowd, along the foot of the Parliament building stood a menacing line of powerful Russian tanks manned by crack Russian troops, whose officers were beginning to wonder if their men had not come to like the Hungarians too much, after long tours of duty in that hospitable land.

In spite of the menacing guns, people began calling for Imre Nagy, to whom they wished to present various petitions. But whenever those behind, like Szigeti, tried to push forward, those in front came face to face with the Russian tanks and pushed back. There were no cries, no menacing gestures, but nevertheless, out of the blue October sky, an AVO sharpshooter atop the Supreme Court building grew nervous and fired a single shot into the crowd.

With fantastic ill luck this bullet hit a baby in the arms of its mother and knocked both the dead child and the mother onto the pavement. In wild grief she raised the baby high in her arms and rushed toward a Soviet tank. "You have killed my child. Kill me." Her anguished protest was drowned by the sound of AVO guns firing more shots into the crowd.

It is absolutely verified that the tank captain, who had grown to like Hungarians, raised his cap to the distraught woman and then turned to wipe the tears from his eyes. What he did next made a general battle in Budapest inevitable, for he grimly directed his tank guns against the roof of the Supreme Court building, and with a shattering rain of bullets erased the AVO crew stationed there. Now even the Russians were fighting the AVO men.

Peter Szigeti was standing near the Ministry of Agriculture buildings, on the opposite side of the square from the Supreme Court, and he could see on the faces of the AVO men stationed above him the horror that overcame them when they realized what the Russians had done. They were more horrified when they saw the Russian tank commander revolve his guns toward them, and with a nest of heavy machine guns they started spraying bullets haphazardly into the defenseless square. They had to fire directly over Szigeti's head, and he could hear the bullets screaming past.

More than six hundred citizens fell in those terrible moments, and after that everyone knew that this fight of the AVO men against the people of Budapest would know no truce.

Proof came when an ambulance, which had been stationed in Bathory Street to the south, rushed its doctors toward the dying who cluttered up the square. No sooner had the doctors moved into the crowd, trying to drag the wounded to safety, than the AVO men cut them down with bullets.

Peter Szigeti, who from the year 1946 had been a fair-haired boy of Hungarian communism, who had reaped the riches that the dictatorship offered, and who could logically aspire to the highest posts, saw this massacre of the doctors with overpowering revulsion. In a kind of senseless rage, something he had learned never to indulge in, he began screaming at the AVO men above him, "Assassins! Dogs! Swine!"

Then, seeing a Russian soldier who had moved away from the line of tanks and who was not firing his rifle, he rushed up to the man and begged for the weapon. The Russian hesitated a moment, then saw the increasing mounds of bodies in the square, and, acting on the spur of the moment in defense of a people he liked, handed Szigeti his rifle.

The chosen young man of communism, unable to stomach it any longer, hefted the rifle to his shoulder and started blazing away at the AVO men in the Ministry of Agriculture.

3   At the Kilian Barracks

When communism faced its first great test in the satellite countries, it found that young people whom it had indoctrinated—like Josef Toth—had turned against it. Next it discovered that once-dedicated intellectuals whom it had pampered with promises of high position—like Istvan Balogh and Peter Szigeti—had not only rejected it but had also taken arms against it.

Russian leaders must surely have been depressed by such evidence of long-range failure, and committees must now be searching for excuses to explain away this major psychological defeat at the hands of those whom the system had reason to trust. But the Kremlin dictators must have been shaken with a mortal fear when they heard how the trusted soldiers of communism reacted when the red system came under attack. For years the red armies had been given special consideration, special pay and special attention from communist commissars. Here is how the soldiers defended communism in its moment of peril.

The city of Budapest, where this test took place, provided a dramatic setting. It is located on the banks of the Danube, some miles below the point where that historic river makes its sudden ninety-degree swing to the south, so that when the river cuts Budapest in half, it is running north and south, not east and west as it does for the remainder of its course.

Long before Roman legions first penetrated to this lonely outpost, a small trading community had grown up on the west bank of the Danube, and it was this inconspicuous village that expanded into a small but notable Roman establishment. Here hot mineral waters gushed out of the ground and allowed the Romans to build fine baths, followed by theaters and spacious public buildings. Thus Buda, on the west bank, became an outpost of civilized Europe. Long after the fall of Rome had called away the legions, and in spite of the inevitable decline of the baths and the buildings, Buda remained a kind of lonely outpost, always tenuously in touch with Europe.

Later, on the east bank of the river, the little village of Pest grew up, and its function was to provide a trading center for the great plains that stretched away eastward toward Asia. For centuries these two settlements stared at each other across the Danube, each expressing a gentle contempt for the role played by the other. Buda was a patrician settlement built on lovely hills and marked by fine trees. Pest was a rustic trading post on the great Hungarian plain. It had little beauty to commend it. Buda, for its part, was an ancient city with narrow streets, houses dating back a thousand years, and historic castles, while

Pest was content to be a thriving commercial city with factories, power and wealth.

Ultimately the two communities joined to form the capital of Hungary, where in the nineteenth century a vivid social life grew up which challenged and in some ways surpassed that of Vienna. Budapest and Vienna were natural rivals. Each was capital of its half of the Austro-Hungarian empire, and they were only a hundred and seventy miles apart. Good trains connected them, as did the famous pleasure boats of the Danube, which drifted down from Vienna to Budapest laden with rich foods and orchestras. Men and women went to Vienna to display their importance, to Budapest to have a good time, and soon the city was known as the little Paris.

Citizens of the dual monarchy delighted in comparing the two capitals. Budapest by common consent had much the lovelier women and the livelier parties. Vienna, on the other hand, was more sedate, and its cultural life, in the formal sense of opera, concert and theater, more illustrious.

Budapest was held to have a better climate, more tasty cooking, finer dancing, more natural vivacity, a wealthier aristocracy and a more oppressed citizenry. Vienna was more religious, had better music, richer desserts and more officials. The architecture of the two cities was about equal, but no one was ever known to claim that Vienna had the natural beauty of Budapest.

Marriages between the better families of the two cities were common, and no stigma attached to the Viennese who was lucky enough to catch the rich daughter of some Hungarian nobleman; but because of the superiority of Viennese opera, theater and museums, Austrians always tended quietly to consider their Hungarian neighbors as country cousins. Actually, in the middle years of the last century Vienna was the rather stuffy imperial center which maintained the pretensions of ruling the Austro-Hungarian empire, whereas in truth Budapest was the scintillating source from which new ideas, new creative impulses and the effective rulers of the empire came. Hungarians were apt to remark, "A sensible man lives in Budapest when he's young and dies in Vienna when he's old." To which the classic Viennese reply was, "Asia begins three miles east of Vienna."

After World War I, Hungary and Austria were split and Budapest became the capital of the larger, more dynamic and potentially wealthier of the two halves. It might have developed into the major capital of Central Europe had not World War II brought about its partial destruction by Russian forces who were attacking German troops that had occupied the city. (It is interesting to observe that Russian propaganda invariably refers to this action as "the Russian liberation of Budapest," whereas the British-American assault on Vienna, which drove out a larger number of Germans with less material damage to the city, is always called "the American destruction of Vienna.")

Under communism the city was rebuilt and resumed its role as a magnificent capital. Anticommunists would be ill advised to ignore the considerable real gains made in Budapest during the first days of communism. Schools and universities were thrown open to the children of peasants, good apartments were made available to those who could not previously afford them, and for a while the benefits which communism is supposed to provide seemed attainable. There were good theater, sparkling ballet and excellent music. Budapest watched new buildings go up, imposing monuments to Russian soldiers, a big, rugged statue of Stalin and a new bridge, dreadfully ugly but serviceable.

Budapest was a unique city, handsomely distributed over the hills of Buda and the plains of Pest. It was dominated by the beautiful Danube, which is probably loveliest at this spot, and whose inviting banks were the center of the city's social life. It was also unique in another way, for it was cut into three concentric segments by three handsome concentric circular boulevards. There was the tight little inner boulevard which started haphazardly in Buda, crossed the Danube on a fine bridge, swung around a tight circle in Pest, and scurried back across the Danube on a second bridge which deposited it in the heart of Buda. There was also a very spacious outer boulevard which accomplished the same journey, but its two bridges were miles apart.

The pride of Budapest was the middle boulevard. It started behind Gellert Hill, which dominated Buda, and after making a wide swing among the other hills of Buda, crossed the Danube on the Margaret Bridge and then formed one of the main thoroughfares of Pest, where it was called in turn Lenin Boulevard, Jozsef Boulevard and Ferenc Boulevard, until at last it came back across the Danube on the famous Petofi Bridge, named after the Hungarian poet, ending in Moricz Zsigmond Square, of which we shall hear a good deal later.

These three circular boulevards thus cut Budapest into a kind of target board, like those used for dart games. Communication was aided by other straight, broad streets which radiated out from the center of both Buda and Pest. Three of these straight streets became famous during the battle for Budapest: Stalin, Rakoczi and Ulloi. They were all in Pest, where the major fighting occurred, and as one might expect, where these fine streets crossed the middle circular boulevard there was bound to be trouble. We have already seen that at the corner of Rakoczi Street and Jozsef Boulevard, where the offices of the newspaper *Szabad Nep* were, one of the first riots occurred, with the destruction of the newspaper building, the burning of the communist bookstore and the humiliation of Stalin's statue.

Farther down, the middle boulevard crosses broad Ulloi Street, and on the southeast corner stands the ancient Kilian Barracks, a rugged brick-and-plaster building four stories high, with walls more than four feet thick. Here, in prewar days, when the barracks was known as the Maria Theresa Barracks, lived the selected soldiers appointed to the defense of Budapest. Under communism, the barracks housed a large administrative staff of tested officers and served as a processing center for recruits from the Budapest area. It was staffed by a small guard of crack soldiers, and although it could in an emergency house about 2,500, it customarily held only about 400, plus members of the labor battalion, who were not armed. It housed no heavy guns or tanks.

On October 23 a delightful, hell-raising sergeant named Laszlo Rigo occupied room 19 on the second floor of the Kilian Barracks. I think anyone would instinctively like this twenty-two-year-old Hungarian farm boy. His friends called him Csoki (Little Chocolate Drop), because his face was unusually tanned. He had dark eyes, heavy eyebrows, wavy black hair which he used to comb in public, a very large mouth and white teeth. He looked like a tough young kid trying to be Marlon Brando, but he spoiled the attempt by periodically breaking into joyous laughter. He had a good time in life and was so lean and muscular that he was always ready for a fight.

Around ten o'clock that night young Csoki was wasting time in the museum park, hoping to meet a pretty girl, when he heard shots over toward the radio station. Thinking some soldiers might be in trouble, he hurried over to find that AVO men in the radio building were firing at the crowd.

"Get away from there!" a stranger shouted, pushing Csoki back toward the museum area. When he recovered himself, he started once more to explore the situation at the radio building, but a fresh volley pinned him in a doorway in Brody Sandor Street and he thought, "I better get back to the barracks and get some guns."

At that point he did not know on whose side he ought to fight, or even what the sides were, but he felt instinctively, "If anyone's going to shoot at AVO men, I'd like to be in on it."

It was only about four blocks to the barracks, and he ran at top speed and shouted, as he leaped up the stairs to the second floor, "There's a big fight on at the radio building. The AVO are shooting people."

He dashed into his room, rumpled things up a bit looking for whatever weapons he could find, and suddenly stopped when he heard a suspicious sound in the hall. Poking his head out gingerly, he saw a man in plain clothes point a pistol at the head of a soldier who was trying to grab him. The civilian fired and the soldier dropped dead.

Sergeant Csoki—his nickname is pronounced as if spelled Chokey—ducked back into room 19, slammed the door and thought, "That must be an AVO man!"

Quickly he grabbed an armful of grenades, pulled the pin on one and, crawling along the floor, opened his door gently and pitched the grenade at the gunman. There was a shattering explosion as the sound of the grenade echoed back and forth along the hallway. Running to the fallen gunman, Sergeant Csoki rifled his pockets and found that he was Major Szalay of the AVO. Shouting at the top of his voice, he warned the rest of the soldiers, "The AVO are trying to take over."

The soldiers instantly mobilized for an AVO hunt, and had they started a few minutes later, Kilian Barracks would have been lost, for they intercepted some hundred and fifty AVO men moving in to take over the headquarters and the ammunition it housed. There was a furious fight, for the AVO men were highly skilled in rough tactics, but in the end Csoki and his companions beat back the assault.

"We killed a good many of them with grenades," the sergeant says. "Some were captured, and if anybody recognized them as particularly bad, we beat them up. Most of them escaped."

Csoki had reason to hate the AVO, for during his army career each unit he had served with had contained several AVO men, and they had instinctively distrusted his jovial attitude toward life. "You've got to be serious when you're a communist," an AVO man warned him. He was not yet a communist, but since he wanted to become an officer, he knew he would have to join the party. So he had held his temper and done what the AVO men told him. Now he was glad to see some of them dead in the hallways.

At this point the Kilian Barracks was infiltrated by a different kind of intruder. Hordes of civilian fighters, driven off from the assault on Radio Budapest, pushed their way into the barracks, crying, "There's a great fight on. We've got to have arms."

The Kilian officers were naturally distrustful of all civilians—it was their job to keep civilians in line—so they rejected the pleas and ordered the civilians out, but one elderly man with blood on his face said sternly, "The AVO are killing us."

A boy wormed his way through the crowd and caught Csoki by the hand. "The AVO have big guns on the roof," he pleaded.

Still the officers refused to issue guns, until a soldier in uniform ran up, shouting, "It's a very big fight. We've got to have some guns."

Csoki and some of the enlisted men shouted, "Let's give them guns!" And under this pressure the headquarters staff yielded and handed out machine guns and ammunition.

When this was completed the crowd withdrew and the men of Kilian were free to contemplate the course they had launched upon. There was no elation, no childish celebration over their defeat of the AVO. "We knew the Russians would attack us in the morning," Csoki says, "and our officers said, 'When they come, they'll come in tanks.'"

This likelihood did not scare the men because, fortunately, the Russian leaders of the Hungarian communist army had taught its men a favorite Russian trick. Said one burly officer, "You can stop a tank even if you have no guns. You do it with gasoline bombs." And he was thoughtful enough to show the Hungarians precisely where a tank is most vulnerable. "If you stand here," he had explained, "the tank's guns can't reach you. Then throw your cocktail in here, and the tank will burn out."

So all that night Csoki and his companions made gasoline bombs. They took bottles, filled them with gasoline and capped them tightly. Then through a small hole in the cap they forced eight inches of cloth tape, which would serve as a fuse when lit by a match just before the bottle was tossed onto a tank. No one in the barracks had any illusions. This was going to be a bitter fight.

At four o'clock that morning the first Russian tank appeared. "Here they come!" a lookout on the fourth floor shouted. "Tanks!"

He was wrong. It was not tanks, but only one. And it was not a tank proper, but a heavily armed reconnaissance car, with machine-gun hatches, plate armor and six rubber-tired wheels. Coming through the darkness—lit only faintly by accidental lights from nearby houses—the armored car seemed more like a boat wandering inland from the Danube. But it was a deadly boat, manned by Russians who were determined to put down any possible rebellion at the Kilian Barracks.

As it drew near the baracks, coming down Ulloi Street from Calvin Square, Sergeant Csoki and six silent soldiers stood in the darkness of the barracks roof, waiting tensely with gasoline bombs ready to be lit and thrown. It was strange, in a way, that they should be there. The soldiers had conducted no formal discussion: "Shall we fight the Russians?" Officers had made no fiery speeches: "We will drive the Russians out of Budapest." There had only been an unspoken, universal understanding: Everyone hates AVO men, Russians support the AVO men. Therefore the Russians are as bad as the AVO men, therefore if you fight one, you've got to fight the other. As for defending Russia, or communism, no one even thought about that.

Sergeant Csoki, waiting breathlessly for the Russian reconnaissance car to come beneath him, whispered to his men, "Now they get it!" At the last unbearable moment they lit their fuses, held the bombs for a moment, then pitched them into the black night air.

In marvelous arcs of sputtering flame they dropped toward the reconnaissance car. The first bomb hit the pavement of Ulloi Street and exploded like a giant night flower blooming suddenly from the asphalt. It must have blinded the Russian driver, for the car lurched toward the wall of the barracks, where it absorbed in quick succession three bombs, which set the entire vehicle ablaze.

Like a foundering boat now, it staggered down Ulloi Street beyond the barracks, where its own gasoline tank exploded. This was the first recorded Russian casualty.

Sergeant Csoki expected that Russian pressure would increase with daylight, and he was right, for at nine o'clock on the morning of October 24 the battle for Kilian Barracks began in earnest. In the next two hours fifteen Rus-

sian reconnaissance cars assaulted the barracks, but with
little luck.

"We couldn't understand why the Russians didn't use
tanks," Csoki says. "Because we murdered the cars. You
see, we had a good position across the street, too. There
was a block of houses and inside the square formed by
these houses there was a big moving-picture house, the
Corvin Cinema. Some of us got on top of this Corvin
block of houses, and my men stayed on the two top floors
of the barracks. With practice we would pitch our bombs
right into the cars, and inside of two hours we had destroyed nine of them."

One car, keeping far to the western side of the boulevard, dodged the bombs and unloaded round after round
of heavy fire into the barracks, and many soldiers were
killed.

"Blow up that car!" everyone shouted, and a rain of
gasoline was showered at it, but the driver was most skillful and dodged his car to safety. From its new position it
lobbed more fire into the barracks, and there were more
demands for revenge, but no one could hit the car, and
after expending all its ammunition, with terrifying results,
it waddled down the boulevard, leaving many dead Hungarians in its wake.

In the silence that followed the end of the Russian attack the soldiers of Kilian met and took a solemn oath: "If
one of us seems about to surrender to the Russians, we will
shoot him." Csoki says, "It was very quiet when we said
this, because we were thinking, 'If a car can do so much
damage, what will a tank do?' " They had not long to wait
for an answer.

But when the tanks did arrive, the young men in Kilian
had on their side a tested leader of enormous courage.
Csoki first saw him on the roof at Kilian, a whip-thin man
with a brown belt across his chest and a Russian-type fur
cap outlining his deeply etched face. It was Colonel Pal
Maleter, a soldier with a wild, heroic background. He had
first been an officer for the fascist Horthy but had drawn
away from such dirty business in disgust, becoming, in

1944, a leader of the underground fight against the Nazis in Hungary. He emerged from this experience something of a national hero and was carted off to Moscow by the Russians as the typical Hungarian army man fighting for communism. More than any other Hungarian soldier, he was petted and pampered by the Russians, but now, when he had seen them driving their tanks against his own people, he had come of his free will to Kilian Barracks to take command.

Sergeant Csoki smiled at his grim, jut-jawed visitor and said, "Lots of gasoline on this roof."

Maleter studied a few of Csoki's bombs and said, from deep experience gained in Russia, "The fuses should be longer for tanks."

"You think they'll send tanks?" Csoki asked.

"Soon," Colonel Maleter said. This brave officer, who was to play so striking a role in the revolution, looked down the silent avenues and said, "They'll come up here, Sergeant. Be ready." And he disappeared down the steps.

But before the first tank arrived, Kilian Barracks received yet another kind of visitor. Tough young kids from all over Budapest, hearing of the battle, insisted upon joining it. Carrying old guns, handmade bombs, even swords, they streamed into the barracks as if reporting for duty. At the same time another large group of would-be defenders took up positions in the Corvin Cinema block, just across Ulloi Street, and these recruits were to be of crucial importance in the fight ahead, for some brave young mechanics dashed from the cinema into Ulloi Street and began dismantling a Russian vehicle that had not been completely destroyed. From it they managed to salvage a high-velocity antitank gun and a quantity of ammunition. Hauling the gun through an archway leading into the movie house, this gang of desperate young men shouted, "Somebody fix it. Then bring on the tanks."

The situation at the barracks was now this. The building stood at the southeast corner of Ulloi Street, one of the major arteries radiating eastward from the Danube, and Ferenc Boulevard, a segment of the middle circular boulevard. Across Ulloi Street, on the northeast corner of the

intersection, stood the block of houses which hid the
Corvin Cinema; but in the middle of the block, and
cutting right through the houses, was a big archway from
which the defenders could fire at the Russians. Throughout
the grim fighting which followed, determined soldiers ran
back and forth across Ulloi Street, at great risk, to assault
tanks from whichever side of the street offered the best
advantage.

The upper floors of the barracks were manned by Sergeant Csoki and men like him. The roof of the Corvin was
staffed by daring young civilians with stacks of gasoline
bombs. And in what was to prove a masterful tactic, the
cellars of each building were jammed with wild-eyed kids
of twelve to sixteen, each burning with desire to destroy a
Russian tank. Obviously, Ulloi Street was going to be
tough negotiating, even for a well-armed Russian tank.

But broad Ferenc Boulevard presented a much different
problem, for here the tanks could maneuver, and as the
battle proved, here a resolute tank commander could
entrench himself, mow down with machine guns boys and
civilians who tried to burn him up, and almost at leisure
pump high-velocity shells into both the barracks and the
cinema. To destroy a tank on the boulevard meant that a
man—or a boy—would have to crawl right up to its mouth
and throw the gasoline in directly under the guns. Only the
very brave need attack a boulevard tank.

For several hours the Kilian men awaited the inevitable
attack, and in time they grew almost impatient to test
their skills. Then a boy serving as lookout on the street
below shouted, "Here it comes!" Hoarse cheers greeted
his ominous news.

Across the Petofi Bridge from Buda came a single creak-
ing, groaning, menacing Russian tank. Once across the
bridge, it turned north and started up the boulevard. It
was armed with two heavy machine guns, thick armor
plate and a huge protruding rifle that waved gently in the
bright afternoon air as the tank rocked back and forth
on its resolute journey. This was a formidable tank, and
although it moved slowly on its ponderous revolving
tracks, it was capable of swift action. Of this tank Sergeant

Csoki says, "Although it made a lot of noise, it seemed to be silent, because we were all silent. And the boulevard was empty. And there was nobody at any of the doors or windows. You didn't even see a boy running anywhere."

Many soldiers from the Ulloi Street side of the barracks ran over to the boulevard side to see the enemy come, and they licked their lips in dry fear as the monster approached, its guns silent. But the watchers had no time for nervous speculation, for now a great shout went up from the Corvin Cinema, where watchers had detected two more Russian tanks coming down the boulevard from the direction of the burned-out *Szabad Nep* bookstore to the north.

And then, to cap the terror, Sergeant Csoki, maneuvering his bomb throwers in the barracks, looked down Ulloi Street toward Calvin Square to the west and there he saw four more giant tanks bearing down upon the barracks. Kilian was therefore about to be brought under direct fire from seven tanks, each thirty-four tons of destructive power.

"Here they come!" Csoki said solemnly. This time there was no cheering.

It was a bright afternoon, and the October sun made the roofs of Budapest shine warmly. Some of the soldiers in Csoki's crew were in shirt sleeves, and they waited tensely, their jaw muscles showing their fear, as the seven tanks drew into position. For the first ten minutes, the Russians had everything their own way. The heavy guns did terrible damage to the barracks and practically shot away one of the corners. More than seventy defenders were killed and at least a hundred and fifty badly wounded. It looked as if the Russians would win.

But at this very moment, when it seemed as if the tanks could stand off with impunity and methodically rip the barracks apart, a street-car conductor, still wearing his municipal uniform, saved the day. For some time this undiscovered genius had been sweating in the interior square before the Corvin Cinema with the sadly wrecked antitank gun which had been rescued from a burned-out Russian vehicle. At first the gun had seemed beyond salvation, but this demon street-car conductor had stayed at his job.

Now he announced tentatively, "I think it'll work." A gang of young mechanics wheeled the gun into position, but the street-car man said, "You better stand back, because it may explode." Then he laboriously trained his masterpiece upon a Russian tank and let go.

Csoki says, "Best thing I ever saw! The tank hoisted up in front, hesitated a minute, and exploded inside."

This action so astonished the Russians that they momentarily withdrew to consider what had happened. Hurriedly scanning the streets, they could see no sign of the Corvin gun, which had been hastily drawn back by scores of young men acting as horses.

Cautiously the Russians advanced a second time, but now determined Kilian marksmen with high-powered rifles started finding weak spots in their armor. There were some deaths inside the tanks, but what was worse, one tank found its way partially blocked by the destroyed tank and two reconnaissance cars which had been killed earlier in the day. For two fateful minutes it hesitated, and in that time Csoki's men launched a gasoline barrage from the roof, while heroic boys from the streets of Pest dashed swiftly under the guns and pitched other bombs onto the tank at close range. There was a giant sigh as the gasoline burned out the tank and left it a smoking wreck.

Five Russian monsters, still hammering away at the barracks, now remained. From Ulloi Street and the boulevard they poured a punishing fire of shells and bullets into the Kilian walls, until portions of the four-foot-thick masonry threatened to collapse.

Again it seemed as if no Hungarian power could reach these tormentors, for tantalizingly they kept out of range of the Corvin Cinema gun. But at this juncture the boys hiding in the cellars put into operation one of the neatest maneuvers of the battle. In preparation for just such an impasse, when their elders would be powerless, these boys had strung a thin rope across Ulloi Street, from the cellars of the barracks to a cellar in the Corvin block, where they had strung together, on one end of this rope, a batch of five large hand grenades.

Now was the time to use their secret weapon. As a tank, after having cleared the upper stories of both buildings with deadly machine-gun fire, started down Ulloi Street, the boys, jockeying their rope carefully from each side of the roadway, tried to maneuver their grenades into the path of the tank tracks. They succeeded. The grenades exploded with a mighty woosh, the tracks were blown off the cogs and the tank ground to a helpless halt.

In an instant, daring men rushed back to the windows of the barracks and rained gasoline down upon the crippled monster. Then a grenade ignited the gas line, and from the cellars boys began to chant, "It's going! It's going!" Finally the burning gasoline reached the interior supply, and the mighty tank erupted in a vast explosion. In ninety minutes of desperate fighting, three Russian tanks had been destroyed.

It would not be correct to say that the men and boys of Kilian Barracks had driven off seven fully armed Russian tanks. It is true that the four remaining vehicles did withdraw, but this was probably because their ammunition had been expended in the furious bombardment of the barracks. But if the fight was not a complete victory—for the barracks were badly damaged internally and the losses were staggering, well over fifty per cent—it must have been a grievous shock to the Russians. They had seen three of the world's most powerful tanks utterly destroyed, largely by hand weapons. They must have realized that the battle for Budapest was going to be costly, long and deadly.

There was another reason why the action at Kilian ought not to be termed a victory, for when the tanks left, the inside of the building was in such precarious condition that some of the floors seemed about to collapse. Accordingly, the soldiers abandoned the barracks, some by a sewer that led to the houses of the Corvin block, where in the cinema they set up what headquarters they could. From here Csoki led a group of soldiers into the street to establish a perimeter within which the daring street-car conductor who had stolen the first antitank gun could dismantle a second from one of the destroyed tanks.

"This conductor was sensational," Csoki says simply.

He got the gun, mounted it on wheels in another angle of the theater, and caught some sleep while awaiting the next attack.

It did not come for a full day, and during the comparative lull Csoki and some of his men said, "It's a disgrace to leave the barracks empty." So they crept back and by means of heavy timbers shored up the collapsing floors.

They were there when the most furious of the Russian attacks occurred. Nine tanks wheeled into position, mostly along Ferenc Boulevard, and started a methodical annihilation of the Corvin Cinema. By a fluke shot, one of their first barrages destroyed one of the two antitank guns, and the street-car conductor was left with only one gun, while the soldiers had only a few grenades and a supply of gasoline bombs to face the full armament of nine determined tank crews.

Nevertheless, they destroyed two of these tanks, held the others off, and protected their one gun. By the time the seven remaining tanks departed, there was more rubble on the ground around the cinema, there were more Hungarian dead, but the Russians still had not achieved victory. As if to prove this, while the seven tanks withdrew, one insolent Hungarian youth ran after them, wound up, and tossed a gasoline bomb at the tail-end tank.

"It was a lovely good-by kiss," Csoki recalls. "It missed, but it was a good idea, all the same."

Two hours later occurred the most dramatic part of the fight. Three Russian tanks rumbled over the Petofi Bridge, clanked up the boulevard and came to the intersection at Ulloi Street, ready for battle. But the first tank had moved too fast, and when it got into the intersection its crew realized that because the five tanks destroyed earlier still cluttered the street, it had no safe place for maneuvering.

At this moment the street-car conductor brought his one remaining gun into position, but before he could fire, the Russians spotted it. Instead of blasting it, the Russians amazed the Kilian men by raising the escape hatch and hoisting a white flag of surrender. The other two tanks, seeing this, turned tail and fled back down the boulevard toward the Petofi Bridge.

Csoki and some of the boys from the Corvin Cinema quickly took over the Russian tank and tried to drive it into the courtyard of the barracks. "We were no damned good," Csoki laughs. They got the tank stuck in the doorway and it remained there for some time, but finally one of the mechanics managed to jam it into reverse gear and dislodged it, running it full tilt backwards until it hit the wall of the cinema block across the street.

Some soldiers, nearly killed by the lurching tank, shouted, "You're doing more damage with that tank than the Russians did."

At last some of the boys who were mechanics got the hang of the controls and wheeled it into position, so that it commanded the intersection. Above them rose the pockmarked walls of the barracks. To the right stood the tottering façade of the Corvin block. Around them lay the dead . . . a boy who had tried to explode his bomb against a tank, a woman killed by accident, a charred corpse and a Russian who had leaped from a burning tank.

And there we leave tough, twenty-two-year-old Sergeant Csoki—Little Chocolate Drop—a wisecracking kid who looked like Marlon Brando. As he sat in the Russian tank, waiting for the next attack, he told the mechanics, "We'll wait till they get close. Then we'll shoot their pants off."

In the fight that followed, additional tanks were destroyed here, making twenty in all plus eleven armored cars, and more soldiers died fighting the tanks with almost empty hands. But the Russians never captured the Kilian Barracks, they never occupied the Corvin Cinema.

The miracle of the fight at Kilian Barracks was not the triumph of Hungarian patriots over Russian tanks. Nor was it the heroism of men and boys fighting without weapons. It lay in this simple fact: Of the four hundred communist soldiers in the barracks on the night of October 23—and they were men both trained and pampered by the Russians —not a single one remained faithful to communism.

Throughout all of Hungary the percentage was about the same. Many experts believe that a similar percentage of soldiers in Bulgaria, Rumania and Poland would, if given a chance, turn their guns on communism. The Czechoslovakian army would, for curious reasons, probably support Russia. Soldiers of the Ukraine, on the other hand, might temporarily side with their communist masters, but probably not for long. And as we shall see later, soldiers from areas like Uzbekistan, Tadzikistan, and the other Central Asian Soviet Republics can certainly not be trusted to remain loyal to Russia.

As a Hungarian soldier who fought against the Russians observed after the battle was over, "Russia won, but they'd better keep two of their soldiers in Budapest for every Hungarian they give a gun. Let the Kremlin sleep on that."

4   Brief Vision

The battle for Budapest, which began on October 23, fell logically into three parts. The first ended October 29, when the Russians, alarmed by unexpected resistance and wishing to withdraw for tactical reorganization, practically surrendered the city to the freedom fighters.

The second phase was brief, but extremely sweet. For five days Budapest delighted in the mistaken belief that Hungary was at last free of Russian domination and that some kind of more liberal government would replace the AVO terror.

The third phase began on November 4, when Russian tanks stormed back into the city in force, imposed a worse terror than the AVO, and horribly crushed the revolution. The Russians not only won; they reveled in revenge.

But during the five days when Budapest enjoyed its brief vision of freedom, the city experienced many vital changes, and from a study of these, one can deduce what characteristics would have marked a free Hungary. To comprehend these days most clearly, it will be best to follow the fortunes of one family, especially from October 29 to November 4.

Zoltan and Eva Pal, an attractive young couple in their early twenties, lived on the top floor of a four-story flat in northern Buda. Their rent, which did not include heat, light or any kind of service, cost them a large portion of their monthly pay. Of course the government owned the building. Mrs. Pal says, "The rule was simple. Any repairs inside, tenant pays. Any repairs outside, government pays. But there were never any repairs outside."

Both the Pals worked, Zoltan as an automobile mechanic, and Eva as a postal employee. If she had not worked, they would have starved. Zoltan says, "I made 1,500 forints a month and my wife made 1,000, so we were rich people. Of course from that 2,500 forints so many deductions were made for the communist party, for insurance, for AVO collections, and for study groups that we had little left. And we had to pay taxes too."

Mrs. Pal, a trim blonde with blue eyes and a pug nose, had at the end of six years' arduous work accumulated the following impressive wardrobe: one coat, two pairs of shoes, one pair of sandals, four dresses, two pairs of stockings and a pair of glasses, whose frames she had bought on the black market. "The eye doctor gives each patient about three minutes for examination. If you want good care, you have to get your doctor's care and dental services on the black market too. Nobody would dare go to the state dentist. As for the state doctors, they simply growled, 'If you aren't dead, go back to work.'"

One thing Mrs. Pal did not have to worry about was make-up. She says, "In each office five or six girls would band together to buy one black-market lipstick and one little flat cake of rouge. So if one of the girls was going to go out with a particular boy, and she wanted to look nice, she was able to use the lipstick and the rouge. Maybe it would be her turn four different times each year. I was married, of course, but I still liked to look nice once in a while, so I helped buy the things. But we married girls mostly left them for the unmarried ones. I looked pretty twice a year."

Since Mrs. Pal worked in the post office, and might have access to secret messages, she was constantly under AVO surveillance. "How many times did I have to fill out questionnaires about myself? As many as the stars."

Getting clothes for a husband was more difficult. Zoltan, thin and wiry like most Hungarian men, but taller than the average, who rarely get enough to eat, says, "In order for us to save enough money to buy me my only suit . . . I used to go around in a windbreaker. Well, it took us six months to save the money, and in that time we were not able to go to one movie. My wife likes dancing, and in six months we were not able to go to one music bar."

Eva says her husband is a good dancer, but points out that a "night on the town," a phrase she picked up from a book, would cost at least 250 forints, or about one quarter of a month's salary, after communist deductions. "We couldn't dance much," she says.

Actually, the Pals knew very few communists socially, for in all of Hungary, which has about ten million people, there were not more than 1,200,000 communists. So out of every eight people the Pals met, seven were not party members. "At the post office all the top officials were communists," Eva says, "and of course the AVO were too. They spoke to me many times about joining the party, but I avoided it somehow or other."

If the party had known that Eva Pal attended secret religious services at the home of her mother, she would have been dropped from her job. "You could go to church, and many people did, but not in a job like mine. Anyone at the post office who was caught going there would be checked by the AVO."

Food was very expensive, but communist books were cheap. And of course things like phonograph records were prohibitive. "Zoltan liked music, and since we couldn't go to music bars or buy records, all we could do was listen to Russian music on Radio Budapest or what we could pick up from western stations."

What disappointed Zoltan most in communism, how-

ever, was the fact that all his life he had wanted to acquire
a beat-up jalopy that he could take apart and put together.
His wife explained to strangers, "Zoltan is very skilled
mechanically. It would be wonderful for him to have an
old car on which he could experiment." Then she added,
"But of course we could never save that much money . . .
not for a car."

Once Zoltan asked me, "Is it true that in America a workman, almost any workman, could save enough to buy himself an old car to take apart?" I nodded, not having the
heart to tell him that in my town most boys of fourteen
have such cars, and it drives their mothers mad, the junk
lying around.

On the evening of October 23, the Pals were at home
listening to the radio, which announced that the secretary
general of the central committee of the Hungarian communist party was going to speak. They knew that whenever
Erno Gero, the top communist in the nation, spoke, it
meant news, and tonight was no exception.

"Dear comrades, beloved friends, the working people of
Hungary," Gero began. "Today it is the chief aim of the
enemies of our people to try to shake the power of the
workers' class, to loosen the peasant-worker alliance, to
undermine the leading role of the workers' class in our
country and to upset their faith in its party, in the
Hungarian Workers' Party. They try to loosen the close
friendly relations of our nation, the Hungarian People's
Republic, with the other countries building socialism,
especially the relations between our country and the socialist Soviet Union. They try to loosen the ties between our
party and the glorious Communist Party of the Soviet
Union, the party of Lenin, the party of the Twentieth
Congress. They slander the Soviet Union. They declare
that our trade relations with the Soviet Union are one-
sided and that our independence has to be allegedly defended, not against the imperialists, but against the Soviet
Union. All this is a barefaced lie, hostile slanders which do
not contain a grain of truth. The truth is that the Soviet
Union has not only liberated our people from the yoke of
Horthy fascism and German imperialism, but she has—

after the end of the war when our country still lay trampled down in the dust—stood at our side and concluded pacts with us on the basis of full equality, and that she still continues this policy. There are people who want to turn against each other proletarian internationalism and the Hungarian national feelings."

"Something's happening," Zoltan told his wife. "When you hear Gero talking like this there's trouble."

"Worker-comrades, workers!" Gero cried with passion. "We must say it openly, now it is a question of whether we want a socialist democracy or a bourgeois democracy. The question is: Do we want to build socialism in our country, or make a hole in the building of socialism and then open the door for capitalism? The question is: Do we allow the power of the working class and the worker-peasant alliance to be undermined or else will you consciously, with discipline and in complete unity with our entire working population, join battle for the defense of the workers' power and the achievements of socialism?"

"I'm going out to see what's happening," Zoltan said. "Gero's in trouble." He caught a trolley car which took him toward the center of the city, and even before he jumped off he heard that students had been meeting, and that there was some kind of rioting at Radio Budapest.

Keeping well back from trouble, he wandered down to the radio station and found a mass of people demonstrating in front of the building. To his horror, shots were fired, and from a vantage point well back in Brody Sandor Street he watched the rapid deterioration of the situation and the ultimate wrecking of the studio.

It was late when he got home, for other riots had disrupted trolley service, but in one way the enforced walk was good, for it showed him clearly how widespread the rioting was. That night he told his wife, "There is going to be a lot of shooting tomorrow. We'd better stay indoors."

But the boredom of staying at home soon grew too great, so Eva Pal went to the post office, where all the communists tried to make believe nothing had happened. "They laughed a little more than usual and there were fewer AVO men than before," Eva says, "but when firing was heard over the river, we stopped pretending and some-body said, 'It sounds as if the riots were continuing.' Sud-denly the communists began talking, and it was clear that a lot of them hoped that the people would keep on fighting. At noon we closed the post office, and I think some of the leading communists hurried off to get guns. Of the seven main communists in my office, at least six joined the revolutionists."

Zoltan Pal had a more adventurous day. He was by no means a revolutionist, nor even the kind of man who sup-ports revolutions emotionally. For example, for a period of ten years he had kept clear of the AVO. At the big garage where he worked he had always given the communist party men enough encouragement to make them think he might make a good party member some day, but never enough to make them actively want him. At thirty he was an inconspicuous, underweight, pleasant man who re-sembled most of the men his age in Budapest.

Yet as he walked along the streets of Buda and heard about the revolution he began to experience deepening emotions. He did not hate AVO men; he merely despised them as inhuman. He did not hate Russians; he merely thought of them as robbers in his land. Only the other night Eva had said of them contemptuously, "In ten years I cannot think of a Hungarian girl who married a Russian, although they have been among us all the time. If one of my friends went with a Russian no one would speak to her. Yet when the Germans were here, there were many mar-riages." At another time she had asked angrily, "Can any-one in the world like a Russian?"

But when Zoltan crossed over the Margaret Bridge into Pest he began to see that it didn't matter whether you liked Russians or not. They were the enemy. Once an armored car whizzed past, firing at another car, and Rus-sians manned the guns. In Karl Marx Square, where Lenin Boulevard enters, a reconnaissance car was shooting at some unseen object, and again the gunmen were Russians.

So by the time Zoltan Pal reached the wrecked offices of *Szabad Nep*, down on Rakoczi Street, he was in a somber mood, which was heightened by the appearance of a powerful reconnaissance car, heavily armed with machine guns. "They're heading for Kilian Barracks!" a boy shouted. "Stop them!"

From Nepszinhaz Street three youths dashed out toward the tank with gasoline bombs, but the alert Russians in the armed car spotted them and easily mowed them down with prolonged bursts of gunfire. Some of the bullets flew wild and smashed windows, so that glass tinkled into the street like children's sleighbells, while the massive car rumbled on. One of the gasoline bombs, its fuse already lighted, exploded in the street, and the dead bodies were enveloped in fire.

Now a Hungarian marksman on a roof fired at the car with a rifle and hit one of the Russians. As the others turned their machine guns toward this roof to destroy the sniper, a fourth young man dashed out from Nepszinhaz Street and pitched his gasoline bomb into the car. But the bottle did not break, and the fuse was too long, so an alert Russian quickly tossed the bomb into the street, where it exploded.

Grimly fascinated by this running battle, Zoltan Pal had trailed down the avenue, intending to watch, but in his excitement he got closer and closer to the actual fighting. He was half running when a young man who had suddenly appeared from a doorway thrust two gasoline bombs into his hands, whispering, "Light them and throw them."

Tucking one of the bombs under his arm, and lighting the other with a match, he increased his speed and dashed out into the boulevard while the Russians were firing at some other roof. With a wild side-arm motion, which made him stop for a moment in the middle of the boulevard, Zoltan delivered his bomb. At the same time two boys who could scarcely have been more than fourteen did the same. This time the bombs exploded, and the Russian reconnaissance car flamed up in a dazzling beacon.

That night the Pals had much to talk about. Eva was terrified by the story of the bombing. But Zoltan said, "It's going to be a major revolution." Eva had seen urgent messages which proved the government was in panic. Each had heard, on October 24, the amazing announcement of

Radio Budapest, now back on the air from improvised quarters, explaining why the Russian soldiers were fighting in the city, and each had been utterly nauseated by the statement:

"Several listeners of the Hungarian Radio turned to us with the question to explain under what conditions and with what task the Soviet units are stationed in Hungary in accordance with the Warsaw Pact. On Tuesday, the enemies of our people turned the demonstration held by university youth into an organized counterrevolutionary provocation, and with their armed attacks endangered the order of the whole country and the life of the population. The Hungarian government, conscious of its responsibility in order to restore order and security, asked that Soviet troops help in controlling the murderous attacks of counter-revolutionary bands. The Soviet soldiers are risking their lives in order to defend the lives of the capital's peaceful population and the peace of our nation.

"After order is restored, the Soviet troops will return to their bases. Workers of Budapest! Welcome with affection our friends and allies!"

Zoltan Pal felt that for the government to make such an excuse for using Russian soldiers to kill Hungarians meant that Erno Gero's gang was in deep trouble and might collapse, but Eva, who sensed more keenly the great power of the communist party, was convinced that they would soon have the insurrection under control. "We mustn't say anything the AVO could remember, don't tell anyone you threw a bomb," she warned. And most of her friends felt the same way.

But when the radio claimed to be reporting from Kilian Barracks, at the moment when that bastion was undergoing a savage attack by a patrol of Russian tanks, "The city is quiet. One or two shots can still be heard on Ferenc Boulevard. The residents remain in their houses!" Zoltan could not contain himself.

"One or two shots! They're blowing up the city. I saw it this afternoon."

The miasma of lies, propaganda and utter nonsense in which Hungary lived under communism became unbearably clear when an unctuous voice on the radio announced that it would now tell the true story of what had happened at Radio Budapest the night before. "Eva!" Zoltan called. "Listen to this!"

"The gravest events of Black Day, October 23," the oily voice began, "took place at the radio station on Brody Sandor Street."

"He's right about one thing," Zoltan agreed. "They were grave."

"What really did happen? In the early hours of the evening when the enthusiastic and orderly group of students demonstrated near the Bem statue, the narrow street before the radio station also became crowded with young people.

"The workers at the radio station welcomed them with the tricolor, placed on the balcony, and with applause. The delegation presented itself to the leaders of the station and declared their demands. They agreed on several points, but when these delegates stepped onto the balcony, the irresponsible elements, who were increasing in numbers, prevented them from speaking. Delegation followed delegation, and it became more and more apparent that there was no question of sincerely presented questions and of their fulfillment. The masses did not even listen to the delegates. Brody Sandor Street was resounding with fascist slogans. The first bricks flew at the windows of the radio building. The station's car, which stood before the entrance with equipment to record the initial, still sober, demands of the demonstrators, was attacked; fire was set to another car.

"When the situation degenerated to this point, the majority of the university students and young workers left in groups; but the masses did not disperse. New groups approached from the boulevard and later armed gangs arrived. Somewhere, the doors of a military barracks were forced open. It was from there they got their arms. The masses at this point forced the door of the radio station open, the guards tried to keep them back with a fire hose and at the same time to put out the fire in the burning car. But when they were unsuccessful, they were compelled to use tear gas. The situation became more and more tense. The windows of the station were broken. The mob passed through the iron bars of the studios facing Pushkin Street. They armed themselves with bricks from a building on Brody Sandor Street and caused extensive damage. Now the slogan was: 'Occupy the Radio Station!'

"The guards fired in the air and tried to frighten away the attackers with blanks. They tried everything to clear the radio building without using their weapons. They did not harm anyone seriously, but more and more shots were fired from the masses. First, a major of the state security authority [AVO] was killed. Later on, during the first hours a total of six [AVO] found death. But the state securty guards still did not fire.

"There was a state of siege in the station, but broadcasting went on without disturbance. When two trucks of armed youth arrived from the direction of Gutenberg Square they occupied the houses opposite and around the station and opened fire on the studio; and it was only as a last step, after many guards were wounded and dead, that the order to return fire was given. The others, however, had machine guns and hand grenades and intensified their attack against the studio. The workers of the station, in spite of the hail of bullets, continued broadcasting to the last moment, and when the masses penetrated into the building the defenders saw to it that the provocateurs did not reach their target, that they did not silence the Kossuth Radio.

"As you are hearing this, dear listeners, the program of the Kossuth Radio is slightly different from the schedule. But the Hungarian Radio, the Kossuth Radio, is still speaking. No counterrevolutionary hordes, not even these well-organized and determined counterrevolutionaries, could silence it. Our studio suffered severe losses. More than one state security guard died a hero's death. Our workers did not face the firing, often machine-gun firing, without loss. But we have been on the air since this morning and remain, even now, Kossuth Radio Budapest.

"Dear listeners, you have heard a report by Gyorgy Kalmar entitled 'What Happened at the Radio Station.'"

As he listened to this extraordinary concoction, Zoltan Pal felt weak. "I was there," he kept repeating, as if one man's witness of incontrovertible fact could somehow outweigh the confirmed lies of a regime. And in this growing realization of the web of falsehoods and terror in which he was caught, Zoltan Pal became a revolutionary.

Zoltan's role in the fighting was not conspicuous—for one thing, his wife kept him at home as much as possible —but when the Russians finally withdrew from Budapest on October 29, the Pals had a right to say to themselves, "We helped free the city." Their contribution was not spectacular, but without the tacit support of millions of people like the Pals, the revolution could not have triumphed.

When relative peace settled over the city, the Pals had an opportunity to find out what had been happening. They were astounded, for example, when they heard that the Kilian Barracks had not surrendered. "When I last saw it," Zoltan said, "I thought it was finished."

The Pals were unprepared for the number of burned-out Russian tanks they saw along the boulevards. "I expected to see only one or two," Eva said.

With embarrassed pride Zoltan led his wife to the first reconnaissance car he had helped destroy, and then to a tank where he had taken part in a gasoline attack. Eva looked at the stricken, shattered vehicle, its treads jammed with steel pipes thrust there by children in order to halt it, and said, "I would not have believed it possible."

All Budapest seemed affected the same way. "Do you mean to say that people with no weapons destroyed all these tanks?" women marveled. And a quiet surge of patriotism possessed the city, for it had been Hungarian patriots, fighting alone and with no help from the world, who had evicted a cruel conqueror, Soviet Russia.

"I can hardly believe we did it," Zoltan reflected. "I don't think they'll stay out," he warned his wife, "but if they do try to come back, the United Nations and America will send us an army." Then he added, "And this one will have weapons."

Eva refused for the moment to contemplate the possibility of Russia's return. "What amazes me," she said, "is that we drove out the AVO too."

This last claim was not quite correct. For several days, isolated groups of AVO men in high-powered cars would rip through the city at eighty miles an hour, spraying machine-gun bullets in sullen revenge. In Pest a queue of women waiting for bread was shattered by such a hit-run blast, and many were left dead.

Food was a major problem. Bakeries tried to open two hours a day, and Eva had to stand in line endlessly to re- place food that Zoltan had handed out to the fighters. However, peasants from the surrounding countryside, feel- ing somewhat guilty for not having participated in the liberation fight, tried to make amends by streaming into the city with all the food they could muster. By truck, by cart, by hand-drawn vehicles, by tractors pulling hay wagons, the country people came with food. Stopping at main thoroughfares, they gave away tons of produce and young pigs and chickens.

There was a kind of festival in Budapest. Nobody stopped to clean up the debris, which littered most streets, nor even to bury the Russian bodies in the burned-out tanks nor the AVO men. Freedom fighters, of course, were buried in improvised graves that lined the public parks, but the hated enemies of the people were left exposed in final and complete contempt.

One of the most touching proofs that freedom had really arrived—and you could see men and women all over the city fingering these proofs with actual affection—was the appearance, almost as if by magic, of many different kinds of newspapers. There were socialist papers, peasant-party papers, labor union papers, and organs proclaiming this or that sure pathway to national prosperity.

"Look!" Eva cried one afternoon. "Newspapers!"

The Pals went up to a bombed-out stand where four different kinds of badly printed sheets were available. They carried mostly rumors, mostly hopes. But they were news- papers . . . at last. The Pals bought one of each. But when they saw that the old *Szabad Nep* of the communist party had the effrontery to use as its new masthead the almost sacred seal of Louis Kossuth, they threw it in the gutter.

The Pals were deeply affected by many trivial things. Sometimes a ridiculous incident, which would have gone unnoticed in another country, would bring them to tears, and they would stand for a moment in the bright sunlight and wonder, "What happened to us?" One day when Eva was walking along the street she was jostled by a man. He stopped to apologize and she realized that he was not a Hungarian. He spoke in a foreign language and they stood looking at each other until a passer-by stopped to interpret. "He is a Frenchman, a newspaperman."

Eva said, "Are newspapermen from abroad allowed in Budapest now?"

"There are hundreds," the Frenchman said. "Everyone wants to know what happened in your city." And for no reason Eva began to cry.

On All Saints' Day, Zoltan was listening to the radio when the announcer said that in honor of the brave men and women who had died winning Hungarian freedom the radio would play music that had not been heard in Hungary for many years. And from the speaker came the golden music of Mozart's Requiem Mass, which was rarely performed in the days of communism. Zoltan sat absolutely quiet during the entire performance, staring at the floor. He felt exalted that he was again able to hear the music of the west.

One of the finest rewards came about in a curious way. In the early days of the revolution, students had demanded that the government shut down its jamming stations, and now the flow of news from London and Paris and Munich could come in strong and unimpeded. It was a luxury beyond analysis to be able to sit and listen to news coming in clearly from the rest of the world. Each of these little things—the coming of strangers, the playing of forbidden music, the arrival of news from Europe—made the Pals think, "We are part of the world once more."

Rumors infected the city, and none was more tragic than the one which claimed that the United Nations would shortly intervene in Hungary's behalf. Eva Pal had long had the habit of listening to the American Radio Free Europe stations whenever their programs were not being blanketed by communist jamming stations. From the messages of hope which she had received in this way, she had unfortunately convinced herself that not only the United Nations, but the United States as well, would land paratroopers in Budapest, followed by tanks and an expeditionary force. When time proved that these rumors were false and that no outside agency had any intention of underwriting the apparently successful revolution, a foreboding sense of having been left isolated crept over the city.

This was partially dispelled, however, by the many jokes which the irrepressible Hungarians circulated. For example, Zoltan Pal took his wife to see the remains of the Stalin statue in Stalin Square. There the two empty boots stood, with a Hungarian flag jutting out of one of them. "We don't call it Stalin Square any longer," Zoltan laughed. "Now it is Bootmaker Square."

Another visitor said, "You know, they didn't pull the statue down at all. They just dropped a wrist watch in front of it, and like any Russian fool, Stalin bent down to get it."

The most appreciated jokes were those which ridiculed the stupidity of the communist government, which had actually broadcast the following plea:

"Persons serving prison sentences for murder, willful manslaughter, robbery, burglary, larceny or theft and who have left prison since 23rd October for any reason without having served at least two-thirds of their sentence should report back immediately to the nearest criminal police headquarters."

Once Zoltan pointed to destroyed machine guns and said, "Those Russian guitars won't play any more music." And the most common joke had in it a large grain of truth: "Imre Nagy says he wasn't really a communist. Janos Kadar says he isn't a communist. In fact, the only communist in Hungary is Nikita Khrushchev."

In this light spirit several profound changes were made in Hungarian life. The word "comrade" was officially banned, and it became very offensive to call another man comrade. October 23 was proclaimed a national holiday, and the Kossuth crest became the great seal of Hungary. Russian language study was dropped as a compulsory subject.

More important, political parties started to function, and nothing pleased the Pal family more. "Now we will be able to vote for the men we like," they said over and over to their neighbors. It was strange how simple things that a large part of the world took for granted gave Hungarians so much pleasure in those brief days: independent newspapers, political parties, a promise of free elections, with a booth in which you might vote in secret.

So joyous was the atmosphere that from all over Hungary delegations of miners and farmers and students came to Budapest bearing lists of proposals for a more democratic nation. They were not reactionary suggestions, as the communists were later to claim, for few citizens wanted to go back to the days of fascism. What they dreamed of, these workmen, was a liberal, middle way of life.

For example, one evening the Pals heard the radio announce the demands of one workers' committee from Borsod County. The requests were simple: Fire the people responsible for the breakdown in what they called the planned economy. Raise the basic wage. Stop undercover price increases. Increase pensions and family allowances. More homes, more loans to builders of small homes. Get the Russians out of Hungary. See to it that Hungarian uranium is sold so as to profit Hungary and not Russia. Arrange some treaty like the one Gomulka got for Poland. Fire the Russians' yes-men in Parliament. Then they added, "We agree with the socialist way of agriculture, but it must be reorganized in the spirit of complete voluntariness and with consideration for the peasants."

At the very moment when such rational demands were being submitted, communists in Moscow and elsewhere were claiming that the Hungarian revolution had been launched by fascists, capitalist elements, reactionaries and those discredited segments of the population who wished to take Hungary back to prewar days. Moscow implied that if the revolution succeeded, Hungary would be plunged back into medievalism or worse.

But the new Hungary, if it had been allowed to survive, would have been a socialist state devoid of absentee land ownership, large concentrations of private capital or private ownership of important industries. One might have termed it a modified communism lacking dictatorship features. It would have been more capitalist than either Poland or Yugoslavia, but it would certainly have been no 1890 feudal oligarchy. Many Americans unfamiliar with developments in Central Europe would have considered the new Hungary dangerously leftist. The world in general would have welcomed the new state as a hopeful step in the gradual decommunization of Eastern Europe, for compared with what had existed up to October 23, 1956, the new nation would have been a model of liberalism.

It should not be suggested that all was order and decency during these five days of freedom. For one thing, many AVO were still at large and some units of the Russian army remained within the city, shooting occasionally at passers-by. Then, too, there were in many sectors bands of revolutionaries who were not yet ready to declare the city safe from possible attack. They were a law to themselves, and in some instances represented a kind of anarchy which if not brought under control might ultimately do the cause of freedom much damage. For the most part, however, the citizens of Budapest were astonished at how well the wild young men of the city had settled down, once the riots had ended in their favor. Especially remarkable was the performance of what Americans call dead-end kids, for it was they who had dashed under the guns of the tanks. It was they who had strung the grenades across the streets. It was they who had fought to the last ounce of their energy. Now they were policing the same streets and putting out unguarded boxes into which people tossed thousands of forints for the care of poor families whose men had been killed in the fighting. All over Budapest, Eva and Zoltan saw these boxes, full of money, standing along the streets. Nobody stole from them, and at dusk each day the dead-end kids collected the money and distributed it.

In these heady days of freedom the Pals thought about the structure of their new nation a good deal. Zoltan says, "At first all we wanted was free elections, no AVO, no Russians, and newspapers. Then we realized that we would have to have some new kind of government, too, and that called for basic changes. Frankly, I didn't know what would be best. About as far as I went was to think that Imre Nagy would form a liberal government and arrange for the Russians to leave. I knew Nagy was a communist himself, but a pretty decent one."

Eva Pal had other ideas. All her life she had been a good Catholic, even when perseverance in her faith cost her much, and now she heard news which thrilled her deeply. The announcement came over the radio one morning at ten o'clock: "Jozsef Cardinal Mindszenty, Prince Primate, who was liberated on Tuesday by our victorious revolution, arrived at his residence in Buda at 0855 this morning."

For Eva Pal there was a kind of exultation in this simple message, for her parents had told her repeatedly that the cardinal was a man to be trusted. In secret she had heard of the trials he had suffered, the punishments and the tortures. Her mother always said first, "Loyal to Hungary." Then she would add, as if she had blasphemed, "And he was loyal to God, too."

During the day, news of his incredible escape from prison swept through Budapest, and Eva heard that on the previous night four officers of the Hungarian army, fighting with the freedom forces, had learned that Cardinal Mindszenty was being held by fourteen AVO men in a mansion outside Budapest. The officers had hurried there without orders, had disarmed the AVO guard and had carried the cardinal away to safety. A few minutes later a Russian tank arrived, to protect the cardinal, the driver said, but Mindszenty was now with his own people.

The next morning these daring officers brought the cardinal to his official residence in Buda. From there the churchman made his first announcement to the Hungarian people:

"I admire what the weapons of the youth, the soldiers, the university students, the villagers, the peasants and the workers accomplished. After eight years of imprisonment, they tore open the door of my prison. These brave officers of Retsag cared for nothing, they came to the house where I was imprisoned and took me along with them. I rested in the barracks. I send my pontifical blessing to the Hungarian weapons. I wish the glory acquired by Hungarian weapons to be multiplied by our peasantry when need comes. I want to be informed of the situation before I do or say more."

For some years Eva Pal, like a good many Hungarians, had kept hidden among her possessions a secret portrait of Cardinal Mindszenty, holding him in her mind as a symbol of resistance against communism and the Russians. Now, as she unfolded the battered portrait and placed it on her wall, the idea came to her that in the days ahead free Hungary would need the leadership of a man like this.

"He ought to be premier," she told her husband.

Zoltan, never one for religion, said, "Maybe not premier. I don't think a cardinal ought to run the government."

"But he ought to be in the government," Eva persisted.

"That might be all right," Zoltan agreed.

And in the next days, when the cardinal's powerful voice was heard speaking gravely of the tasks ahead, Eva Pal became more satisfied than ever that the unwavering churchman ought to help run Hungary. She argued with her husband, "Otherwise we have no leader. Who can really trust Nagy Imre?" In Hungarian, names are given in reverse order, and the communist leader's name, when Eva spoke it, sounded like Nodge Imry, but all in one word.

"I like Nagy Imre," Zoltan said. "He's a man of great courage."

"Why not a government of Mindszenty and Nagy Imre?" Eva suggested.

"Maybe, if Nagy Imre were premier," Zoltan grudgingly agreed.

Eva saw nothing strange in her proposal for a Hungarian government based on Nagy, the old communist who still adhered to the economic theory of communism, and

Mindszenty, the prince of the church. When she suggested this strange team to her neighbors, she found that many of the women approved.

Zoltan, however, talked mostly with workmen, and while they agreed that a towering moral symbol like Mindszenty should have a place in the government, they felt that even Imre Nagy was too old-fashioned. "We'll make him president, since everyone respects him, but we want younger men, the ones who led the revolution, to run the government." And they spoke of a middle-of-the-road system which would preserve the main outlines of the 1945 socialist state that had replaced fascism, but which would be based above all else on respect for human dignity.

"I know two things," Eva said. "Mindszenty ought to be in the government, and the AVO should be thrown out."

"And the Russians, too," Zoltan added.

On the evening of November 2, exciting reports circulated through Budapest detailing the terms which Cardinal Mindszenty had insisted upon as those under which he would agree to participate in the government. Eva Pal was relieved to know that arrangements were being completed, but the workmen with whom Zoltan talked were most apprehensive. "The Russians will hear of these terms," they argued, "and they'll have an excuse for coming back to Budapest. You watch. They'll claim the revolution was run by priests and reactionaries."

Zoltan talked about this fear with his wife, but she reasoned that since the revolution had already succeeded before Cardinal Mindszenty was even out of jail, such Russian arguments would be ridiculous. "I think we're going to have a wonderful new country," she repeated hopefully.

The vision of an honorable Hungary, free from Russian domination, seemed to bring out the best in many kinds of people, for additional proposals on how to organize the new nation came from all parts of the country and showed a greater statesmanship than the initial series. For example, Zoltan was deeply impressed when he and Eva listened to the sober plans which a committee of farmers had initiated for abolishing collectivized farms in Hungary. The reforms were not reactionary, nor were they stupid. The farmers said, "Our basic principle is that only those collectivized farms which produce surpluses and whose members want them to remain in operation should be continued. Those that cannot stand on their own feet, or whose members object, should be ended. But liquidation must be carried out gradually, after the completing of the autumn sowing and at the beginning of spring. Where a collectivized farm is liquidated, the land should be distributed among the peasants. This winter experts should study what size farm would be best, thus enabling the farmers to begin spring planting on their own lands. If a collectivized farm is continued, its norms and the way each farmer's work is evaluated must be changed to insure more justice. For the time being, the present system of collectivized farms may have to remain, but control must be reorganized, and all of us must get a more just opportunity to use the machinery."

Men who ran factories were making proposals of equal responsibility. Political leaders were suggesting ways of combining powers to form a stable government, and the philosophers of the country were beginning to talk about the genesis of a true national spirit that would reflect Hungary's love of freedom, her courage and her determination to exist as a sovereign power. There was a great deal of talk about making Hungary the Switzerland or the Sweden of Eastern Europe. "I like the idea," Zoltan said. "We are a small country. We should be neutral." And he found that Eva agreed with him heartily.

In fact, in these great sweet days of freedom, the people of Hungary talked good sense, and it seemed as if a basis were being built for a powerful and dedicated nation. "Certainly we have earned the right to be a nation," Eva told her friends.

Then came ominous news from the east. A boy came running into the street crying that hundreds of Russian tanks were in motion at the airport. "Not little ones like before. Big ones."

Men confirmed the evil news. "It looks as if the Russians were going to come back in force," a soldier said. "And those new tanks! They have extra machine guns that point down between the treads. You can't blow them up."

There was a rumble to the east, a cold wind blowing from the steppes of Russia. At four o'clock the next morning, on Sunday, November 4, Budapest was awakened by the shattering sound of Russian tanks tearing the city apart.

The tanks did not reach northern Buda till late, but when they did they rolled up the street where Zoltan and Eva Pal lived and methodically began to blow apart a house where a sniper had been seen. It was not the house in which the Pals lived, but, huddling together by the shivering window of their fourth-floor apartment, the young couple knew that theirs might be next. The glorious days of freedom were ended. The five brief days which had provided a glimpse into a different kind of future were over. Even the memories were being destroyed by the Russian tanks.

5 The Russian Terror

At four o'clock on Sunday morning, November 4, the Russians returned to Budapest. With a terror unparalleled in recent years they destroyed a city, and in doing so they stood unmasked before the world for the aggressors, the murderers, the insane fanatics that they are.

In the rubble of Budapest, in the graves of women and children mowed down by machine guns, and in the unrelieved terror of Soviet revenge lay buried Russia's claims to friendship with the satellite countries who live within her orbit. In eight hellish days Russia proved that she holds Poland and Bulgaria and Lithuania and many of the Central Asian Republics by cold, brute force.

Budapest was a dreadful price to pay for such knowledge, but if the knowledge is widely disseminated among those who were unaware of it before, and if Russia's cynical and disgraceful lies are laid bare to the rest of the world, the death of this noble city will not have been in vain.

The Russians were quite brave in their assault on the unarmed city. First they took command of Gellert Hill, a rocky height which rises 770 feet in one sheer sweep up from the western shore of the Danube. To the top of this Buda hill the Russians sped mobile heavy artillery and enormous stores of ammunition. Shells from these guns, which landed with terrifying force in apartment houses and government buildings, measured nearly four feet long and were vastly destructive.

From Gellert Hill, the highest point in Budapest, the Russian artillerymen could command the entire city. The guns, which were established near a monument erected to Russian soldiers who had helped drive Hitler out of Budapest, looked directly down at the eight main bridges that spanned the Danube and connected Buda with Pest.

To the north the powerful guns could fire into the old town of Buda, whose Castle Hill was a handsome collection of narrow streets, quaint houses and historic sites. The Russians knew that with enough high-explosive shells they could blow the old town completely apart.

East of the river, the great guns could pinpoint university buildings, railway stations, museums, the radio studio, the factories in Csepel and one particular spot whose continued resistance infuriated the Russians: the sagging, gutted remnants of Kilian Barracks, where some soldiers and officers still held out.

In fact, these massive guns on Gellert Hill could by themselves have destroyed Budapest. But they were, in some respects, the least weapon in the Russian commander's arsenal. He had in addition about 140,000 of the most ruthless foot soldiers in the Soviet army, plus another 60,00 available in the immediate vicinity, if the going got rough. Each soldier was equipped with a submachine gun and huge supplies of ammunition that could be momentarily replenished. These soldiers had been given one simple order: "Shoot!" It did not matter whether the moving target was a student with a gasoline bomb or a housewife with a loaf of bread. "Shoot!"

Next came four thousand new tanks. These were not the vulnerable, old-style T-34s, with high turrets and machine guns which could not deflect, like the kind Sergeant Csoki had destroyed in the first days of fighting. These were low-slung, swift, superarmored and well-gunned T-54s with a turret from which shells would deflect because of its sloping sides. They could do forty miles an hour, and run over a trolley car or crush an automobile. They carried in addition a powerful gun which could fire semi-automatically and deliver a punch that would destroy a house. The Russians brought two thousand of these tanks into the city and kept an equal number in reserve.

In the air, jet planes and propeller-driven bombers were called in to hit specific targets or to bomb whole areas. These planes were usually armed with rockets carrying enormous concentrations of high explosives, and one rocket could rip out a factory wall. Since the Hungarian rebels had neither planes of their own nor more than one antiaircraft gun, nor the ammunition if they had had the guns, the Soviet pilots flew courageously and accomplished great damage.

On the ground there were rockets, too. Nests of rocket launchers could be wheeled into position behind fast-moving trucks and discharge in rapid-fire order six giant rockets against a building that was attempting to hold out. Usually one volley was enough to collapse a building and kill all occupants.

But even these formidable weapons were not enough for what the Russians had in mind. Squads of men with flame throwers moved throughout the city, burning down large areas and incinerating the inhabitants. There were also armor-piercing batteries in case Hungarian freedom fighters turned up with armor or captured tanks. There were anti-tank guns to deal with the latter, bazookas in case of extreme trouble, and a new kind of baby tank that was extremely mobile and well armed. In addition they had an intricate system of communications, flares, walkie-talkies, reconnaissance cars and armed jeeps. Most important, for this second assault each Soviet soldier had been issued a new type of sub-machine gun twice as effective as the old Russian guitar.

Against this concentration of Soviet power the Hungarians had some homemade gasoline bombs.

Even so, the Russians were not willing to take any chances. Before launching their attack, they lured into a phony meeting the one Hungarian who might have defeated them. Colonel Maleter, now a major-general because of his amazing skill in defending Budapest and driving out the Russians, took the Russians' promise of safe passage at its face value and went to a meeting "to discuss the withdrawal of all Soviet troops from Hungary." The Russians, stalling for time so that their last gun could be drawn into position, made concessions which amounted to a total Hungarian victory.

Hardly able to believe what he heard, Maleter accepted the Russian surrender. "Come back later and we'll sign the papers," the Russians said. "In the meantime, no fighting."

During the truce thus obtained, the Russians consolidated their strangle hold on the city, and when General Maleter returned for the subsequent meeting, safeguarded by a flag of truce, the Russians promptly brushed aside the flag, arrested the hero of Budapest and whisked him off to prison, possibly in Siberia.

In the dreadful days of fighting that were to follow, the young men of Hungary marched out almost unarmed against the Russian tanks, without a leader, without generals and without lines of communication. What these young patriots accomplished against their Russian oppressors is an epic of human endurance.

The heroic Russians spent Sunday shelling the city from the safety of Gellert Hill and sending out squads of swift tanks to shoot up the boulevards. They kept their foot soldiers in reserve and tried to terrorize the Hungarians so completely that on Monday mopping up could begin.

They made a bad guess. The Hungarians stayed indoors during the worst part of the shelling, and tried to dodge bullets during the swift tank forays. Even so, courageous freedom fighters did find time to erect barricades across many of the streets of Pest, and there were some teams of young boys and girls who tackled any tank that slowed down. At one important intersection, Moricz Zsigmond Square, in Buda, a college student who had been forced by the communists to study military science cried, "It looks to me that if we can hold this square, the Russians will be tied up. Let's barricade it."

Assuming command, he devised a masterful defense plan, but before he could complete his work a boy shouted, "Here come five cars of soldiers!"

The college student ordered his best men onto the nearby roofs, and when the reconnaissance cars swung into the partially barricaded square, he gave a signal and brought the cars under very heavy fire. Sixty-seven Russians were killed, and the three cars that were able to turn about fled back toward Gellert Hill.

Before the next Russian attack came, the college student directed his forces to overturn all the street cars in the area. They interlaced the street cars with timbers, and blocked themselves in. He gained unexpected support from some Hungarian soldiers who delivered two captured Russian tanks to the square, and these formed the main artillery of the defense.

Russian retaliation was not long delayed. Seven large tanks came screaming down from Gellert Hill, and as they came, machine guns sprayed bullets into all the surrounding houses. Out of range of the fighters in Moricz Zsigmond Square the tanks halted, rounded up twenty street boys and executed them in one titanic burst of bullets.

Inside the square the college student said to his men, "We will die here today."

The seven swift tanks, having completed their first act of revenge, now rushed at Moricz Zsigmond Square, but the defenders were so well dug in, so well armed and so daring that all the tanks were destroyed. The November Sunday then settled down into a brutal battle between more and more tanks and the fiery young men inside the square. It was here, facing youngsters, that the Russians learned that their grand plan for a quick humiliation of

Budapest was not going to work. They would have to dig out the Hungarians man by man.

Among the freedom fighters inside the barricades at Moricz Zsigmond Square was a twenty-year-old youth, tough as nails but almost boyishly eager to be a story-book hero. His name was Imre Geiger, and his great sorrow was that throughout the entire revolution he never acquired any weapon larger than a rifle. He felt that if he had been able to get hold of a machine gun the outcome of the fighting might have been different.

Geiger was a handsome fellow, dark, chunky, with fine teeth and jet-black hair which he wore in a crew-cut. He wore a turtleneck sweater, kept a cigarette dangling from the left corner of his mouth and tried to talk in a snarl. He was on duty when five fresh Russian tanks whipped up to clean out the square.

"They didn't succeed," Geiger reports. "I don't know how we did it, but we killed one tank in the battle and drove the rest off." In the hours that followed, two more Russian tanks were destroyed at Moricz Zsigmond Square, and in the dull hours of night the Russians had to accept the fact that the second battle for Budapest was going to be tougher than the first. As if to prove this conclusion, Geiger and his men held their square against the full might of the Russian attack for thirty-six hours. At one point they were under fire from Gellert Hill, from tanks lining the perimeter of the square, from armor-piercing mobile guns that methodically shot down the buildings of the square, and from mortars that lobbed phosphorous incendiary bombs all over the fighting area. Even so, the young Hungarians withstood this massed assault for two hours, and retreated only when there was no square left to defend. "They didn't get much," Geiger says. When the Soviets finally marched in, the streets nearby were so blocked with crushed streets cars, burned-out tanks, ruined vehicles, and collapsed houses that it was not worth having. As for Imre Geiger, he had squirmed his way out to fight at a more important post.

After the capture of Moricz Zsigmond Square, the Soviets turned their attention to a more difficult target.

North of Gellert Hill they could see the old castle which dominated Castle Hill. Most of the streets leading up to it were on a steep incline, with treacherous turns, and here a group of dedicated young Hungarians, including many college students, had gathered to defend Buda to the end. After the fall of the square, they were augmented by a handful of experienced fighters who had already tasted all that the Russians had to offer. But the fight at Castle Hill was different from that at the square in one respect: here many young girls assisted in the fighting. They were to prove heroic.

The cautious Russians approached the problem of Castle Hill as if it were defended by the most powerful enemy in the world, rather than by a bunch of young men and girls with no weapons. In classic sequence the mighty guns on Gellert Hill laid down a merciless barrage of high-explosive shells for about an hour. It seemed unlikely that any human being could have lived through this destruction.

But not wishing to take any risks, the commander next sent in tanks to annihilate any remaining organized opposition, and these were to be followed by companies of foot soldiers with machine guns. Their job was to wipe out isolated survivors.

But the soldiers didn't get there—not just then. For as soon as the sullen barrage had ended, boys and girls mysteriously appeared from their hiding places and under impromptu supervision took steps which would make the defense of Castle Hill a memorable page in the history of military improvisation.

Among the recruits which Castle Hill acquired from Moricz Zsigmond Square was Imre Geiger, still lugging a rifle and still burning for a fight. "We had a simple problem," he says. "How to destroy tanks.

"There were three main ways," he explains. "The first way was to make them slip sideways and crack up. Sometimes we were able to do this when they were going uphill. Girls would spread liquid soap on the street, and the tank's tracks would either spin or slide. Maybe the tank would jam into a building, and then we would pounce on it.

"A man who worked in a garage showed us how to smear

grease and oil at corners, and a tank might slide sideways into a tree or a building, and we would have it trapped.

"Our second trick was to make them stop for a minute. Anything to make them stop. One clever girl spread brown plates upside down, and they looked exactly like land mines. The Russians would come up to them, hesitate and then start to back up. That's when we got them. A workman thought up a very smart idea. From a soda-water plant he got a truck load of empty oxygen tanks. He spread these on the street and you should have seen the tanks rolling around. Some little boys strung grenades on strings, and jockeyed them back and forth until they came under the tracks of the tanks. The explosions stopped the tanks and we killed them. But the bravest were the young boys and girls who just dashed out and stuck lengths of plumber's pipe into the tracks, making them jam. You never saw such kids.

"The third way," he explains, flipping his drooping cigarette up to a better angle by twisting his lips, "was to lure some tank into a dead-end street. Once we got it there, we had a good chance to kill it. Girls would put broomsticks out windows, and the tank crews would take them to be snipers' guns, and they would nose into the dead-end street. Too bad for the tank. Or we propped up old empty guns in doorways, and tanks would come after them, get bottled in the dead-end street, and we would kill them."

Getting a tank stopped, of course, was merely the easy part of the battle, for even a trapped tank could spit fire from its three heavy machine guns, all of which could seek out attackers by revolving in almost a complete circle. In addition, the Soviets were quite prepared to fire their heaviest cannon point-blank at even a single Hungarian, if by so doing they could prevent an attacker from reaching the tank with a gasoline bomb.

The young people of Castle Hill were equal to the occasion. They discovered many ways to kill a wounded tank. One energetic worker filled an entire depression in the cobblestone pavement at the top of a hill with gasoline. He just left it there and hid in a doorway until a tank reached the middle of the gasoline. Then he pitched a grenade into the open gas, and engulfed the tank in a wall of flame.

Another worker ran a high-tension electric wire onto a tank and electrocuted the occupants. At the bottom of a hill a determined motorman set his trolley car in motion, got it up to high speed and leaped off just before it rammed headfirst into a tank, which was then set ablaze.

But ultimately, the monstrous Soviet tanks were destroyed by incredibly brave young men and women who got close enough to them to douse them with handmade gasoline bombs. "I didn't think girls could do what I saw them do," Imre Geiger says. "They would hide in doorways with one bomb apiece. If the tank went by in good shape, they didn't move. Some of them, of course, were killed by machine-gun fire when such tanks shot into all the doorways they saw. Many girls were killed.

"But if the tank slipped, or ran into a wall, or was stopped in any way, out would dart these girls and blow it to hell." A Presbyterian minister who saw the fight on Castle Hill says simply, "I have never known such heroism as the girls of Budapest displayed."

It fell to the lot of one twelve-year-old boy whose name is not known to achieve the ultimate in his fight against the Soviets. He lashed grenades to his belt, carried others in his arms, and ran into the tracks of the lead tank in a column, blowing its tracks and himself to pieces, but he stopped the column for older fighters. The same minister says of this child, "It should not have happened. Somebody should have stopped such a child. But he knew who he was fighting against."

In the end, of course, the Russians captured Castle Hill. A full two days behind schedule the ruthless foot soldiers marched up as planned, and finished the mopping up. But as they marched, cautiously and with the maximum weapons, they passed the burned-out hulks of more than a score of Russia's finest tanks. Not one heavy gun had been used against these tanks . . . only the hands of young Hungarians who were fighting for personal and national freedom.

When the victorious Soviets finally entered the castle itself, the final bastion, only thirty young Hungarians remained to walk out proudly under the white flag of surrender. For three days they had withstood the terrible concentration of Soviet power, and they had conducted themselves as veritable heroes. The gallant Soviet commander waited until they were well clear of the walls; then with one burst of machine-gun fire he executed the lot.

Arcoss Budapest the same terror prevailed. Early in the fighting the Soviet army had evolved a simple rule of thumb: "If there is a single shot from any house, destroy the whole house. If there are many shots from a street, shoot down every building in the street."

From then on this clear-cut rule was applied with savage force. No part of Budapest was safe from the tanks, and if any commander heard a single shot, he would stop his tank—it was now safe to do this—maneuver it into position and shoot off the upper coping, so as to kill any snipers on the roof. He did not then fire at the upper stories, but only at the bottom one, pulverizing it with heavy fire until the house fell down upon itself. In this way thousands of Hungarians were buried alive.

Had the Russians been fighting a people who had never co-operated with them, such barbarism might conceivably have been understood. Or had they, in their fanaticism, been warring against a reactionary people, their uncontrolled fury might also have been acceptable as a part of the communist ideology when considering the lot of noncommunist regions. But in Budapest the Soviets perpetrated their horrors upon a people who had originally been their peaceful associates, who had once been good communists, who had co-operated to the point of sacrificing their own national interests. In Budapest, the Russians destroyed with cold fury the very people who had in many ways been their best friends in Eastern Europe. They were not fighting reactionaries. They were not fighting capitalists. They were not fighting antique elements trying to turn back the clock of history. They were annihilating people who had once been communists.

But the worst barbarism was still to come. In areas already subdued, Russian tank crews ran wild and roared their tanks through the streets, firing on any groups of civilians they saw. There were three instances in which women in queues were shot to death.

Ambulances and Red Cross workers—probably because the Soviets themselves use these internationally recognized welfare agencies as blinds for military action—were mercilessly shot down. Nurses attending the wounded were executed by point-blank, single-rifle fire.

All the blood and blood plasma at the Hungarian central depot on Daroczi Street was confiscated by the Russians and taken to the Szabolcz Street hospital, which they had reserved for themselves. As a result, Hungarian doctors were reduced to using only saline transfusions, which often killed their patients. As a result, thirty-five per cent of all leg wounds ended in amputation.

Children were killed, hospitals were fired upon, and young men were executed merely upon suspicion. Crimes against inanimate objects were as bad. A squad of flame throwers attacked the National Archives and burned it out. When patriotic firemen tried to save the building, they were shot. A house across from the Protestant seminary was set ablaze by another squad, and when a boarder in the house tried to protect his possessions, he too was shot. Stores were completely looted, even though the Russian troops did not need the food. And on the third floor of 46 Nepszinhaz Street, three Soviet soldiers knocked down door 23 and smashed into a jewelry shop which operated there. Shooting the owner, the soldiers scooped up all the watches and then sprayed the store with bullets.

The sack of Budapest was senseless and unnecessary. It was an act of blind revenge because the people of the city had grown tired of Soviet lies, Soviet terror and Soviet expropriation.

But when the ruin was complete—when the girls and young men were liquidated—there remained two unsubdued Hungarian outposts whose existence must have especially galled the Russians. On Ulloi Street the battered and torn Kilian Barracks still held out. One corner of the thick-walled building had been completely blasted away, leaving all the good fighting positions exposed to machine-gun fire. Much of the interior flooring had collapsed; the rest was propped up by improvised timbers. In a few places even the massive walls had begun to crumble, while inside the shell the defending soldiers had few guns, little ammunition, no food and no water. Still these amazing men of Kilian resisted.

Against it the Russians wheeled up tanks and mortars, rockets and flame throwers, generals and privates, plus a grim determination to wipe the defenders off the face of the earth. Armor-piercing shells and high explosives practically demolished the barracks, so that on the night of the second full day of bombardment it seemed that the Russians had won, for from the staggering walls a group of officers came out to surrender the building. But as they approached the Russians, their own determined men inside the barracks shot them dead, and the fight continued.

The battle for Kilian did not end heroically. In fact, no one was aware that it was over, for after three days of resistance beyond the capacity of man to endure, the nameless fighters simply dispersed. Some went through sewer pipes to the Corvin Cinema and slipped into the crowd there. Others waited for nightfall and slipped out back ways of their own. On the fourth day the Soviets occupied it, a gaping shell from which the blood of freedom had mysteriously, but not cravenly, vanished.

The last major center of resistance must have been in some ways even more infuriating to the Russians than the Kilian Barracks had been, and it was to this final redoubt that cocky young Imre Geiger, lugging his rifle and his drooping cigarette, went in the early morning of November 7.

Just south of the city and only a quarter of an hour away by high-speed railway, lay the big island of Csepel, thirty miles long and crowding the center of the Danube River. On the southern end of the island were the vegetable gardens in whose rich soil grew most of Budapest's produce, but the northern end was a special ward of the communist governments both in Budapest and in Moscow, for this was Red Csepel, the sprawling industrial center where the heavy industry of Budapest was concentrated. This was the heartland of communism, the center from which the Soviets had captured Hungary. Communist orators could grow tearful when they referred to Red Csepel, and it was almost a requirement for any red Hungarian orator to cry "Csepel is Hungary and Hungary is Csepel." Communist philosophy preached the doctrine that it was upon the workers in heavy industry that the movement must ultimately depend, and in no satellite country was this held to be more obvious than in Hungary, where the powerful workers of Csepel were the absolute hard core of the communist movement. One Hungarian communist philosopher said, "If the red men of Csepel ever turned against communism, it would be like the cardinals of the Vatican turning against the Pope."

If this communist analysis of Csepel was correct, why was a young freedom fighter like Imre Geiger lugging his rifle there during the last gasp of the revolution? He was heading there to make a last-ditch stand because Budapest had found that the communist propaganda about Red Csepel was one hundred per cent wrong. In fact, in none of their high-blown philosophizing were the communist leaders so completely wrong as in the case of Csepel.

For the men of Csepel, the workers in heavy industries, not only refused to fight for communism; almost all of them fought against it. And now, when there was no slightest hope of victory, when only certain death awaited any man who defended a factory on the side of freedom, the Csepel men had their finest hour.

In Chapter Seven I propose to examine why the men of Csepel behaved as they did. Now I shall only state that these appallingly brave men gave communism its gravest blow both physicially and morally.

The revolution was proposed by the writers and philosophers of the Petofi Club. It was initiated by daring students. It was maintained by determined young boys and girls who wrestled with tanks barehanded. But it was made effective by the men of Csepel, and when every other section was beaten into submission, these plain workmen, the propaganda darlings of communism, retreated to their island and maintained a defiance that startled Russia and the world.

When young Imre Geiger and his futile rifle reached Csepel an acute ear could have heard the death rattle of freedom. The workmen, barricaded in great factories that had been the pride of Josef Stalin, had little ammunition. They possessed one antiaircraft gun, a few cannon, a lot of gasoline, for the oil cracking plant was on their island. Most curiously, they possessed no inspiring leader, no grandiose ideas. In fact, they had only one substantial weapon: their unreasoning hatred of Russians and their stooges, the AVO.

Hardly a man in Csepel had avoided some kind of contact with the AVO. Spies were everywhere and punishments were severe if these spies even suspected disloyalty or a lack of enthusiasm. Harassment was the order of the day, and spies kept lists of even the slightest infractions. The Csepel men had had enough, and they had torn the regime apart. Now they were prepared to give world communism a lesson that will be marked in history.

From the moment when the big guns on Gellert Hill began bombarding the city, one of their favorite targets had been Csepel. Into it they pumped many tons of high explosives, and it was against the sprawling workshops that the Russian jets directed most of their rockets; but these weapons were no more successful in subduing the Csepel men than they had been in cowing college students. So the Soviets were faced with the dismal job of going into the island with tanks and infantry.

The tragic story of the other centers of resistance was repeated here, but with many strange overtones. Because the Russians had a special hatred for the Csepel workers who had turned against them, the assault was particularly bitter, and because the Csepel men knew that surrender was impossible, the defense was extremely tough. For example, when the main attack came, one Csepel worker rigged up a high-power hose that sprayed gasoline over tanks, which were then ignited with grenades. Another determined worker had rebuilt an antiaircraft gun captured from the Soviets, and this he used in one spectacular burst of glory, shooting down a low-flying jet which had assumed it had unchallenged control of the skies.

In the brutal fighting young Imre Geiger had a weird experience. He was busy making a fresh supply of gasoline bombs when he stopped to stare at a young man who was working from the same barrel. "God, he looked funny," Geiger says. "I thought he was a new kind of Russian soldier who had slipped in with us. You know what he turned out to be? A North Korean. After the Korean war the Chinese communists sent several dozen selected North Korean communists, who had fought against America, here to study in our factories. Every one of them turned against communism and fought on our side."

Geiger's next encounter was of a more pathetic kind. On the line where the Csepel men handed out their meager stores of ammunition, Geiger met up with two boys of eighteen who could speak little Hungarian. "They could hardly make themselves understood. But they wanted to talk to me and give me something. They had two letters to their families. They wanted me to mail them if I got out. And what do you suppose those letters were written in? Greek. They said there were several Greek kids in the factories. These were the ones the communists kidnaped from Greece during the civil war there. They were made into good communists and given everything they wanted . . . the best jobs in Csepel. But when the chance came, they fought against the Russians."

In its last stages the fight for Csepel became a horrifying contest between unparalleled mechanical power on the one side and bare human determination on the other. The defenders of Csepel tried everything. When the Soviets swarmed onto the island the Csepel men ignited the gasoline plant to fight them off and writhing pillars of fire illuminated the deathly scene. But it was no use. Huge Soviet guns sent volleys ricocheting through gaunt, empty factory buildings. Railroad cars were blasted by low-flying rocket planes, and everywhere the mournful whooomp! whooomp! of red mortars brought destruction. The time came on the eighth day of battle, November 11, when further resistance was simply not possible.

Then, like the last weary defenders of Kilian, the men of Csepel quietly vanished into the vegetable patches, or swam the river, or crept inconspicuously into the crowds. They did not surrender. They lived on to participate in what was to be the bravest act of the revolution, one which would forever prove to the world how completely Soviet Russia had lost control over its men in the heavy industries. I shall discuss their action in Chapter Seven, but for the moment they were defeated, and as they slipped away, young Imre Geiger went with them.

The battle for Budapest was now officially over, but the terror continued. Russian tanks had been superb against revolvers; they were even better when the populace had no arms at all. They paraded their might by roaring through the city and firing at random. After a few days of unchallenged triumph they subsided and foot soldiers took over.

With their arrival shocking stories began to circulate throughout Europe, for the savage troops patrolling Budapest were found to be Mongols from the Central Asian Republics. They behaved like animals, and the murders they piled up were frightening.

Why had they been brought in to terrorize the city? Because the original troops, from Russia proper, had been garrisoned in Hungary, under the terms of the Warsaw Pact, so long that they had become too human and could not be depended upon to shoot civilians. There were several confirmed instances, in addition to that of the tank commander at Parliament Square who had shot the AVO assassins, of Russians' voluntary siding with the Hungarian freedom fighters. One of the reasons for the five-day peace was to provide Russian army commanders with time to replace these disaffected troops with uncontaminated Mongols. Rumors, unconfirmed, claimed that many of the original occupation troops were either shot or sent to Siberia. At any rate, they vanished.

There is one aspect of this use of Mongol troops against the Hungarian population that must not be overlooked. In World War II troops from these very republics were thrown against the Germans on the eastern front. In most instances they went over to the enemy en masse, announcing that they hated Russians so much they wanted a chance to shoot them. When the Germans interned them in prison camps, the wild men of the steppes begged to be put into German uniforms and set loose against the Russians, even though they knew that in such circumstances capture meant certain death. A regiment of such troops was organized under German command, and it fought with terrible fury against the Soviets. From this it would appear that Russia has adopted a Draconian policy of never using troops in their own native countryside, but always moving into disaffected areas shock troops from remote parts of the empire, knowing that troops from any given area cannot be trusted to massacre their own kin. It is doubtful if troops from Russian areas near countries like Bulgaria, Rumania and Hungary will ever again be used in those countries. They will be used to massacre Asian populations, if the need occurs.

The Russian terror was able to operate successfully in Budapest in spite of the fact that the entire Hungarian army fought against it. Why were the Russian troops so successful? Why did the Hungarian army not use its heavy guns?

First, the quick and dishonorable capture of General Maleter through trickery deprived the Hungarian army of its leadership. Second, during the five days of peace the army studiously refrained from any military build-up lest it invite Russian retaliation. Third, on the night of November 3 the Russians tricked some of the best units into moving out of Budapest by issuing false orders for these troops to reconnoiter in a nearby village. Fourth, just prior to the initial bombardments at 0400, Russian storm units captured a good many Hungarians in bed. But all of these reasons are subsidiary to the major explanation. The Hungarian army brought over no big weapons because the Russians never allowed them to have any. Even before the Hungarian uprising, the communist army lived in fear of what its satellite troops might one day do, and nations like Hungary and Bulgaria were studiously deprived of big guns, modern tanks, large backlogs of ammunition and communication equipment. In Hungary this policy paid off, and we can suppose that it is now being enforced even more rigidly in the other satellites, and in the minor republics of Central Asia. In other words, from the day the Budapest revolution started and for as far as one can see into the future, Russia must live in a state of fear, not fear of what the democracies might one day try to do to her, but fear of what the satellites will do if they get the chance.

After the Russians had won the military victory in Budapest, they still had to win a propaganda victory. They therefore launched a world-wide attempt to prove that the United States triggered the revolution and that it was participated in only by reactionaries, former Horthy fascists, armed refugees smuggled in from Germany, Cardinal Mindszenty and enemies of the working classes. Russia is already claiming that true communists, honest workmen and intelligent students remained loyal. These lies will be repeated endlessly, and in some parts of the world will probably be believed.

During the height of the revolution the freedom fighters were aware of this likely charge and did all within their power to keep the revolution uncompromised. I know of several instances in which fighters said to political prisoners, or to sons of good families, "We appreciate your help, but please stay away. We want this revolution to be absolutely clean. Only communists and workers must do the fighting. In that way the Soviets can't charge us with being fascists."

One poster, which appeared widely in Budapest, took cognizance of the Soviet lies. It read, "Nine Million Fascist Counterrevolutionaries, All Former Factory Owners, Bankers and Cardinals Are Hiding in the Country!! Their main hideout is the aristocratic residential district of Csepel. Luckily there were still six true Hungarian communists who formed a government in order to save the country." The one time the street boys selling the new communist newspaper *Nep Szabadsag (People's Freedom)*—a typically communist juggling of the former name, *Szabad Nep (Free People)*—hawked their wares by shouting, "Today's most recent complete lies, all for only half a forint."

The true news of the revolution was disseminated by heroes. On an inadequate hand press they printed a newspaper called *Truth*, which contained digests of radio news gathered from American and British broadcasts. Every article and poem appearing in *Truth* was signed by the writer's real name. Each day of the battle, these treasured newspapers were handed to brave youngsters who on bicycles and afoot scurried from one outpost to another with the broadsides. One fighter has reported, "We never missed an issue, but many boys were killed bringing us the news. Strangely, we did not grieve over them, for they had died fighting for what we were fighting for, the right to know the truth."

The revolution was unique in that not only the freedom fighters got the news; for one tragic day the entire world was free to eavesdrop upon the battle. In the old *Szabad Nep* building at the corner of Rakoczi Street and Jozsef Boulevard, an MTI (Hungarian Press Agency) reporter was sitting at a teletype machine when the Russians began their Sunday assault on his area. By a most unlikely coincidence, he had an open wire to the Associated Press offices in Vienna, 178 miles to the west. For several hours this brave young man typed out his report on the death of his city. Deservedly, his words were printed all over the world, and there must be few readers who are unacquainted with them:

"At the moment there is silence. It may be the silence before the storm.

"We have almost no weapons, only light machine guns, Russian-made long rifles and some carbines. We haven't any kind of heavy guns.

"The people are jumping at the tanks, throwing in hand grenades and closing the drivers' windows. The Hungarian people are not afraid of death. It is only a pity that we can't stand for long.

"A man just came in from the street. He said not to think because the street is empty that the people have taken shelter. They are standing in the doorway, waiting for the right moment.

"One Hungarian soldier was told by his mother as she

said good-by to him: 'Don't be a hero, but don't be cowardly either.' "

"The tanks are nearing, and the heavy artillery. We have just had a telephone report that our unit is receiving reinforcements and ammunition. But it is still too little, we need more. It can't be allowed that people attack tanks with their bare hands. What is the United Nations doing? Give us a little encouragement."

"We will hold out to our last drop of blood," he said over the Telex. "The government has not done enough to give us arms. Downstairs, there are men who have only one hand grenade."

"I am running over to the window in the next room to shoot, but I will be back if there is anything new or you ring me."

When informed by Associated Press in Vienna of a Washington dispatch that Cardinal Mindszenty had taken refuge in the United States legation in Budapest, the *Szabad Nep* informant asked: "Is that all they have achieved?"

"Russian plane just fired a machine-gun burst. We don't know where, just heard and saw it.

"The building of barricades is going on. The Parliament and its vicinity are crowded with tanks. We don't know why, but it certainly is not a good sign. Planes are flying overhead, but can't be counted, there are so many. The tanks are coming in big lines.

"Our building already has been fired on, but so far there are no casualties. The roar of the tanks is so loud we can't hear each other's voices."

"They just brought us a rumor that the American troops will be here within one or two hours."

"A shell just exploded nearby. At 1020 now there is heavy firing in the direction of the National Theater, near us in the center of the city."

"Send us any news you can about world action in Hungary's behalf. Don't worry, we burn your dispatches as soon as we have read them.

"In our building we have youngsters of fifteen and men of forty. Don't worry about us. We are strong, even if we are only a small nation. When the fighting is over we will rebuild our unhapppy, much oppressed country."

At ten-thirty that morning the last message came through, and then the correspondent in the *Szabad Nep* building was heard no more. Appropriately the message read: "Just now the heaviest fighting is going on at the Kilian Barracks. There is steady artillery fire."

But before this young man vanished he Telexed a personal message to a relative who had escaped to England: "Sending kisses. We are well and fighting at 0920, CET, 4 November." Later in the day the *Szabad Nep* building was fired at point-blank by Russian guns.

When the rape of Budapest ended, some freedom fighters tried to cast up a report of what had happened. Their figures must of necessity be haphazard, and I would not want to swear that they were accurate, but it seems likely that something like this happened. One hundred and forty thousand armed Russians swept through the city. They were backed up by at least four thousand tanks and armed vehicles plus ample supplies of all the other accouterments of modern warfare. They totally destroyed eight thousand houses, and shot out about sixty per cent of all the windows in the city. About thirty thousand Hungarians were killed or wounded, plus another ten thousand who were buried alive in collapsing buildings, but many Hungarians insist that total casualties numbered about eighty thousand. The Russians lost not over eight thousand men and about 320 tanks. This last figure could probably be revised about fifty per cent either way, so that we can say that the Hungarian freedom fighters, with little equipment, destroyed at least 160 but not more than 480 tanks. From the reports I have studied and the pictures I have assembled, I would guess that the figure inclined somewhat toward the latter number. A city was ravaged.

And all this was accomplished by Russia in pursuit of her announced policy of friendship and peace: "We Soviets have intervened not as enemies but as true friends of the Hungarian people, and our own interest is only to help in putting down the revolt of fascists and criminal elements."

At the height of fighting, when students and writers and workers and young girls were laying down their lives, Soviet apologists in Budapest had the effrontery to offer the following explanation of what was happening in Hungary: "Ferocious fascist beasts wanted to restore the power of capitalists. We are convinced that the Hungarian people in order to protect peace will possess sufficient strength to crush the fascist gangs. All over the world, led by the Soviet Union, the unity of the countries of the socialist bloc has the greatest significance. If Hungary will restore order with the help of the Soviet Union then it will again return to constructive socialist work. The rapid victory won against the antirevolutionary forces proves that these antirevolutionary forces consisted only of the scum of the nation. It also proves that they were not supported by the masses."

There was to be, however, a more honest and a more honorable requiem for the people of Hungary. From an unknown freedom radio station, an unknown fighter cried to the conscience of the world: "Civilized people of the world, on the watchtower of 1,000-year-old Hungary the last flames begin to go out. The Soviet Army is attempting to crush our troubled hearts. Their tanks and guns are roaring over Hungarian soil. Our women, mothers and daughters are sitting in dread. They still have terrible memories of the Army's entry in 1945. Save our souls. S-O-S. S-O-S.

"People of the world, listen to our call. Help us—not

with advice, not with words, but with action, with soldiers
and arms. Please do not forget that this wild attack of
Bolshevism will not stop. You may be the next victim.
Save us. S-O-S. S-O-S.

"People of Europe whom we defended once against the
the attacks of Asiatic Barbarians, listen now to the alarm
bells ringing from Hungary.

"Civilized people of the world, in the name of liberty
and solidarity, we are asking you to help. Our ship is sinking. The light vanishes. The shadows grow darker from
hour to hour. Listen to our cry. Start moving. Extend to us
brotherly hands.

"People of the world, save us. S-O-S.

"Help, help, help. God be with you and with us."

After this there could be only silence.

6   The AVO Man

During the five days of peace, freedom fighters indulged in
a group of incidents which did great damage to the revolution and which are difficult either to condone or to explain.
Unfortunately for the good name of the revolution, photographers were present at some of these bloodly incidents,
and the resulting pictures were flashed around the world.

These photographs were quickly pounced upon by the
Soviets as proving that the fight for freedom in Hungary
was nothing but a reactionary attempt to press down upon
the brow of honest workmen a crown of capitalist thorns.
Before Soviet tanks had ceased firing point-blank at residential buildings so as to bury the inhabitants alive, Soviet propagandists were preparing booklets which featured
these grisly photographs and were distributing them
throughout Europe and the world.

But what the Soviets were not distributing, along with

the photographs, were accounts of what had led up to the incidents thus portrayed, and it is these missing background accounts which I now propose to provide in reporting the history of a typical AVO man. His portrait —which by necessity is a composite drawn from all I could learn from many sources about the character and behavior of AVO personnel—is not pleasant to look at, but the events on which it is based are all meticulously true.

Tibor Donath was a country boy. He was born in 1925 in a small village near the Russian border. Unfortunately, he was an unpleasant-looking child with washed-out blond hair, weak eyes and a prominent chin. His parents were distressed when he did not do well in school, even though in the protection of his home he showed a quick ability to learn. The priest assured the Donaths that their son would "grow into a man" when he became interested in games.

This never happened, partly because Tibor remained underweight and gawky, partly because the other boys did not like him. He was able to withstand these disappointments, but in late adolescence he discovered a much crueler fact: girls did not like him either. Again the priest said, "When he's older, and his complexion clears, everything will be all right."

But with Tibor Donath things never were to be all right. In 1943, when all his friends were called into service, he was rejected as being badly underweight. That was what the doctor said, but among the real reasons was a strong suspicion that the boy was not well balanced. Proof of this came when, in 1944 under the German occupation, he formed a lasting attachment to a German lieutenant, who was shortly thereafter killed on the Russian front.

With the coming of peace Donath, now twenty years old, faced numerous difficult decisions. He could not find a job. He could not find a girl. And he could not find any sense of security or meaning in an aimless life of sitting at home while his mother lectured him. Once he said, "You know what I'm going to do? I'm going to Russia!" But his mother laughed at him. Then he proposed going to Germany and living with the family of his dead lieutenant.

Finally he found a niche, not an important one and not one which paid him the money he felt he needed. But it was a substantial niche, nevertheless, and gave him for the first time a sense of accomplishment. He achieved all this by joining the communist party.

His first jobs were unimportant, for the smart top party men recognized him instantly as poor material, but they did allow him to participate in supervising life in his own small village, and this was for Tibor Donath a great delight. He could now speak up to boys who had abused him and walk with girls who had ignored him. He found that his new position afforded many petty ways of obtaining small personal revenges. For example, he informed the communist party leader that one of his boyhood companions was probably a fascist, and when he saw this boy four months later, he observed with relish that his former enemy was much subdued.

It was after he had provided the party police with several such tips, some of which turned out to be accurate, that Tibor Donath, now a little heavier at age twenty-four but still with a bad complexion, was casually approached by a visitor from Budapest.

"They tell me you'd make a good special policeman," the stranger said.

"I never thought of it," Donath replied.

"You'd have a uniform, important duties," the man explained, but Tibor noticed that he wore civilian clothes.

"Could I work some place else?" Donath asked.

"Possibly," the stranger replied. And that was all Donath heard about special police duty for nearly six months. Then suddenly, in late 1949, he was ordered to report for immediate training to a barracks in central Hungary. Here he met a group of good-looking, tough, able young men, most of them, like him, from rural districts. Their officers, however, were from Budapest.

His lessons at the barracks were simple and direct. Said the instructor, "The way to break up a riot is to use guns."

He taught them how to shoot, how to drive military vehicles, how to repair armored cars and how to fight if an assailant attacked unexpectedly in the dark. "There are enemies everywhere," the instructor warned.

At the end of three weeks, the same stranger who had visited Donath in his village appeared in camp, wearing polished boots, flared trousers and a crisp khaki uniform with blue metal decorations. He was attended by several men about Donath's age, who were also in uniform, but with fewer decorations. "Men," the visitor said, "on you Hungary is going to build its greatest defense. You are to be national heroes, watching day and night. You may have to engage in frequent battles. Your first task is to seal the frontiers hermetically and transform our border regions into real fortresses."

From then on Donath's training increased in intensity, and soon he was given the khaki uniform of the border guard, with flaring pants, polished boots and green metal decorations. "We will make it very difficult for enemies to get into Hungary," the eager young men pledged.

But when Tibor and his class were sent to the frontier they found, somewhat to their astonishment, that they were not concerned about people trying to get into the country. Their job was solely to hunt down Hungarians who were endeavoring to escape. For example, Donath was sent to the Yugoslav border, where one might have expected Tito bandits and murderers to try forcing their way into Hungary, but instead he found hundreds of Hungarians fleeing into Yugoslavia.

"We'll soon put a stop to that," Donath's commander said sternly.

On the first night Tibor and his men simply shot any would-be escapees, and after word of this policy circulated through the countryside the stream of refugees diminished. Then barriers were set up and a band of border land thirty yards wide was plowed up so that footmarks could be tracked. Next a barbed-wire fence was constructed at the most likely points of escape. But the commander was not yet satisfied, for he gave Donath a special job which occupied him for three months.

Throughout the plowed strip, Tibor carefully planted mines that would explode if touched by an unwary traveler seeking escape. Sometimes he wired eight or ten of the mines together, so that if one escapee accidentally tripped one of the mines, all the others would explode and catch additional members of the fleeing party.

At strategic points wooden watchtowers more than thirty feet high were erected, with solid bases for heavy machine guns and powerful searchlights which scanned the escape routes all night, every night of the year.

In spite of these precautions, some Hungarians nevertheless managed to slip through the lines and this infuriated the heads of the special police in Budapest. A top officer inspected the frontier and told the guards, "These enemies of the state are inhuman. They catch cats, put them in bags, and carry them to the edge of the mine fields. They release them there and the cats scamper into the mines. They're blown to bits. Then the enemies of the state creep through unharmed. This has got to be stopped."

So a standard order was passed: "If you hear any cats, rake the area with machine guns." This tactic often succeeded in either killing or wounding fugitives in places where no one would otherwise have suspected them, and Donath found real joy in tracking down with dogs some crippled enemy who was attempting to drag a wounded body across the line. Tibor never asked himself, "Why do we never have anyone trying to get into Hungary? Why is it always out?"

When Tibor caught a wounded man, it was his trick to jam the butt of his rifle into the man's stomach, double him up with pain, then strike him with all the weight of his right fist in the face. He would march the captured man, who might be bleeding from gunfire, back to the area headquarters, where he and several other men in green insignia would begin their questioning of the prisoner.

Each of the men in green had some special way of making prisoners talk, and often by beatings, nail pullings, smashing rifle butts onto insteps and other tortures, they forced a single escapee to tell them about others in the area, and when these were caught, they could be beaten and bullied into betraying still others.

"Never stop trying to uncover the whole escape apparatus," Donath's superiors had ordered, and he became so adept at squeezing out of prisoners their last hidden secrets that he was marked for special promotion to a better job in Budapest. When news of his good luck reached him on the border, he was about to set forth on night patrol with his team of dogs, and as he walked through the starry night, he had occasion to reflect upon his good fortune.

"It'll be good to get away from this shooting business," he mused. "I don't mind shooting some man who is trying to escape just punishment, like real enemies of the government. But so many of these people have been women."

He thought particularly of one husband and wife he had shot down some months before. He could not forget them because they resembled in many ways an average farm couple from his own village. The woman, given a few years, could have been his own mother, and after their bodies were dragged in from the mine fields, he had spent some time speculating on what crimes they had committed against the government. It never occurred to him that they might be what they appeared to be: two farm people who simply wanted to leave communism.

He could not imagine anyone wishing to leave Hungary. "The fields are so perfect in early summer," he thought. "And Budapest is such a magnificent city, with the Danube, and the big restaurants and the people."

In the cool night air, with the stars of his homeland over him, he contemplated the kind of job he might get. "I know I have a good record," he reflected. "The captain said so, and so did the other men."

Dreaming of the good things to which he felt he was now entitled, he dared to propose for himself specific jobs. "What I'd like," he said softly, "would be a job driving a big automobile. I'd drive it all around Budapest and sometimes take important people down to Lake Balaton." He spent some time imagining himself at the wheel of his big car, but it seemed so remote that he began to consider other possibilities: "Maybe a good, clean job keeping records somewhere. I like things to be in order and I'd be good keeping records."

His dogs howled at some unseen object in the mine fields, but on this night Tibor Donath was in an expansive mood, and he did not stop to shoot at any vague or imagined figures. "I'd like to get away from the shooting part," he told himself again. "And beating people up. I've proved that I'm as tough as any of the men. Now I'd like . . . well, maybe driving a big car." And he spent the rest of that starry night dreaming of a young man in a handsome uniform, whipping around the boulevards of Budapest.

But instead of driving a car, Tibor Donath was put to work in a job which he did not particularly want, but for which, as events proved, he was admirably suited. One block in from the Danube, on the Buda side, ran Fo Street, the main thoroughfare of the right bank, and on its handsome flank, where the Kossuth Bridge crossed from Pest, stood the prison headquarters of the AVO. It was housed in a sprawling complex of buildings whose five-story façade was nearly four hundred yards long. The first two stories were heavily barred, giving it the appearance of a prison; but it was another feature, not visible from the street, which made this building particularly attractive for the purpose to which it had been put. It had two deep cellars.

It was in the upper of these cellars that Tibor Donath, exchanging the green markings of the border guard for the more important blue insignia of the true AVO man, reported for work. Hiding his disappointment, he went down into the cellar.

"Your duty is to protect the communist government of Hungary from its fascist, capitalist, reactionary enemies," he was told. In a solemn ritual he swore allegiance to the communist leaders of Hungary and then listened in a kind of stupefied amazement as his superiors told him of the many enemies who were daily operating in Budapest. His new job was obviously more important than his last.

"But we shall stamp the enemies out," his officer shouted. "It is our job to track down every one of them. You men have been promoted from the border guards because you have shown that you know how to do this job."

At first Tibor Donath had the naïve idea that he was going to prowl the streets of Budapest searching for enemies of the state, but he quickly learned that lesser AVO men were doing that, and that his job was to accept these enemies when they were brought to his cellar on Fo Street. His job was to exact confessions.

But again he was somewhat disappointed, for interrogations were not entrusted to him. "You're too dumb to outwit a real enemy," his superior told him bluntly. "You get the prisoners in shape for the experts to talk to." These experts were older men, often not in official AVO uniforms, but extremely intelligent. Donath marveled at the skillful way in which they were able to lead prisoners into important confessions.

His job, on the other hand, was to accept prisoners as they came in off the street and to see to it that they were willing to talk by the time the experts got to them. His procedure was direct. When a new prisoner in Tibor's cellar arrived, frightened and uncertain of his future, Donath found it effective to explain to the man in absolutely unqualified phrases that he was beyond all hope of rescue. "No judge can reach you down here," Tibor would say coldly. "Your family won't know where you are. We definitely will not let you correspond with anybody for at least a year. Nobody but me can say how long you will stay here, and I don't care if you stay here till you die. I can beat you, starve you, torture you till you're senseless, and nobody will hear you cry or ever know what I've done. I want just one thing from you. Information. But before I have the inspector ask you for any, I'll soften you up for him first."

Always when Tibor said this, the prisoner would cringe, as if he were to be beaten, but that was not the plan. Tibor led the man to a solitary cell just big enough to hold a cot; it had no windows, no water, a steel door with peep holes, and one brilliant light that was never turned off.

"You stay here alone," Tibor snarled. "You sleep on your back, no other way. You keep your hands always flat on the blanket, no other way. And if your back is turned to the door at any time, the guard will shoot." Prisoners were allowed no shoelaces, no belt, no tie. "If you die in here," Tibor explained, "we'll do it."

The softening-up period had been devised by earlier guards and had been found almost miraculously effective. It consisted first in breaking down any sense of time a man might be trying to maintain. Sometimes a day would be nineteen hours long, the next one fourteen, then one of thirty-six, then a night of three hours. And always the flaming light burned in the eyes. When time had been destroyed, the rest came easily.

After thirty or forty days of this, the prisoner would be moved into a cell with the same inescapable light but with no room either to sit or to sleep. He would be kept here without food for three days, going to the toilet as he crouched and then standing in the excrement. Then, when he was starving, he would be fed with heaps of greasy food, which would make him violently ill, and very salty food, which without water would drive him to torment. Often he would be forced to go to the toilet in his own food dishes. This broke down many men.

At the end of this period, he would again be hauled before Tibor Donath, who would point sullenly to a line of steel-cored rubber hoses on his wall. "Pick the one you want," Donath would mumble. Then, taking the chosen weapon, he would beat the man senseless. At such moments Tibor, who resented the inferior position in which he was still kept, became a gasping maniac, thrashing the weakened prisoner about the head, in the crotch, across the mouth. His eyes would blaze with some inner fury, and then, while he still gasped for breath, he would throw water over the fallen prisoner. When the man could get to his feet, Donath would say coldly, "Next time you'll meet the inspector, and you better talk."

Then he would remand the prisoner to the same routine of meaningless days, blazing lights and total humiliation. Sometimes Tibor's merciless beatings broke bones or wrecked kidneys, but that was not his concern. If bones had been broken, they were free to mend as they wished, and on Fo Street you often saw men with arms jutting off at queer angles, for there were no doctors in the cellars. And if a prisoner died, Donath was empowered merely to close the books on him without any further questions from anyone.

But if the prisoner managed to survive the cellar and graduated into the general compound, then Tibor and his colleagues had terrifying ways of making his life unendurable. There were daily tortures, prolonged beatings, water cures and psychological pressures that were most effective. And there was also Sunday.

Partly because Sunday was a holiday for the guards, and partly because the AVO studiously wished to defile a day still held in affectionate memory by most of the prisoners, Sunday had become a day of special terror. On that day, the guards, after lunch, would idly call out half a dozen prisoners and play games. Tibor was irritated by one of the games, since his inherent lack of strength left him at a disadvantage, but he nevertheless looked on with a kind of savage pleasure when some recalcitrant prisoner had to stand up, his hands at his sides, while a guard would exhibit his prowess by knocking him flat on the floor with a gigantic blow to the mouth. Of course, since the prisoner was forbidden to move, the guard could aim his swing from far back and be sure of landing it on the prisoner's mouth.

On some Sundays Tibor would watch this game, and others, until he became quite excited. Then he would shout for the junior guards to bring out some especially offensive prisoner and he would begin to scream at him and then beat him over the head with the steel-cored hose. Often he would knock the man completely senseless and then kick at him until his face and head were bleeding.

It was Tibor who invented one of the cruelest Sunday punishments. The guards would bring in a dozen prisoners and stand them facing a row of bright electric lights. "Now stand on one foot!" he would command. The combination of intense light and one wavering foot brought forth unexpected reactions. A man would begin to scream, another would faint, a third would start dancing. But no matter what happened, if any prisoner made so much as a single move, all the others would be savagely beaten. Not the one who moved. He was safe. Tibor noticed that when a man on one foot would begin to faint, he would utilize every ounce of physical and moral energy at his command to save his fellow prisoners from another beating.

"There he goes!" the guards would shout. And they would beat the prisoners left standing until they all collapsed.

"There they all go!" the guards would shout as the prisoners fainted and screamed and went mad.

Tibor's other contribution was both extremely simple and extremely effective in subduing difficult prisoners. He stood the man facing the wall where a bright light shone into his eyes. Against the man's forehead he would place the point of a pencil, putting the other end against the wall. "If you let that pencil fall, you will be beaten to death," Tibor warned his prisoners. And there the man would stand, pressing the pencil against the wall with his forehead, trying not to faint because of the bright light in his eyes. Sometimes when a man left this punishment after a couple of hours, the pencil would go with him, imbedded in the thin flesh of his forehead.

There were other aspects of Sunday that even Tibor, when he subsided from his fearful rages, preferred not to think about. Since his early youth he had not cared much for girls, but in the house on Fo Street he began to hate them. Because on Sundays the women guards, who always seemed to Tibor more vengeful than any man could ever be, would drag to their own quarters some male prisoner and force him to undress. Then they would torment him in hideous ways that most of the men guards refused even to talk about. The AVO women used knives and hairpins and cigarette lighters, and the things they did to the male prisoners made even their male colleagues shudder.

"Somebody ought to stop them," Tibor said one day, and this was his undoing, for a spy within the Fo Street prison reported this uncommunist remark to the head of the prison, who called Donath before him.

"Did you speak against the women guards?" asked the official, a thin man with a sharp nose and penetrating eyes.

"I only said—"

"Shut up! Liar!" the thin man screamed. Rushing up to Donath, he shoved a report under his nose. "Look at this!" he shouted hysterically.

He showed Tibor a study of confessions, and it proved that almost twice as many enemies of the government confessed after a Sunday afternoon with the women guards, as confessed following treatment by Tibor and the male guards.

"Are you an enemy of the government?" this man shouted.

"No," Tibor pleaded. "I've had a good record."

"Yes, you have," the thin man agreed in a surprise move which caught Donath unawares. "And for that reason I'm not going to dismiss you. But you've got to learn that meaningless sympathy for criminal elements who oppose the government is in itself a crime against the government. I'm sending you to Recsk."

Tibor, trained in hardness, stood firm. "Yes, comrade," he said without blinking.

"A year or so at Recsk will prove to you," the thin man said softly, "how despicable and unworthy of the least sympathy are the enemies of our government. You'll come back a better man."

When Tibor Donath returned to his quarters he looked with eyes of incalculable hatred at each of his colleagues. One of them had betrayed him. One of them had caused him to be transferred to the worst prison in Hungary, a place terrible for the imprisoned and the guards alike. For a momentary advantage some foul friend had betrayed him, yet such was the system that he dared not even speak of the betrayal, nor allow his manner to admit that it had happened.

"One of them did it," Donath swore silently to himself as he surveyed his friends. "Some day I'll find out which one, and I'll slowly strangle him, I'll gouge his eyes out, I'll . . ." He had to stop his phantasmagoric dreams lest he fall into a screaming rage.

"I'm going to Recsk," he said simply. He had to speak to relieve the unbearable hatred.

None of his friends reacted to the statement, some lest they be reported for having shown undue sympathy with what was, on the surface, merely a routine shift in assignment, and one because he did not wish to convey his sense of joy in the punishment for which he was responsible. In terrible hatred, Tibor Donath completed his arrangements. That night a truck picked him up for the fifty-mile ride to northeast Hungary, where the infamous prison of Recsk stood.

As he left the headquarters on Fo Street, his friends stood stolidly in the doorway watching him go. Still not a flicker of human emotion crossed their faces, and he in turn sat stiffly in the truck without turning his back to try one last time to penetrate their masks and uncover the man who had spied on him. "I'll find him," Donath swore. "I'll cut his heart out." Indulging in such fantasies, he allowed the full fury of his hatred to consume him, and by the time he reached Recsk he was practically a maniac and well prepared for his new assignment.

The truck that sped Tibor Donath to his disciplinary assignment in Recsk also carried, cooped up like an animal in a quarry box, a political prisoner named Ferenc Gabor, who was also on his way to Recsk, but for discipline of a much sterner kind. Even as he rode he was doubled up into a tight knot, the walls of his cage pressing in upon him on all sides. He had a gag in his mouth and his hands were bound by iron chains. His crime, if he had committed one, had been forgotten. He was identified merely as a man who would not talk, and the last words his brutal guards at the headquarters on Fo Street had flung at him were, "Well, Mr. Silent, you'll talk at Recsk."

I now propose to describe the horrors of this ultimate AVO prison in the words of Ferenc Gabor, a broken man of thirty-five when I met him in Vienna. This is what he said his years in Recsk were like.

"Five kilometers outside the little village of Recsk, northeast of Budapest, we entered the main gate of the notorious prison where I was to live for three years. I was handed a uniform which had to last me as long as I lived there. It consisted of an old AVO suit from which the official leg stripes had been removed, to be replaced by wide red bands which could be seen from a distance. Shoulder patches and other marks of rank had been cut off. I was a figure in khaki.

"Recsk formed roughly a square, one thousand yards on each side, and was known as escape proof. At least only one group of prisoners ever escaped from it. Around the prison grounds ran an intertwined barbed-wire fence nine feet high and charged with electricity. Thirty yards outside that ran a second fence, also charged with electricity. Fifty yards further out was a third fence. These fences might conceivably have been penetrated by a determined prisoner with a rubber-handled wire cutter—except for the fact that between the first and the second the ground had been carefully plowed and harrowed so that footprints would show, and hidden beneath the fresh soil were numerous powerful mines. In addition, the middle fence was studded every fifty yards with tall watchtowers containing machine guns and searchlights.

"On the inner fence, facing the prisoners, were signs which read, 'Warning! If you touch this fence, you will be shot.' On the outer fence, facing any accidental tourist or villager who might wander toward the prison, was a similar warning: 'Government property. Trespassing forbidden. You may be shot without warning.'

"But it was not the fences that made Recsk intolerable. It was the life inside. Only the most hardened AVO men were assigned here, and since duty at Recsk was for them a kind of punishment, they made our lives so hellish that we often prayed for death. Believe me, what we experienced at the headquarters in Budapest was nothing compared to what we went through at Recsk.

"Toward one end of the compound there was a small granite outcrop which rose about 280 feet in the air. We were given the job of reducing this hill to gravel which would pass through a small sieve. Each prisoner was required to produce two hand trucks full of gravel each day. Since we had no goggles, many men lost their sight from flying fragments, but this did not excuse them from work. The food was kept inadequate to support such work—

they didn't care if we died. During the first year the average prisoner lost about seventy pounds in weight.

"If I did not make my quota of gravel each day, I was forced to stand in a clammy cell for the entire night with cold water up to my knees. Then, if the guards wanted to play with me next morning, after I had no sleep, they would make me carry a hundred-pound rock up and down a ladder fifteen times. If I fainted, they resumed the game when I recovered.

"But the worst thing about the punishment was that we knew the AVO were able to corrupt our fellow prisoners. They had planted among us spies who would inform on anything we said, or even seemed about to say. For this the spies got extra food.

"We worked from four-thirty in the morning until nightfall with only a brief rest for lunch, and after work we were marched back to our quarters, which consisted of two compounds containing small rooms, into each of which eighty men were jammed. For three years we were allowed no books, no papers, no pencils, no radio news, no newspapers. We could have no visitors, no mail, no parcels of food, and we were not permitted to tell our families where we were. We did not know for how long we were there, nor for what reason. We lived a life of blank terror, in which we could not even discuss anything with our fellow prisoners, for fear the AVO would know of it.

"Month after month we lived lives of utter exhaustion, too weak to work and too tired to sleep. The only break in our schedule came when the AVO summoned us at night for interrogation or games. Then we were beaten and abused and humiliated. They screamed at us to talk, but they never said what about.

"One night when a sallow-faced guard with pasty yellow hair, whom the others called Tibor, had beaten me with unusual cruelty, one shouted, 'Let's make him the white mare.' To do this, they inserted a broomstick under my knees, then doubled me up into a tight ball, lashing my wrists to my ankles. We were deathly afraid of this punishment, for it placed such a stress upon the stomach and heart that we knew no man could bear it longer than two hours. And if the AVO were particularly playful they sometimes made a man into the white mare and forgot him. Then he died without anyone's caring.

"But even normally, this treatment was almost unbearable, for after a man had crouched on his knees for some time in this position, while his taut muscles were beaten with rubber hoses, he would have to fall over, and then new portions of his body would be exposed to the hoses.

"On this night they had another man and me for the white mares, and after they had beaten him until he was numb all over, he rolled against the hot stove, and his left hand had become so insensitive that he was not aware that it was pressing against the fire. In this way he burned off two fingers and half his palm. He became aware of what was happening only when he smelled his burning flesh. Of course the AVO men knew, but they were laughing.

"One of the cruelest tricks they played on us, however, was a psychological one which cut deeply into one's sense of reason. Each month we were paid a good wage for our work on the rock quarry. When we got our wages the AVO always lectured us, 'This proves that communism does not make slave labor of its prisoners, the way capitalism does.' Then they charged us for our food, our barracks, our electric lights, and for the services of the guards who protected us. We were left enough for one package of cigarettes a month. But on any report sent out from Recsk there appeared the reassuring fact that its prisoners were being paid regularly at the going rate.

"I said that one group escaped from Recsk. There was a tailor who by diligence manufactured out of his old AVO uniform one that looked real. Then from scraps he painstakingly built up a cap, and ornaments, and when he was properly fitted out, he assembled a group of daring fellow prisoners and with a make-believe tommy gun in his arms, boldly marched the whole contingent out the main gate.

"'We're bringing in some dynamite,' he told the guards, and off his crew went into the woods and freedom.

"The AVO response to this was diabolical. Without making any fuss, they quietly rounded up 250 prisoners, anyone who had been seen talking or loitering at meals or laughing. Those who had fallen below their quota at any time during the last two weeks were also grabbed. It was a sickly time, because the prisoners knew that something terrible was about to happen, and everyone seemed eager to spy upon his neighbor in hope of escaping the dreaded and unknown punishment.

"At first the retribution was simple. The 250 prisoners were herded into a special prison within the prison. Expecting all sorts of extreme punishment, they found what happened to them less than what they had expected, but after a week of constantly increasing pressures—beatings, wormy food, unusual and hateful punishments centering on the sexual organs—it became apparent that the AVO at Recsk had decided to reduce these 250 men gradually to the level of screaming animals.

"They succeeded. The experience of that prison within a prison was so horrible, so far beyond the imagination of man either to conceive or to accept, that within two months there was not a sane man left. And each day when the guards threw the animals their meat, laughing at them as they fought and tore at one another for the inadequate chunks, a voice would announce over the loud-speaker, 'You are in here because your friends escaped.'

"The hatred that was thus built up against the clever tailor and his brave crew was terrifying, but perhaps not even the guards knew how inhuman it had become, for when they caught one of the escapees, some three months later, as he was trying to flee Hungary, they brought him back to Recsk and led him into the prison within a prison. The voice in the loud-speaker cried, 'Here is one of the men whose escape caused you your misfortunes.'

"Within two minutes after the recaptured prisoner was thrown among his former mates, he was torn to pieces."

Among the AVO men who conceived this plan was Tibor Donath. His years at Recsk had hardened him to the point where he was totally incapable of the softness he had once displayed in Budapest. During the long dreary nights in the barrenness and cruelty of Recsk, pairs of guards formed attachments for each other, and whenever a new batch of young guards arrived, the older men would study them attentively. On one such occasion Tibor noticed a handsome young man from one of the country districts and promptly made overtures to him, but the new guard repulsed him, and that week the young man was mysteriously reported for holding out for himself some of the cigarette money collected from the prisoners.

The new guard was severely punished, for he had been in trouble before arriving at Recsk, and when he returned to the AVO barracks Tibor saw with great inner glee the manner in which the young man tried to penetrate the basilisk stares of his friends, endeavoring vainly to determine who had spied upon him. But Tibor's moment of triumph was not unmixed with fear, for the young man seemed so choked with hate that Tibor thought, "I'll have to be careful of him." But before long some other friend secretly reported the young man for some other offense, and he disappeared from Recsk, to what ultimate punishment Tibor never knew.

Sometimes in the guards' games with prisoners Tibor would stand aloof for a long time, watching, with a fascination he did not comprehend, the punishment of some especially recalcitrant enemy of the government. He would not take part in the beatings or the torments, until suddenly one of the new prisoners would remind him vaguely of some schoolboy associate, and in great agitation he would grab a rubber hose, and, in blows twice as fast as any other guard used, he would thrash the bewildered victim until the man almost fainted with agony.

"Speak! Speak!" Tibor would scream, dancing about the man like a demon.

But in spite of his moments of apparent aberration, Tibor Donath was far from being insane. He knew what he was doing, and when the wild beatings were ended he would sometimes sit alone in his quarters and feel resentful over the fate that had sent him to Recsk. "What's the use of beating prisoners up?" he mused to himself. He was not sorry for the prisoners. As enemies of the state—and never once did he question that they were members of the criminal element that was trying to destroy Hungary—

they deserved no pity. It was what such endless punishment did to the guards that bothered Tibor.

"I'd like to get a desk job," he often told himself. "In Budapest. I'm orderly and enjoy keeping things straight. I'd be good in a desk job." Then the poisoned dream would return and he would have to acknowledge to himself how unhappy he really was. "What I'd really like would be to drive a big car." His shoulders would weave as if he were turning smooth corners fast and he would steer with his hands. In dreams he would be hastening down the boulevard with someone very important in the back seat, and he would be happy. Then a bell would ring, and he would have to admit that he was not in Budapest, but in Recsk.

At such moments he had learned to stay away from prisoners. "If I saw one of their dirty faces now, I'd kill him," Tibor admitted to himself. And he had no special desire to kill anybody, for although no embarrassing questions were asked when a prisoner died, it probably got onto a man's record somehow, and Tibor had learned that in Recsk the most important thing was never to give anybody—not even your closest friend—a single thing to report to the command. Because in Recsk everybody spied constantly on everybody else.

It was while brooding about his exile to Recsk that Tibor Donath discovered a fact which he had not previously admitted to himself. "I'm going to be an AVO for the rest of my life," he mused one day. "And why not? I get good money, the best things in the stores, and if I ever get back to Budapest I'll be able to have a car of my own. This is a pretty good life, and nobody'll ever get anything on me again." He forgot the inconveniences of Recsk and thought of the good days ahead, when he could be more of his own master. "I'll have a good apartment in Budapest and a car and maybe an officer's rank. What would I have had if I'd stayed in the village?" He laughed at the comparison and whispered to himself, "Recsk can't last forever. Then . . . fun."

It was therefore with a sense of real relief that Tibor Donath learned that his disciplinary sentence to Recsk was ending. His assignment was to the provincial capital of Gyor, where he quickly became one of the ablest sergeants. The brutality of the Gyor headquarters was famous in that part of Hungary, and he did nothing to diminish the reputation.

Finally, in the spring of 1956 he was given a second chance in Budapest. He still did not get the desk job he wanted, but he did buy a car with his increased pay and he did find the acceleration of life in the capital as exciting as he had hoped. "We have got to be on special guard," his officers told him. "Something's happening in this city, and we've got to know about it."

Arrests were much more frequent now than when Tibor had first served in Budapest, but the crowding in the cells had become so critical that prisoners had to be released more quickly. What this meant to a man in Tibor's job was that he was left a shorter time in which to exact confessions, and was therefore inclined to use more brutality and to use it sooner. To add to the congestion, infamous concentration camps like Recsk had been abandoned, so that again the pressure to discharge trivial prisoners was increased, and Donath found himself setting men free whom in the old days he would have kept for incredible tortures.

The general agitation which marked the summer of 1956 escaped Tibor's attention, for the elite AVO spies did not bother to tell him anything, while choice political prisoners who might have something to divulge by-passed his authority. All he knew was what he was told: "Something's happening. Find out what it is." But he found nothing, for the dismal procession of students, petty agitators and fools brought before him had nothing to tell.

Therefore, one of the Hungarians most astonished by the events of October 23 was the farm boy, Tibor Donath. "They're firing at the radio station!" an underling reported, and with mouth agape Tibor watched a truck load of reinforcements leave his building for that battle.

When others departed for Stalin Square, "where a big riot is taking place," and to the offices of *Szabad Nep*, "where they're destroying the paper," Tibor felt that all

Hungary was falling apart. This feeling increased during the twenty-fourth, when sickening reports of the previous night's doings filtered down to his level.

"They murdered AVO guards at the radio station," an AVO man who had been there reported. "Murdered them!"

"What for?" Tibor asked.

An officer appeared, ashen-faced, to announce, "The whole city's in revolt. It's got to be put down. If you see anyone who even looks suspicious, shoot him."

Assignments were then made and another officer said, "We're going to surround Parliament Square. Weak-kneed politicians will probably make promises if people gather there. We'll make our promises with machine guns. Have you heard what happened to our men at the radio station?"

As the gruesome news accumulated, Tibor Donath fell into a dull panic. "Why doesn't the government do something?" he asked himself over and over. Noises in the city terrified him and he began looking frantically into the faces of his friends, wondering which one had betrayed him into such a dreadful plight. But in their no longer stolid faces he saw panic like his own. Night was particularly bad, and he ordered all the lights on. When he heard noises from the cells below his office, he thought for one fearful moment that perhaps even his prisoners were joining the frenzy, and he shouted, "Go down and see what's happening."

He was pleased, therefore, when direct action became possible, and on the morning of the twenty-fifth he hauled a machine gun to the top of the Ministry of Agriculture building overlooking Parliament Square. As masses of people carrying flags began to come within range of his gun, he whispered to his companions, "We ought to fire now," but they said, "We will, later." But the wait allowed his sense of confusion to deepen, and it was not until the man on his left nudged him that he felt a sense of stability.

"Look at those tanks!" the man whispered.

Tibor Donath stared down at the line of massive Russian tanks, their huge guns pointing at the crowd. "They'll keep order," he said reassuringly.

The other AVO man nodded eagerly, and it was with sadistic relief that Tibor and his friends saw the AVO men on the Supreme Court roof finally begin firing volleys into the crowd. His sense of reality was restored.

"Now we shoot!" he yelled, releasing the safety catch on his own gun.

Before the next command could be given, Donath with dumb amazement saw a Russian tank turn its heavy guns and deliberately aim at the AVO men on the opposite roof. "What are they doing?" he half screamed. The man on his left gasped, and there was a dull roar as the tank fired. Tibor could see the AVO men on the Supreme Court roof fall backwards from the force of the blast, and he was too weak to fire his gun.

Then, as his horrified eyes watched the Russian guns slowly change direction and end their traverse facing him, he began to scream, "They're going to fire on us!"

The AVO man on his left did not bother with words. Deserting his gun, he dived for shelter, but Tibor stayed where he was and began firing. Forgetting the impending doom of the Russian guns, he madly sprayed machine-gun bullets into the crowd below him. Each human being in that crowd he personally hated. Somehow they had caused this idiotic, this outrageous falling apart of the world.

A tremendous explosion shattered the walls about him, but in a terror which consumed and yet directed him, he shifted to the abandoned gun on his left. More bullets were sent into the stampeding crowd, while a second blast of Russian shells tore at his security.

When the gun was emptied, when the rubble had collapsed about him, he dumbly rose and stumbled across the roof. Looking down for the last time in stupefied amazement at the Russians and at the dead Hungarians littering the square, he left his post. "What's happening?" he muttered to himself.

With the instinct of a clever animal, Tibor ripped off all AVO insignia as he descended the Ministry stairs. He did not depart by the main door, but slipped into an alley and

The AVO Man   111

then another and on down a back street far from the
Danube until he came at last to Koztarsasag Square, a most
ill-named square, considering the use to which it had been
put: Republic Square was where the communist party of
Hungary had its headquarters and where the AVO had
one of its most diabolical underground prisons.

Tibor Donath remembered having visited this headquarters once when things were going well in Hungary.
Then everything had seemed neatly ordered, with intelligent men directing the nation. Now there was chaos. A
man in a gray suit was shouting to no one in particular,
"Damn Rakosi and Gero. They've taken a plane to
Russia."

"Where's Rakosi?" another man yelled, not having
heard the news.

"What are you doing here?" a communist official asked
Tibor.

"The Russians fired on us," Donath said.

"Everybody's firing on us," the official snapped. "Our
own police, our own soldiers, our own people."

"What's happening?" Donath asked weakly.

"You damned AVO are all crazy," the communist
shouted. "Go down in the cellar where you belong."

Bewildered by the confusion in which guns were being
hauled into window emplacements by men who knew
little about guns, and in which orders were being shouted
where there was no one listening to carry them out, Donath slipped down into the cellar, where he was to spend
six days of increasing terror.

About two hundred other AVO men were there at one
time or another—the number fluctuated—and many prisoners. Occasionally an ashen-faced AVO man would appear with shocking news, "They hung one of our men at
the Petofi statue."

"But I was there only a few minutes ago."

Or some super-tough AVO man would swagger into the
cellar with a captured freedom fighter, and he would begin
beating the boy until an older man, aware of the desperate
situation in which they found themselves, would growl,
"Get back on the streets."

Among the prisoners who suffered a special hell in this cellar were some women and children, and one day Tibor saw that some of his wiser colleagues were staying close to the women.

"What are you doing that for?" Tibor asked.

"When the time comes for us to leave this cellar," the older AVO men explained, "one of these women walks out ahead of me."

"Do you think there'll be shooting?" Tibor asked.

"Look!"

From a window which could be peered through if one stood on a box, Tibor saw with horror that all the riffraff of Budapest—the kind he used to thrash with rubber hoses—had gathered in Republic Square. "Why don't the tanks drive them away?" he wondered, but then his last memory of how the Russian tank had behaved recurred, and he concluded that if the world had gone mad his job was to save himself.

"Do you think they'll let you through?" he asked the AVO man who planned to use the woman as a shield.

"Of course," the older man said. "They always do."

But Tibor had a better plan. Looking again at the wild-eyed fools in the square outside, he had a premonition that perhaps they were going to shoot if any AVO man appeared. So he went over to another group of prisoners, who flinched in expectation of a beating, and said to one about his own size, "I'll take your clothes."

He was not a minute too soon, for through one of the front windows a hose was thrust into the cellar and water began flooding the refuge of the AVO men. Another was jammed through a second window, and it was clear that if the flood of water continued long, those in the cellar would have to evacuate, whether the men standing guard outside intended to shoot or not.

At this point Tibor Donath slipped out a back door and down another series of alleys, but he was so fascinated by what was going to happen in the square that he rashly doubled back toward that point, standing inconspicuously in his new civilian clothes at the edge of a crowd that was about to witness one of the major events of the revolution.

It was these events in Republic Square to which I alluded in the opening paragraphs of this section. They were a blot on the revolution, and since there are incontrovertible photographs of what transpired, Soviet Russia had the opportunity of reproducing them in a white paper which attempts to prove that decent officers of a decent government were callously murdered by capitalist criminals.

As the waters rose in the cellars of the communist headquarters, whose upper floors were already occupied by freedom fighters, the trapped AVO men had no alternative but to drown or surrender. They chose the latter, and from the front doors of the ominous building there issued forth about a dozen typical AVO men. They had been guards at Recsk, where they had doubled men up into white mares and killed them with kicks. They had been watchers in the deep prisons at headquarters, slashing and beating with rubber hoses. They had been border guards, shooting and tracking down with dogs men who would be free. They were the sadists, the monsters, the perverts and the murderers.

A dreadful silence greeted them as they stepped into Republic Square. Men who had suffered under their terrible ministrations looked at them. No one moved forward to touch them. Instinctively the crowd moved back, as if still terrified by the power of these inhuman jailers.

It is possible that the tragic massacre of Republic Square might have been avoided—although this is only speculation on my part—if a young freedom fighter had not spotted, in the rear of the AVO procession, the prisoners who had been kept underground for months and even years.

"Look at what they do to us!" the young man shouted.

And from the prison came women and children starved nearly to death, men too crippled to walk, men with blue welts across their faces, and men whose minds were deranged. A ghastly sigh went up, the pathos of a generation.

Then one of the older AVO men appeared, pushing a woman in front as a shield, and this set loose the awful fury of the crowd.

Some of the AVO men were clubbed to death. Others were shot. A few tried to run but were caught and killed. Some of the dead were strung up by their heels. An outraged society had suffered enough at the hands of these inhuman monsters, and its revenge was overwhelming.

For days no one would bury the dead AVO men. Buckets of lime were thrown on them by health patrols, but even this decency was not accorded two fat bodies that lay in Republic Square for a week. People came to see them and workmen would stand over them and weep bitter tears of frustration, recalling the ten years of fraud and terror under which they had labored to support such AVO men.

The reason these two bodies were not disturbed was that across their chests had been pinned, for the public to see and know, documents found on the men when they were shot. The first body was that of a major whose papers stated that for his meritorious service to the communist party his monthly salary was being raised to 18,000 forints.

"I get 800," a man from Csepel said as he looked at the document.

The other man was not an officer, and his pay slip read 10,000 forints a month.

Nothing that was said about the AVO caused more bitterness than these two official documents. Workmen were outraged to discover that men who had contributed nothing but terror to the nation had regularly received more than twelve times the salary of a man who made bicycles, or bread, or shoes.

I cannot condone the massacre at Republic Square, but I can understand it. The great revolution of Budapest would have been cleaner if Republic Square had not happened, but it would have been too much to expect men and women who had suffered the absolute tyranny of the AVO not to have retaliated. One of America's finest and gentlest newspapermen, the dean of our corps in Middle Europe, said bitterly after he had reviewed far less of the AVO terror than I have reported, "I was in Budapest at the time, and although I believe that revengeful death accomplishes little, I devoutly believe that the human race would have been better off if Hungarians had assassinated every one of the 30,000 AVO. The world's air would have been a little cleaner."

But beyond revenge lies the necessity of trying to understand why communism requires an AVO to perpetuate its system. From what I have seen of communist regimes, I am satisfied that each communist country has its exact equivalent of the AVO. The reader can be absolutely certain that a similar force operates in Russia, in Bulgaria, in Latvia, in North Korea, in China and wherever else communism has been in operation for over one year. Evidence from escapees who have fled these countries is unanimous in defense of this contention.

Why must communism depend on such dregs of society? We must answer either that communist philosophers are inherently evil beyond the capacity of a normal imagination to conceive—which I am not willing to claim —or that no matter on what elevated plane communism begins its program of total dictatorship, it sooner or later runs into such economic and social problems that some strong-arm force is required to keep the civil population under control. It is this latter theory that I accept.

What happens is this. When communism is wooing the workers in Csepel, all kinds of exaggerated promises are made if they seem likely to awaken men's aspirations and their cupidity. These promises are couched in such simple terms and such effective symbols that they become immediate goals of the revolution, and I think we have seen in Hungary how eagerly the fulfillment of those goals was awaited when communism did triumph.

But the promises were so vast and unrealistic that there never was a chance of attaining them, and probably the organizing communists who made the original promises knew then that they were totally beyond any hope of realization.

Review briefly what communist agitators had once promised the Hungarians who appear in this book: consumer goods such as they had never known before, increased wages, increased social benefits, shorter hours of work, improved education for everyone, a greater social freedom, and a government directly responsible to the working classes.

Under communism such promises were never even remotely capable of attainment, for although Hungary had the natural wealth wherewith to produce the new consumer goods required under the communist plans, the communists lacked either the organizing ability or the honest intentions needed for the translation of raw materials and labor into consumer goods. Any system—either state socialism or enlightened capitalism—would have had to work intelligently and hard for at least ten years to achieve what the communists promised. Under communism, with its irrational production, its gross favoritism and its downright incapacity in management, there was never a chance of success. Within two years the people of Hungary realized that the promises which had seduced them would never materialize, and that instead of freedom they had purchased only tyranny.

When an awakening of such magnitude begins to spread across a nation, the communist leaders, who from the first have been aware of the impracticality of many of their promises, must take steps to silence the protests that naturally begin to arise. At first this is simple. The police pick up and sentence to long years in jail those intellectuals who begin to see through the empty promises.

But when this relatively simple task has been completed, the police must next begin to arrest workingmen who are asking when their pay increases will begin, and housewives who want more bread and cheaper shoes for their children, and clergymen who have started to protest the earlier round of arrests. Soon the ordinary police begin to balk at such senseless arrests, so a special police must be organized.

I find it difficult to believe—and for this reason some Hungarians say I am naïve—that when an AVO is first instituted in a communist country, its communist leaders intend it to become an instrument of national torture. I rather think that frightened bureaucrats call it into being with the firm intention of controlling it and keeping it a rather simple force which will operate to protect their position. Later, like Dr. Frankenstein, they find that they have created an uncontrollable monster, which ultimately entangles them in its evil grasp.

"Not so," reason my Hungarian friends. "When communism took over our nation, every important leader had already been trained in Russia. Rakosi and Gero were Soviet citizens. In Moscow they had been carefully taught that communism must rely on terror, and when they arrived to take control in Budapest, they already carried in their pockets precise plans for the AVO. When they built it, they knew what it would become. For they knew without it communism could not exist. Proof of our reasoning goes beyond the personality of those horrible men, Rakosi and Gero. Proof is that our first AVO officers were trained in Russia. Our terror did not mature, as you suggest. It was transplanted, fully grown and ready to operate.

"Furthermore," reason my friends, "if any communist leader in Europe succeeds in taking his country into communism, he will have to rely upon his own special AVO. And it will not occur by accident. It will be organized carefully, and its initial cadre of officers will definitely have been trained in horror in Moscow."

I am not sure who is right, I in my belief that an AVO matures by a process of inevitable deterioration in a communist society, or the Hungarians who point out that Lenin preached the introduction of terror and the liquidation of opposition in the first days of a communist regime as a calculated strategy of power. In either event the end is inevitable total terror.

But what I am sure of is this: If Japan were to go communist tomorrow, as some of its citizens desire, within a year it would have one of the world's most terrible communist secret police. If Indonesia goes communist, it will know the same sullen fury as Budapest knew. If the communists I have known in India succeed in taking that vast land into communism, they should realize that with the inevitable collapse of their cynical promises will have to come a secret police that would terrorize Amritsar and Delhi as they have not been terrorized since the day of Tamerlane. I am sure that communism must have an

AVO to silence the protests of the people it has defrauded.

From what has been related so far, we can see how subtly the presence of an AVO poisons the entire life of a society. The process is one of interlocking incriminations. In a factory a spy ring reports on each workman. Within this spy ring, inner spies report on the work of lesser spies. The AVO itself is ridden with spies, and even the upper circles of the communist control groups are checked constantly by their own spies. There was in Hungary no prison cell so remote but what the man in the next cell might be a spy, there was no AVO post so insignificant but what some other AVO man was spying upon it.

One of the awful aspects of interrogating Hungarians regarding their life in communism is their admission that they had to take into constant consideration the fact that their neighbor, or their schoolteacher, or their butcher was an AVO spy. The number of men and women I have met who were betrayed into weeks of brutal AVO treatment by intimate friends was a constant shock to me. In fact, this studied tearing down of the fabric of normal society was perhaps the AVO's outstanding contribution to Hungarian life. Their goal was to incriminate every living Hungarian, and many of the dead. When everyone was incriminated, then any normal social relationship was impossible, and only the AVO could thrive. It is against such a conclusion that we must judge the men and women who gathered in Republic Square that November day and finally came face to face with the evil which had corrupted the entire nation. That an outraged citizenry should have risen to smite their tormentors should be no surprise.

In studying the AVO dictatorship in Hungary, I repeatedly found that my senses had been numbed by the magnitude of the story and that, like the world at large, I had reached a point of cynicism at which I muttered, "Well, the camp at Recsk was probably bad, but not that bad." Any mind has difficulty in focusing upon the planned corruption of an entire nation.

But on three occasions, when I had reached such numbness, I found that some trivial question of mine would lay bare a minor story of such intensity that it would illuminate the entire subject, and I would for a moment perceive what communism in Hungary must have been like. For when the mind has abused its elasticity in trying to engorge a horror of national magnitude, it can still accept the limited story of one man.

One Sunday afternoon in Vienna I was talking with a sturdy Hungarian coal miner about conditions in the mines at Tatabanya. We discussed wages, working conditions and how a miner qualified for a paid vacation at Lake Balaton. ("Never the miners, only the bosses.") This big workman was so clear in his answers and so unemotional in his attitude toward Hungary, that at the end of a most rewarding interview I pointed to his rugged physique and said, "Well, at least one man seems to have prospered under the regime." I thought that had ended an excellent interview, but it was the phrase that actually launched it.

"You should have seen me when the AVO got through with me," he said.

"Did they arrest you?"

"Yes. They held me for thirty-three days. When they let me go I could barely walk, and my wrists were as thin as this."

"They give you bad treatment?"

"The worst," he said simply and without rancor.

"What for?"

"They saw my suit."

"What about your suit?"

"It was an American suit. An old one, but the only one I ever had."

"Where did you get an American suit?" I asked.

"That's what they wanted to know."

"What did you tell them?" I pressed.

"The truth. During the war I had been deported by the Germans as a forced laborer. I wound up in Linz, where the Americans found me. Before I could get back to Hungary I worked for them for a while, and an American engineer bought me this suit at the PX."

"So what did the AVO do?"

"They said that any man who had an American suit must be an American spy."

"Then what?"

"They beat me every day for thirty-three days, and starved me."

"And all because you were wearing an American suit?"

"Yes."

"You mean to say an AVO man could pick you off the streets and hold you in prison for thirty-three days simply because he didn't like your suit?"

"He could have held me for thirty-three years."

Even more deeply moving was a casual conversation which to me still epitomizes the AVO terror. More than anything else I stumbled upon, this accidental account remains in my memory. I was interviewing a Hungarian housewife whom I had met at the border and whose fine, warm face had led me to think, "There's a woman I'd like to talk to. I'll ask her how women faced the revolution." During our discussion she gave me much valuable information which I have used in the section dealing with housewives during the days of peace. She was eminently sensible about everything, so free from a spirit of revenge and with such a warm good humor that I was congratulating myself upon having found a woman with a perfectly average story, free from all emotional complications.

But as I was putting away my notebook I happened, by the merest chance, to look down at the woman's right hand and casually I asked, "What did you do to your hand?"

"The AVO broke it," she said simply.

"Those fingers?"

"They broke them with a rubber hose."

"And those two holes in the back?"

"Lighted cigarettes."

"Why?"

"A friend of mine escaped over the border."

"Did you help him?"

"It was a girl. I didn't even know about it."

"But they arrested you?"

"Yes."

"What for?"

"On the chance that I might know something."

"Was it pretty bad?"

"When I said I didn't even know the girl was going they shouted, 'You liar.' Then a man punched out my teeth."

There is no point going on with her story. It was cruel to the point of nausea—thirteen months of endless brutality and persecution—yet there was nothing unusual about it. Other prisoners had their hands broken and their teeth punched out. But there is one aspect of Mrs. Marothy's story which was different.

Most of the names in this book are fictitious for the reason that the people involved are still terrified that the AVO will track down their friends and relatives and torture them endlessly. Each of the people whose stories are told here will recognize himself, for in each instance at the end of the interview I said, "Now you make up a name for me to use." They understood and did so.

But when I finished talking with this particular woman she said boldly, "Go ahead and use my name. It's Mrs. Maria Marothy. I suffered so much at the hands of these beasts that this can be my only revenge. Let them know that in freedom I hold them in contempt." Mrs. Marothy found a new home in Ohio, and I can imagine her walking into a store in some small town and shopping in broken English. But I fear that if the storekeeper, or one of the other customers, were to ask her, "What happened to your hand?" no one in Ohio would be prepared to believe her answer.

There was one feature of Mrs. Marothy's story which I myself was unable to believe. After she had explained her broken hand, she added, "Maybe another story would show you how much we despised the communists. Who do you suppose is going to come out with us?"

"Is it someone I might know?"

"You know him."

"Who?"

"Imre Horvath, Jr."

It is difficult to explain to an American the profound shock this simple statement made both on me and on the listeners at our table. We were stunned. Because Imre Horvath, Sr., was probably the most universally detested Hungarian communist. During the height of the Budapest revolution this shameless diplomat had the gall to rise in the United Nations plenary session in New York City and claim that the Russians had a right to return and that all good Hungarians welcomed them, since the uprising was merely a civil disturbance engineered by fascist warmongers. When news of Horvath's pronouncement in the United Nations reached Hungary the rage against him was extreme. Many refugees told me that they would have killed him if they could have got to him. He was unquestionably their most despised enemy.

"Is his son leaving Hungary?" I asked.

"Indeed!" Mrs. Marothy assured me. "He lived in our apartment house. He knew what the AVO had done to me, and he was ashamed of his country. When he heard about his father's speech in the United Nations he swore he would leave Hungary forever."

"Did he do so?"

"Can you keep a secret?" Mrs. Marothy asked.

"Of course."

"He has left Budapest. He will join us tomorrow."

It seemed so unlikely that a young man of Imre Horvath's, Jr.'s, significance would be allowed to escape that I showed my disbelief. Mrs. Marothy saw this and said, "Believe me, all decent Hungarians are mortally ashamed of what Horvath, Sr., did to us. His son most of all. Believe me, he will come out."

But days passed and he did not appear. I left the border and he was still not among the refugees. Back in New York I kept watch on the headlines and Imre Horvath, Jr., did not appear among the list of refugees, so I concluded either that Mrs. Marothy had never known him and had made up the story, or that she was mistaken about his intentions.

Then, on the last day of my work on this book, at the last moment when changes could be made, news came that Imre Horvath, Jr., had fled to the west. He said little, but what he did say provided one of the worst indictments of the system which had driven him and Mrs. Marothy into exile: "I was especially shocked when I talked to my

father about the fate of Laszlo Rajk [nationalist communist leader executed by Stalin's order in 1949]. I said everybody in Hungary knew that scores of innocent people were
being tried and executed. He replied, 'It is better to
liquidate hundreds of innocent people than to let one
guilty person remain in the party.' "

The most revolting story I stumbled upon was told by
a man whose name would be recognized throughout much
of Europe and America, for he was for some years a world
champion in an exacting sport. I had been trying for some
time to check the charge made by many refugees that
athletes were given special treatment in Hungary and that
they had no cause to fear communism. As one refugee had
explained it, "The communists figured that athletes were
big and dumb and would never cause political trouble, so
they were fell fed and pampered because if they won
against the democracies, it gave communism good public-
ity."

It was among a group of refugees at the border that I
found this world champion, and we had a delightful talk.
He was very quick and lean and had laughing eyes which
let you know immediately that he knew why you were
asking so many questions.

"Sure, we had it much better than the average man," he
admitted. "Nobody ever bothered us much, once we
signed the agreement."

"What agreement?" I asked.

"Well, when they took you out of the country, say, to
England or France, you agreed that if for any reason you
ran away from the team and didn't come home, the police
would arrest your whole family and keep them arrested
till you did come home."

"What if you didn't have any family?"

"Then your friends."

"So you signed?"

"Oh, sure. You knew they would apply the rule anyway,
so there was no reason for not signing."

"Would you say that athletes were used for propaganda
purposes?"

"Certainly. What else? It gave us a big thrill in Paris

when we beat the Frenchmen. We players were thrilled because we had beaten France. But the AVO were thrilled because we had beaten noncommunists."

"Were there AVO with the team?"

"With every team. They were very strict outside the country, because if one of us ran away, it would be the AVO's neck."

"But no rough stuff?"

"Oh, no. Athletes were special."

"Why don't you compete any more?"

"The two bullets in my shoulder."

"What two bullets?"

"The ones the AVO put there."

"On a trip?"

"No," he explained. "After several trips to England and France I suddenly said to myself, 'Hungary is a hell of a place to live. I'm leaving.' But at the border they shot me down."

He showed me the huge indented scars in his shoulder and I said, "How'd you get such big scars? They operate on you with a shovel?"

And he replied, "Dum-dum bullets. They explode inside."

He proceeded to tell the same old story of beatings, indignities and three years of slave labor in a filthy, deadly coal mine. Only two features were new, and by this time I was so deadened to what I knew was coming next that I took only desultory notes: "The AVO man who supervised our team testified that in Paris the English referee had spoken to me twice, so this proved I was a spy. I got my three-year sentence for spying, not for trying to escape." And the other note in my book reads: "In twenty-one months at coal mine 50 killed, 250 crippled. Drownings, pit gas, cave-ins. Nobody gave a damn."

Then, as so often happened, as we were about to part, this clean, happy, wiry champion said almost gaily, now that he had gained freedom and had left the evil behind, "But I'm not a crybaby, remember that. When things were worst I always told myself, 'Well, anyway, you missed Major Meat Ball.'"

"Who was he?"

"It was a she."

"Major Meat Ball? An AVO?"

"Of course. It was only the AVO that you remembered."

"Where'd you meet Major Meat Ball?"

"Her name was Piroshka, which is Russian for meat ball. I met her in the AVO torture cellars at 60 Stalin Street, in Budapest. I can describe her exactly. Anybody who ever saw her could. She was a redhead, plump, about thirty-five years old. She was pockmarked and had fat lips. She was about five feet two and not bad-looking except for the pockmarks. Everyone knew she was a horrible sadist.

"I say I missed her, that means I missed the worst part. But I had enough. She went into the cell next to mine with a bottle and told the man, 'Urinate in it.' Then she brought it in to me while it was still warm and said, 'Drink it.'

"Once she drew a little chalk circle in my cell and told me to walk around it. I did so for eight hours.

"With women prisoners she was unbearable. She did things to them that even now I can't describe. But as I said before, I was forever grateful that I missed her. The man in the next cell didn't. She came in to see him one day wearing only a dress. 'You must get hungry for a woman,' she said, nuzzling against him. 'Well, I get hungry for a man, too. Tonight I'm going to take you up to my quarters.' So that night she took him to her quarters and got undressed. But just then an AVO burst into the room, shouting, 'You rapist. Messing around with my wife.' This AVO called some other AVO, and they began beating my friend almost to death. They ended by holding him down and ramming a thin, hollow glass tube up his penis. Then they beat him till it broke into a million pieces. That was how Major Meat Ball operated."

Weakly I asked, "How do you know?"

The world champion said simply, "I had to hold the guy when he went to the toilet."

A stranger to Hungarian history is tempted to say of the AVO terror that it was the worst in the experience of this long-troubled nation. But in certain respects that statement would not be true, for Hungary has known six major terrors, and the communist one is merely the last in an ugly line.

Between the two epoch-making battles of Mohacs, the first (in 1526) a notable Turkish victory over Hungarians and the second (in 1687) a triumph of Hungarians over Turks, Budapest and its surrounding countryside lay under Turkish domination. At intervals, this Ottoman terror was brutal, but when the dominance of Muslim rule was finally accepted by the Hungarians, the Turkish dictatorship relaxed into a kind of heavy-handed, corrupt occupation. In both extent and stupidity, this Turkish terror was a dreadful experience and a deterrent to Hungarian progress.

In 1919, in the midst of the chaos that accompanied the end of World War I, Hungary experienced a native-born terror about which confusion and debate continue to this day. In that year, Admiral Horthy, of the old Austro-Hungarian fleet, became regent of Hungary and instituted a reactionary dictatorship that lasted until 1944. Life in Hungary during this period was not exactly pleasant, but it probably never reached the levels of debasement screamed about by communist agitators, who refer in almost every speech to the "Horthy fascist terror." Nevertheless, Horthy must be blamed in part for Hungary's quick surrender to communism. Invoking his memory, the communists had easy entry into Budapest.

In 1944 Hungary entered into a one-year Nazi terror, which can be precisely defined. If one was an average, well-behaved citizen, the Nazi occupation was not too bad. Everyone testifies to that. It was disagreeable, and Hungarians came both to despise and to ridicule the Germans, but life was not intolerable. But if one was Jewish, the Nazi terror was hideous beyond description, and the worst accomplished by the AVO fell short of what the Nazis did. It was this German terror that was automatically extended by the home-grown regime of Ferenc Szalasi for a brief period in 1944.

In addition to these three terrors which extended over the entire nation, there were two others of sometimes awful character that touched only parts of the country. In Transylvania, to the east, mixed populations consisting of Hungarians and Rumanians have frequently in history been shifted back and forth between those two nations. When Rumania controlled Transylvania, Hungarians living there had a miserable life, and when the converse was true, Hungarians proved that they could be just as beastly overloads as the Rumanians had been the year before.

The same situation prevailed along the southern border, although this time it was Hungarians and Serbs who bedeviled each other, and if the worst incidents of both the Transylvanian and the Serbian troubles are collected, they surpass in horror the AVO terror.

Therefore one would not be well advised to use careless superlatives in describing the AVO terror. It has had its precedents in Hungary.

But the peculiar horror of the AVO terror and the characteristic which sets it apart as particularly loathsome is this. In each of the preceding terrors there was little sanctimoniousness or abuse of truth. Turks had come to Hungary to convert the citizens to Islam or to rule them harshly if they rejected the new religion. When Hungarians refused to accept Islam, they knew what to expect, and there was no mouthing of platitudes, no corrupting of speech to prove that what was happening was pleasant for the Hungarians.

In the Nazi terror a grim power which had occupied Hungary handed down simple rules for the governing of a nation and the occupation was not labeled an experiment in brotherhood. It was a cold-blooded, efficient military operation, and if one happened to be a Jew, it brought death.

Even the Horthy dictatorship avoided the worst abuses of the AVO terror, and certainly it fell far below communism and its perversion of common sense. It did not defraud the peasants on Monday and then try to convince them on Tuesday that this was to the peasants' benefit. It was a calculated policy of repressing large areas of the population, and it ended as it had begun, in revolution.

And of course the Transylvanian and Serbian miseries

were the openly declared retaliations of people who had been at enmity for centuries. No oily words could have glossed over the hatreds that exploded in those areas.

It remained for the communist terror, as administered by the AVO, to debase Hungarian life and at the same time to announce that this was being done as an act of friendship. When Russia introduced her terror into Hungary she stole the produce of the land and called it "elevating the peasants." She victimized the workers and called it "the dictatorship of the proletariat." She corrupted every institution of government and called it "the new society." She stole from housewives, contaminated children, allowed the old to die in poverty and called it "world brotherhood." And through the AVO she declared war on every Hungarian citizen and called it "peace."

The first five terrors in Hungarian history were honest brigandage and murder. The Soviet terror was a sanctimonious cynicism. It remained for Russia to introduce into the terror business a completely new dimension: hypocrisy.

For this reason the AVO terror can be termed the worst in Hungarian history, since it did the most damage to the social institutions by which any nation must be governed. It is this crime of loathsome sanctimoniousness which will do Russia the greatest damage in her future intercourse with nations like Italy and India. The fundamental hypocrisy of her position has been laid bare.

As one of the Hungarian intellectuals has said, "Terror as terror is cruel, but terror clothed in hypocrisy is really unbearable. Our revolution proved that."

I talked with well over a hundred Hungarian refugees and was always careful never to be the one who first brought up the question of the AVO, yet in almost every conversation the dreaded name was mentioned. At such times I tried casually to follow the diabolical avenue wherever it led. Under no possible circumstances can I accuse myself of having sought out stories of AVO bestiality. They grew out of any normal discussion of life under communism.

This naturally led me to query the foundations upon which the AVO was built. I found that the non-officer personnel was often from backward rural areas. ("This brute was so illiterate that when he was sent to bring ten of us out of the compound he didn't trust his own ability to count. So he made us lie down on the ground, one by one, so that he could go back and forth checking his figures.")

Many were homosexual, some had been petty criminals and a surprising number had minor physical defects which they tried to hide. One characteristic of the AVO damns communism and makes it doubly hypocritical: the typical AVO officer had been a bully boy for the Horthy regime, a servile tool of Hitler's Nazi occupiers, and a brutal operator for the Szalasi dictatorship. These were all fascist governments, and fascism was supposed to be the deadly enemy of communism. But when the Soviets assumed control, they adopted into their system the worst elements of the fascist police force and called them good communists. Many of the AVO didn't even know what communism was.

Some officers, however, were dedicated party members and many had acquired good educations. Those who progressed most rapidly in the system were apt to be graduates of the Moscow school of terrorism, and their loyalty to Russia was unquestioned. There is no record of any of them having betrayed the Soviets during the fight for freedom.

AVO men were selected at first with scrupulous care, their loyalty to communism being the prime requisite, their ability to administer punishment impersonally being the next. But in the later years, when the corps was expanded to more than 30,000 uniformed members plus untold spies, some diminution of quality undoubtedly took place, and there are verified accounts of young men who were impressed into AVO services against their wishes.

A young university student told me the steps whereby a friend of his was converted into an AVO spy who would report on professors and fellow students. "In 1952 the AVO said to this fine young man, 'You will be our operative in the University.' My friend refused, so the AVO said, 'If you don't, we will kill you.' He was a man of principle, so he said, 'Go ahead.' And they added, 'We will also kill your father and your mother and your sister.' So he became, unwillingly, an AVO spy.

"But he was not a good spy. He wouldn't report all he saw, so they devised a most diabolical trick. They said, 'We have placed a second spy in your classes . . . to check on you.' Then you see what his problem was. If Janos Balint makes a suspicious argument in class, must I report him? If I do, he gets beaten up by the AVO. But if I don't, perhaps Jonas Balint is the second spy and he is saying these things only to test me. It was after such confusion that my friend considered suicide, but with fiendish cleverness the AVO were able to judge when a man would think of suicide and they called him in. 'If you commit suicide,' they warned him, 'we will kill your entire family.'

"So for five years my friend went through this spiritual agony. He had to tell enough to keep the system going. He had to judge every incident as to whether the offender was the second spy. And he had to try to guess whether there was indeed a second spy. But do you know what was cruelest about it all? I was his closest and dearest friend. He had trusted me all his life and I grew to be his only safeguard against insanity. We would analyze these things together and if ever there was a man in trouble who could trust another man, he should have been able to trust me. But there would come moments, unexpectedly, when he suddenly looked at me in terror. Something I had said had made him ask himself, 'Is he the second spy?'

"Then we would look at each other in silence. And the terrible veil of suspicion that communism clothes us all in would descend between us, and after a while he would begin to weep, not because he had distrusted me but because the AVO had so corrupted all of life that a man could no longer trust even himself."

When the revolution struck, most AVO men remained loyal to the Russians, but this did not prevent some of the more wary from escaping into Austria and seeking refuge in countries overseas. At least two got to Canada, and I suspect that more than four reached America. On December 7, Hungarians queueing up for visas at the American consulate in Vienna spotted an AVO man standing boldly in line, waiting for his clearance to the States. He disappeared when challenged. In late December, an American businessman appeared on the border in a daring rescue mission which saved several Budapest Hungarians from the AVO. Later, while he was celebrating in Vienna with some of the people he had rescued, they suddenly froze to silence. A dark figure had passed near the group, and the frightened Hungarians whispered, "That man is an AVO." But before the accusation could be checked, the accused had flown to the United States.

Any figure on the total number of AVO men can only be guesswork. Most commonly heard is a total of 30,000 plus 2,000 top-secret plain-clothes men and another 5,000 loosely attached spies. From all reports that I have heard, probably not over 200 were killed during the revolution, in spite of the national fury against them. This means that about 36,800 survived to be used again by the new communist regime.

After the Russians had reconquered Hungary, the Soviets undoubtedly sent some AVO men to intermingle with the refugees and to make their way into Austria, where they were to establish some kind of discipline and a grapevine between Vienna, Paris, Montreal and New York. On the night of December 6, such a team struck boldly in Vienna and severely beat up a leading Hungarian refugee from whom they needed information concerning the whereabouts of one of the Esterhazy family. On that same day Austrian police tracked down a clandestine radio with which the AVO cell in Vienna was maintaining communications with their Soviet-controlled headquarters in Budapest.

The AVO mentality was so alien to normal experience that observers frequently asked, "Were such men peculiar to Hungary?"

They were not. We know that similar organizations operate in all communist nations surrounding Russia and in Russia itself. It is one of the dismal characteristics of humanity that in any society there is an irreducible minimum of men and women who enjoy sadistic work and who would volunteer for it if the opportunity arose. Communism is the form of government which surrenders its governing obligations to such men.

If communism attained power in any nation in the world tomorrow morning, by tomorrow night it would have initiated its own AVO of psychotics, murderers and sadists.

And lest Americans smugly think that they are exempt from such a danger, let me be specific. If communism in America required an AVO—and it would—we could easily find men and women who would enjoy kicking a Negro to death or shooting down small businessmen as they tried to flee to Canada and freedom.

But what happened to Tibor Donath? After he had spied in horror upon the retribution in Republic Square he hid out for ten days, until he was certain that the Russians would recapture the city and establish a new communism. Then he smartly reported for duty at headquarters, where he sustained a great shock. "The AVO had been disbanded," he was told. But he regained his composure when he found that a new special police group was being formed.

"In view of your record, you can be an officer," the communist official assured him. "You'll have a car. Your job will be just about the same, but this time you'll wear a blue uniform, and we're going to call you 'R Troops.'" It is these "R Troops," the former AVO, who now patrol Soviet-occupied Hungary.

7   The Man from Csepel

A few months before the Budapest revolution, the communist government of Hungary published an official guide to the country, composed by devoted communists and fine-tooth-combed by a board of strict AVO censors, whose job it was to see that it contained only material hewing to the party line. In view of what was shortly to take place, the passage on Budapest's industrial section of Csepel was ironic.

"Csepel," wrote this apologist in early 1956, "is the largest of all these industrial areas. . . . The Rakosi Metal Works of Csepel includes eighteen factories and one hundred and fifty shops. The radial drills, vertical boring and turning mills made here are exported to many countries of the world, as are Csepel motorcycles, bicycles, sewing machines, kitchen utensils and pumps. In Csepel are also an oil refinery, a leather works, a felt mill and a paper mill. Along with this industrial development has gone the building of department stores, a hospital and clinics, and a splendid sports hall. A statue of a worker reading in the park of the housing estate is a symbol of the new Csepel—a result of the long struggle of the workers of 'Red Csepel,' who, in 1919, were the first to join up in the workers' battalions to defend the Republic of Councils. The Csepel workers remained faithful to their traditions also later on; by resisting the evacuation order of the Nazis in 1944, they saved the important factories and their equipment."

If, when erecting their statue of the happy communist worker reading his Karl Marx in the cool of the evening, the Russian leaders of Hungarian communism had wanted an ideal subject to pose for the statue, they could have selected no one better fitted than Gyorgy Szabo. At thirty-five he was an unusually handsome skilled worker in the Rakosi Bicycle Works. He was about five feet ten, a lean, rugged, gray-eyed, dark-haired workman with deep lines in his face showing a resolute character and a dimple in his chin showing a love for the good life. He had a sturdy wife and three healthy children. Szabo describes himself more simply. "I was," he admits, "the classical type of communist worker. I even looked like one."

From the age of seventeen, Gyorgy had worked in Csepel, as had his father before him, and his mother. Since he was a son of proletarians, he was not only attracted to the secret communist party of the 1940s; he was also the kind of workman the reds were seeking. Accordingly, he began to listen to the subtle invitations he and young men like him were beginning to receive.

"It sounded good to me when they said, 'When we take over, you won't work like a slave.' Our life in Csepel in those days was very hard and we liked their next promise: 'When we run this factory, you won't work for a man in a big automobile. It'll be the workers who own the automobiles . . . and the factory too.'"

Szabo was also intrigued by the promise that under communism there would be committees, formed only of workmen, who would determine work loads and pay. "That made sense. Under capitalism somebody in the office simply handed out decisions, and we had to obey them. The communists also said that each year we workmen would get paid vacations at the swanky resorts on Lake Balaton, where in those days only the rich could afford to go. We were promised better houses. And before long every man was going to have a motorcycle."

The promises of communism were so inclusive and so cleverly worded that in 1944 Gyorgy Szabo, who was then exempt from military service because he was working in the munitions part of what was later to be renamed after the contemporary communist leader, the Rakosi Metal Works, secretly joined a cell of communists. In this exciting and dedicated group of men, Szabo imagined himself to be working for a communist Hungary in which the vast promises of his party would be fulfilled.

In the spring of 1945, when Szabo was twenty-four years old, the communists launched a major propaganda drive which was destined to end in their controlling Hungary. Szabo says, "It was very exciting. Of course, we understood that not all the promises could be put into operation right away, because Hungary had to be rebuilt after the destruction of the war. And it was explained to us that we needed Russian guidance for some years, since they knew what communism was and we didn't."

So although Russian planes and guns had destroyed much of Hungary in freeing it from the Germans, Gyorgy Szabo and his communist friends had to buckle down under Russian leadership and repair the damage. Promises were also suspended because of the various economic plans, during which every worker had to work about one-third more time each day for no extra pay, just in order to fulfill the plans.

Szabo, a good communist, understood the necessity for such overtime. "We were told that we had only a short time to make ourselves strong before the capitalists and reactionaries would try to capture Hungary and revive the bad old days."

Nor was Szabo immediately disturbed when he realized that each month the norms which determined how much work a man should do were being quietly upped. "I didn't worry about it because I had become a Stakhanovite and had even won a medal for doing more work than any of the men on my shift."

Looking at Szabo's powerful hands and strong physique, you can believe that he led the pack. He would be a good worker under any system, and with little imagination you could picture him at the Boeing works in Seattle or on the Ford assembly line at River Rouge.

"I have always loved my job," he admits. "It was good work, and until I got married I didn't realize how little money I was getting paid. But when I did take a wife, I asked for a vacation and was told I was too valuable and could not be spared. Then I saw that all the people who got the paid vacations at Lake Balaton were the same types that used to get them before. The managers got the vacations, and the Russian advisers, and the AVO spies and the party bosses. But the workers rarely got there.

"And the same types of people had the automobiles, and the fur coats, and the good food. I did not speak to anyone about this, for I was beginning to be afraid of the AVO spies. But one day a friend of mine from the Rakosi Bicycle Works, without saying a word to anyone, escaped to Austria. The AVO picked me up on suspicion of having helped him, and for two days it was pretty bad. They beat me almost all the time, but in the end I convinced them that I had nothing to do with his escape. After the beating they gave me a little card with three phone numbers, and if I ever heard anything about my friend, or anything else,

I was to call one of those numbers and report it. Every once in a while the AVO would check to see if I still had the card."

By this time Gyorgy Szabo had discovered that being a member of the party really didn't help him very much. He was forced to work harder than ever before in his life, for less money, and with less chance to make a protest. Nor did being a good communist protect him from AVO beatings. It didn't get him vacations on Lake Balaton. It didn't get him a better house.

"In fact," he asked himself one day, "what does it get me?"

Only more work. Sometimes two or three nights a week he would have to stay in the plant after work to hear long harangues about the glories of communism. "Always things were going to be better in the future," he says ruefully. "What made me angry was that we were always harangued by men who weren't doing any work themselves."

Then there were the enforced protest meetings. "We marched for the Rosenberg trial, for the workers of Paris, for the Koreans. During the Korean War we had to contribute four extra days a month of unpaid work to help the Chinese communist volunteers, and we protested against the American use of germ warfare.

"There were some weeks," Szabo says, "when I hardly saw my family. And when I did see them, I had hardly a forint to give them. For all this work I received only 1,000 forints a month, not enough for a suit of clothes—I could never even save enough money ahead to buy one suit of clothes." Gyorgy Szabo's meager funds—his rewards from communism—went mostly to buy his children's clothing.

Inside Gyorgy's family a quiet protest had begun against such a defrauding system. It had been launched accidentally by Gyorgy's wife, who had begun to ask questions. "Why is it?" she first asked. "You're a good communist. You attend party meetings and march in parades. Why can't we buy in the good stores?"

"You can buy anywhere you like," Gyorgy said. "Only have enough money."

"No, I mean in the good stores, where the prices are cheaper."

"Look," he snapped. "If you want to go into the big stores in Pest, you can go."

"But the stores I mean are here in Csepel." And she told him of the three good stores into which she couldn't go. First there was the very good store for Russians only, and here the best things produced by Hungary were on sale at eighty-per-cent reductions. Second were the stores that were almost as good, for Hungarian officials and AVO men, where the reduction sometimes amounted to seventy per cent. Next came the stores for minor officials, where the goods were of fine quality and the prices reasonable. "And when everything good has been used up by those stores," Mrs. Szabo complained, "what's left is placed in stores for us workers, and we pay the most expensive prices. Why is this?"

Gyorgy said, "It's that way with everything, I guess."

But his wife persisted, "I thought you told me that in communism everybody was going to be equal."

"After they get things properly worked out, everybody will be equal."

"Until then, Gyorgy, will you please see if we can buy in one of the better stores?"

But in spite of his good record and his unquestioned loyalty to the party, Gyorgy found that no ordinary worker could possibly buy in the good stores. "They're for the big bosses," he was told. "You wouldn't feel at home in big stores like that."

That night Gyorgy spoke to his wife in the secrecy of their home. "We're worse off than we used to be," he confessed. "Before, we never had any money either, but we could dream, 'When I get a lot of money I'll go into the biggest store in town and buy one of everything.' But now they don't even let you in the stores."

One of the most moving stories of the revolution concerns the manner in which this hard-core communist finally took arms against the system. It was not because he was a reactionary, for he had fought in defense of communism. It was not because he was a devout Catholic, for he never bothered with the church. Nor was it because he had intellectually weighed communism and found it to be a fraud. It was because of a football game, and as one listens to his account of this memorable game, one suddenly realizes that all over Hungary, in those bitter days, men were discovering the nature of the deception that had been practiced upon them . . . but always as the result of some trivial occurrence.

"It was a fine day in Budapest," he recalls, "and I was walking down Voroshilov Street to the big new stadium. Even if a man didn't have enough money for a new suit, he set aside a few forints for football, because it was a pleasure to go into the stadium. You cannot imagine how beautiful it was. It was about the only thing the communists accomplished. I have been told it's the biggest in Europe and the most beautiful in the world."

Hungarians' love for sport is legendary. In a nation with about the same population as metropolitan New York City, a completely disproportionate number of world champions has been produced in fencing, swimming, riding and track. For example, in the Helsinki Olympics of 1952, Hungarians copped an improbable number of first places and as a team ranked third among nations. But in recent years it has been soccer which gladdens the heart of a Hungarian, especially the Csepel man. This intricate game reached Hungary long after it had thrived in England and France, yet in the matter of a decade the Hungarians were world champions, sometimes thrashing their more famous competitors by such large scores as to lead one foreign expert to charge, "If magicians were driven out of England at the time of Merlin, I know where they went. To Hungary."

"This day there was a great game," Szabo recalls. "A championship team had come over from Vienna, and we won. Of course, we usually win, but what was unusual at this game was that I sat behind some visitors from eastern Austria who spoke Hungarian and I told them their team was going to lose. We talked a little and I said,

'If you have come all the way from Vienna, why do you sit in the cheap seats?'

"They said, 'We're workmen, too.'

"And I asked, 'But how can you afford such good suits?' Then I asked many more questions. 'How can working-men save the money for a trip all the way to Budapest?' 'Where do you get so much extra food?' And there were other questions that I didn't ask them—why they weren't afraid of the policeman who came by, and why they laughed so much, even though their team was losing." Big, tough Gyorgy Szabo stares at his hands and adds, "From that football game on, I never stopped asking questions as to why dirty capitalists in Vienna could have such things whereas good communists in Budapest couldn't."

When Gyorgy Szabo returned to the bicycle works after the football game, he began asking new questions. "Where do all these bicycles go that we are making?" They went to Russia. "Am I making more money than when I worked for the capitalists?" He was making less. "Have the prices of things gone up or down?" They had gone far up. "Why are all these Russians still here?" They were here to police Hungary.

Finally he asked the most damning question of all: "Am I any less a slave now than I was then?" The answer was terrifyingly clear: "Then I was free. Then I was not afraid to laugh or to speak my mind. It is now that I am a real slave."

From then on Gyorgy Szabo, "the classical communist worker," began to speak openly. He found that most of the men in the Rakosi Metal Works felt as he did. He says, "We said to hell with the AVO. If they arrested all those who complained, they would have to arrest us all."

He stopped going to party meetings. He refused to march in fake processions. He allowed his work norm to drop back to what a human being might reasonably be expected to perform. And he began to tell his children that they, and their father and mother, were caught up in a hopeless tragedy. "I taught them to hate the regime," he said. "It sits on the necks of the workers."

It was in this frame of mind that grim-lipped Gyorgy Szabo heard, on October 22, 1956, that some students were going to stage a demonstration against the government. Without telling his wife where he was going, he went into the heart of Pest and made inquiries as to where the meeting was to be. He was told that some students had gathered in the Technical High School in Buda. He crossed the river and walked up to the brightly lighted building. Inside, he listened in dismay as one clever young man after another delivered what seemed to be pointless talks, and he thought to himself, "This won't get anywhere."

But then, from the rear of the meeting, a man in a brown windbreaker like his own rose and said, "I should like to ask one question. Under what right are Russian troops stationed in our country?" The question electrified Szabo, and in the following minutes he was overjoyed to hear young men who spoke well expressing all the doubts and hatreds he had accumulated against the regime.

"Something big is going to happen," he muttered to himself, and then another workman, from another part of the hall, spoke Szabo's mind for him. "I don't have the good language you men have," this man said haltingly. "I'm a worker, from Csepel. Men like me are with you." At this announcement there was cheering, and that night Gyorgy Szabo went home determined that if "something big" did happen, he was going to play his part.

Late the next afternoon he was working at the bicycle shop when news arrived that students had begun marching in the streets. Instantly he told his fellow workmen, "There'll be trouble. They'll need us." The same thought had struck many workmen in Csepel that afternoon, and at dusk they marched forth. Of 15,000 workmen in Szabo's immediate area, all but 240 ultimately joined the revolution. Of these 240, two hundred were assigned by the revolutionists to guard the plants against sabotage, meaning that out of 15,000 workmen on whom communism depended for its ultimate support, only forty remained loyal.

It would be repetitious to recount in detail Gyorgy Szabo's actions during the three stages of the revolution.

In the attack on the radio station, it was a truckload of arms and ammunition that he had helped dispatch from the Csepel ordnance depot which turned the tide. The young fighters who holed up in the Corvin Cinema used Csepel guns and were in large part Csepel workers. The Kilian Barracks, having little ammunition of its own, depended upon Csepel equipment and Csepel men to use it. Throughout the victorious battles of those first days Gyorgy Szabo and his fellow workmen provided the sinews of the revolution. Gyorgy himself was shot at many times, helped burn tanks, and in general proved himself to be the firebrand that most once-dedicated communists turned out to be when they finally took arms against their oppressors.

In the second, peaceful stage, he performed an even more important task, for it was under his guidance—he being an older man than many of the Csepel workers—that the Csepel workers developed their plan for the utilization of the Rakosi Metal Works in the new Hungarian state. Their plan was certainly not reactionary, and many people in America would surely have deemed it arch-communism, but for the Hungary of that day it seemed a logical and liberal solution. "What we proposed," Szabo says, "was a nationalized factory, owned by the state and supervised by it, but run in all working details by workers' committees. Our engineers would set the norms in terms of what a human being should perform. Norms would not be handed down by some boss in an office. There would be no AVO, nor anyone like an AVO, allowed in the plant. And any of the good things, like vacations and doctors, would be shared equally. We were very certain about that."

By the afternoon of November 2, Gyorgy Szabo and his committee had concrete proposals to offer the government. Szabo also had suggestions for what pattern the government itself might take. "We thought a liberal-labor party would be best, one which stressed the production of things for people to use and to eat. No more munitions for Russia. We wanted personal freedom, courts, political parties, newspapers and a free radio. And we insisted upon one right which we wanted very badly, the right to travel to other countries. We wanted to see what workers were doing in other countries." As for the general spirit which ought to guide the new Hungary, Szabo proposed, "We don't want the aristocracy returned, or any selfish capitalists like the kind we used to know. If the Church won't meddle in politics, it ought to come back the way it was before. We should all work for a decent government and we should try to be like Austria or Switzerland or Sweden."

When these fine dreams were destroyed by the Soviet batteries on Gellert Hill, whose shells ripped through the Rakosi Metal Works, Gyorgy Szabo found himself in the middle of the prolonged and bloody battle which marked the third part of the revolution. It was a determined workers' army which faced the Russians, for Szabo was joined by every available Csepel man, and this sturdy group of workers was to give the Soviets their toughest fight in the battle for Budapest. Szabo himself used guns from the Csepel armory, helped spray Csepel gasoline on Russian tanks, lugged ammunition to the antiaircraft gun that knocked down the Soviet plane, and thought up one of the neatest tricks of the campaign. Whenever a group of Csepel men found an isolated tank which they could not destroy, some young workers of incredible daring would leap upon the turret, where no gun could fire at them, and plant there a Hungarian flag. If the Russians inside opened their hatches in an effort to dislodge the flag they were killed and the tank immediately destroyed. But if they allowed the flag to fly, the next Russian tank they met would blaze away at a supposed enemy and blow it apart. Obviously such a trick could work only a limited number of times, but until the Russians caught on, it was a beautifully simple maneuver.

But finally the Soviets triumphed, and with the annihilation of Csepel the situation of Gyorgy Szabo and his men was desperate. As we have seen, they quietly melted into the countryside and escaped capture. What they did next forms a heroic chapter in the battle for Budapest, and in order to appreciate their heroism we must pause to analyze the situation they faced.

The Russians dominated the city, and through a puppet government made decisions of life and death. All food supplies were under Russian control, and only those Hungarians whom the Russians decided they could pacify were fed. The Russians also controlled the police, the health services and every operation of the city's existence. Anyone who dared oppose this Russian control ran the risk of starvation, imprisonment or execution.

In addition, the Russians had another horrible weapon, one which the Hungarians feared more than any other. On the afternoon of November 6, while the fight for Csepel still continued, Russians began rounding up Hungarian men, tossing them into trucks, and carting them off to secret railway depots where they were herded into boxcars for shipment to perpetual slavery in Siberia. Possibly by plan, Russians allowed a few such deportees to escape so that news of this inhuman punishment could circulate throughout Hungary. To most Hungarians, such deportation to Siberia was truly worse than death, and many resisted it to the death, as their bullet-riddled bodies were later to testify.

So all of what Gyorgy Szabo accomplished in the days following the termination of actual fighting he did under threat of death, starvation, imprisonment by the reincarnated AVO and deportation. Here is what he accomplished.

On November 11, the workers of Csepel reported for work. Both the Hungarian government and its Russian masters had made earnest entreaties to the workers in heavy industries to resume production lest the country collapse in a runaway inflation. Communist leaders tried to cajole miners and electrical workers into producing their prerevolutionary norms, and were promised food and full wages if they did so.

Szabo met these government enticements by helping to organize a general strike. He was only one of many to whom the idea occurred at roughly the same time, but in his factory he did have the courage to stand forth clearly as the leading spirit. He knew that the AVO spies who had been replanted in the works would report him as the instigator, but he no longer cared. "We will work long enough to replace the 3,000 bicycles stolen from freedom fighters by the police," he announced, "then we will quit."

In other plants similarly brave men stood up and made similar proposals. All over Hungary the strike proved to be amazingly successful, even though the leaders were constantly threatened with death.

The economic life of the nation was brought to an absolute standstill. Trains were halted and no industrial electricity was provided during critical hours. Truckers refused to bring food into the starving city if it had to be turned over to the communists for distribution, and women would not work at cleaning buildings. Factories in Csepel lay idle, and those in nearby Kobanya worked only enough to provide minimum essentials to the workers themselves.

The government raved and made new threats. Then it pleaded tearfully, "Dear workers, please go back to work. Don't let inflation destroy us." When this appeal failed, wage increases were offered, then additional issues of food to "workers who were loyal to the cause of workers' solidarity and world peace."

No appeal made the slightest impression on the men of Csepel, and with consummate insolence they even refused to answer the government's proposals. Szabo says, "We had reached a point in which not a man cared if he was shot or starved to death. We would not co-operate with our murderers." They even published a poster which read, "Wanted. Six loyal Hungarians to form a government. The only requirement is that they all be citizens of Soviet Russia."

Day after fatal day the strike continued. From Csepel it spread to other regions of the city, and from there to the countryside. In no section of Hungary was greater bravery shown than in the coal mines of Tatabanya. Here men who could be easily identified for future retaliation and torture refused to go into the mines to bring out the coal required for heating and lighting the new communist paradise. Against these miners the frantic Russians brought their full power of coercion. Food was cut off from Tatabanya, and any stray young men who wandered from the crowd ran the risk of being picked up for Siberia. Troops were moved in, and tanks, but to no avail. The mines stayed shut. The Soviets, having run out of ridiculous promises by which to lure these stubborn miners, resorted to threats of death, but the miners replied, "Shoot one man and we'll flood the mines."

At this point it is appropriate to consider the meaning of this general strike. There had always been, during the three stages of the Hungarian revolution, a chance that Soviet propaganda might eventually turn a crushing moral defeat into a shabby victory. They could claim that reactionary forces had led the revolution. They could tell uncommitted nations in Asia and Europe that broken-down nobility had tried to engineer a coup d'état. They could and did point to Cardinal Mindszenty's speeches as proof that the Church was about to seize control of Hungary. And they could claim, legalistically but spuriously, that a legitimate Hungarian government—the Janos Kadar puppet regime—had specifically invited them back into Hungary to put down a counterrevolution. They could also claim, spuriously, that under the terms of the Warsaw Pact of 1954 they were not only entitled but also obligated to return. Finally, in order to explain away the participation of students, writers, youths and workers in the actual fighting, they could, and had already begun to, feed out the official line that the students were impetuous, true, but underneath it all really dedicated communists; that the writers were nervous types who didn't know what they were doing; that the youth were misled by evil adults; whereas the workers acted on the spur of the moment out of hot-headed but understandable patriotism. I regret to say that such excuses would probably be accepted in India, parts of France, parts of Italy and Indonesia, where they would accomplish great harm.

But no propaganda, no matter how skillfully constructed, can ever explain away the coldly rational, unemotional strike of the Csepel men. It was conceived by workers, and by workers in heavy industry. It was carried out without the aid of writers, students or churchmen. Of greatest importance was its duration and determination, proving that it was neither hastily conceived nor emotionally operated.

The Csepel strike was a solemn announcement to the world that the men whom communism is most supposed to aid had tried the system and had found it a total fraud. Most of the leaders of this Csepel strike were members of the communist party. They had known it intimately for ten years and had, in some cases, even tried to help direct it along the promised channels. There was not, so far as I can find, a single excited intellectual or daring philosopher of freedom involved in this strike.

This was communism itself, rejecting itself. This was a solemn foretaste of what communists in India or Italy or France or Indonesia would themselves conclude if they ever had the bad luck to live under the system. This was, for Soviet communism, a moral defeat of such magnitude that it cannot be explained away.

When the world propagandists for communism have explained everything to their satisfaction, how will they explain the fact that of 15,000 workers in one Csepel area, only forty remained true to the system? How will they explain the fact that the other workers fought Soviet tanks with their bare hands? And how will they explain the behavior of a man like Gyorgy Szabo, who, when there was no hope of further resistance, was willing to stand forth as the leader of a general strike against the Soviet system?

For example, what sensible man, knowing the facts of Budapest, could possibly accept the following explanation which the trade unions of Soviet Russia offered to fellow workers in Europe as an excuse for the massacre of a city? "You know, dear comrades, that Soviet troops upon the request of the Hungarian government came to its help in order to crush the counterrevolutionary forces and in order to protect the basic interests of the Hungarian people and peace in Europe. The Soviet armed forces could not remain aloof because to do so would not only have led to further bloodshed but would have also brought tremendous damage to the cause of the working class. The Soviet trade unions wish to bring to your attention the fact that the Soviet army has never fought for an unjust cause."

When such lies became intolerable to the man of Csepel, and when the puppet government dared to announce that all the trouble in Budapest had been caused by discredited members of the nobility who were trying to impose their will upon the simple communist workers, Gyorgy Szabo and his men could stomach the nonsense no further. They had posters made which announced, "THE 40,000 NOBLEMEN OF CSEPEL, EACH WITH A CASTLE NEAR THE RAKOSI METAL WORKS, AND WITH NUMEROUS SERVANTS, DEFY THE GOVERNMENT." Then, to make their intention crystal clear, they announced, "We have mined the buildings in Csepel and if you try to take them over or to make us work, we will blow them to pieces."

The importance of the resistance in Csepel did not lie, however, in the unparalleled heroism of the workers. Rather it lay in the slow and methodical manner in which it was conducted. The world had time to hear of it and could marvel at the total rejection of communism voiced by these men of communism. Had there been no strike, the Soviets could have argued, as indeed they tried, that although there had been an unfortunate uprising, no real workmen were involved. If the revolution had ended abruptly or in obscurity, any reasonably logical interpretation could have been promulgated in Rome and Paris and New Delhi. But with men like Gyorgy Szabo doggedly striking, and in the very teeth of communism, day after day until the stoppage lasted a month, and then on into the second month—that could not be brushed aside as accidental. That was a rejection of communism which was irrefutable. As this book goes to press, toward the end of January, 1957, the methodical, unemotional workers of Csepel are still showing the world what they think of communism. They have now entered their fourth month of protest.

In my recent life I have witnessed many brave actions—in war, in Korea, in municipal riots, and one which I shall speak of later when I write of the bridge at Andau—but I have never seen anything braver than the quiet, calculated strike of the men of Csepel. I have long suspected that raw courage, like that required for blowing up a tank, is largely a matter of adrenalin; if a man gets a strong enough surge of it he can accomplish amazing feats, which the world calls courage. But courage such as the workers' committees of Csepel exhibited is not a matter of adrenalin, it is based on heart and will. Voluntarily these men signed manifestoes, although they knew that their names were being collected by the Russians. Without protesting they permitted themselves to be photographed, although they could be sure that these photographs would be filed and used to identify strikers for later retaliation. They were willing to stand forth undisguised and to demonstrate their contempt for their Soviet masters. I call that the ultimate in courage.

On November 22, when the strike was at its height, Gyorgy Szabo returned home from an exhausting meeting in which he had publicly argued for a continuation of the strike "no matter what the Russians do."

As soon as he entered his grubby home he realized that his wife was distraught. "Gyorgy," Mrs. Szabo said in a trembling voice. "The Farkas boy was deported last night."

"Sooner or later we'll all be deported," he said, sinking into a chair.

Mrs. Szabo twisted her hands nervously, then blurted out, "I think we ought to escape with the children to Austria."

Gyorgy said nothing. Dropping his head into his hands he tried to think. For some days he had known that this question was going to come up, and twice he had forestalled discussion of it. Now he said bluntly, "I'm a Hungarian, not an Austrian."

His wife's voice rose in both pitch and intensity. "I am too. But I can't bring my children up in Hungary."

"This is my home," Szabo argued stubbornly.

"Gyorgy," his wife pleaded, her voice growing urgently gentle. "They need men like you in Australia. Today the BBC said America was taking refugees."

"I don't want America—" he began.

His reply was interrupted by a terrible scream. Mrs. Szabo had risen from her chair, her hands in her hair, and was shouting hysterically, "I can't live here any longer! I can't live here and listen with dread for fear an auto will stop outside our house at night and the police—" She fell back into her chair and sobbed, "Gyorgy, in a few days they'll take you away."

One of the children, hearing his mother's screams, had come into the room. "You must put your clothes on," Mrs. Szabo said in grimly excited tones. "And tell your brothers to put theirs on, too."

Gyorgy Szabo, the good communist, the trusted worker in heavy industry so dear to communism, looked stolidly at his wife. There was no arguing with her now, so he stalked into the cold night air.

The scenes about him were familiar and warm. This was his Csepel. He had defended it against capitalists, against Nazis and against the Russians. He had grown up here as a boy and had grown to love the sprawling buildings and the things they produced. This factory in the darkness, he had helped to build it, helped to protect it against the Soviet tanks. Within its ugly walls he had known much comradeship and happiness. This was a good island and a good land. Maybe things would work out better . . . later on.

A car's lights showed in the distance, and instinctively he drew into the shadows, for under communism an auto meant danger. Only the police and the party bosses had automobiles, and such men usually meant trouble. Flashing its spotlight here and there, the car approached and Gyorgy could see the glistening rifles of police on the prowl. He remained very silent and they failed to spot him. Slowly the car went about its duty, and in the darkness Szabo acknowledged finally how terrified he was.

"I was afraid," he admitted later. "For many years I had been living in a world of bleak hopelessness. I had no chance of saving for things I wanted to buy. No chance at all. But worse was the emptiness inside. All the big promises that I had lived on as a boy were gone. Not one thing the communists had promised had ever been fulfilled. You can't understand how awful it is to look into a hopeless future. At the start of the revolution lots of us were brave, but do you know why? Because we didn't care whether we lived or died. Then we had a few days of hope, and we spoke of a new, honest system, but when the Russians came back I knew the bleak days would start again. That time I was brave because I didn't give a damn about Siberia. It couldn't be any worse than Csepel, because in Siberia you admit you're in prison. That's why, when I hid in the shadows afraid of the automobile and heard my wife's screaming in my ears, I finally said, 'If there's a better life in Canada or Australia, I'll go.' I was afraid."

A man who had destroyed tanks by spraying them with gasoline from a hose, a man who had stood forth as the announced leader of the strike, beat his face with his hands and said, "I was afraid."

Using only the shadows, he returned to his home, where he found his wife and the three boys bundled up in all the warm clothes they could muster. Mrs. Szabo was no longer crying, for she had made up her mind to leave Budapest this night and walk to the Austrian border whether her husband joined her or not—to do anything to escape the terror under which her children had been living and would live for the rest of their lives if they remained in Budapest.

Szabo looked at his wife, reached for his own heavy clothes and said, "We'll leave right away."

So Gyorgy Szabo and his family left Hungary. They carried with them one small handbag of food for their children. After ten years of dedicated service to communism this gifted workman had as his worldly possessions one small bag of food and a legacy of fear. When he fled from Csepel to the mainland and then across the bridge from Pest into Buda, he did not bother to look back on the beauty of Pest, for he knew that it had been destroyed.

8   A Poem of Petofi's

Of every hundred Russian tanks burned up in the streets
of Budapest, about eighty-five were destroyed by young
people under the age of twenty-one.

To appreciate the staggering impact of this fact, one
must understand what the life experience of a twenty-
year-old Hungarian youth had been. Born in 1936, such a
child would have known no politics until the age of five, at
which time the dislocations of World War II hit Hungary,
and life became a perpetual crisis. At eight the child experienced the rigors of Nazi occupation and at ten entered
the relative calm of communism.

It is important to remember this, for a twenty-year-old
Hungarian could not, like some of his elders, look back
nostalgically upon a happier world. His early years had
been spent amid deep uncertainties, and communism
brought security. In his early years he knew hunger, but
communism brought food. In addition, since communist
theoreticians based their state on the belief that a child
properly indoctrinated will never defect from the system,
communism made great efforts to ingratiate itself with
children. More effort was spent on them than upon any
other segment of the population, and children had every
opportunity to become familiar with communism and to
love it.

For example, a ten-year-old boy was allowed to join the
Hungarian equivalent of the Russian Pioneers, in which
he was given a red scarf and two hours of indoctrination a
week, long talks about how wonderful it would be to live
in Russia, and free passes to propaganda movies. Many
things which his family could neither afford nor find, like
chocolate candies and oranges, would be freely distributed

by the communists, always with the injunction, "This comes from your good friends, the Russians."

At fourteen he joined the Hungarian equivalent of the Soviet Komsomol, in which he studied the theory of communism. Special emphasis was placed on hating the west, and his instructors assured him that one day he would have to protect sacred Hungarian soil from American fascists who were waiting in Austria to destroy Hungary.

Soon he moved into the Freedom Fighters Association, where he studied intensively such exciting subjects as military drill, how to use a revolver, how to break down a long rifle, and how to read a map. His instructors said, "You must know these things in order to destroy the American invaders." Hating the west was a major requirement in this course, but there were also pleasant occupations like singing military songs and marching in formation. Promising boys, who proved that they hated the west and were ready to lay down their lives fighting America, were given a special course: how to destroy an American tank with homemade gasoline bombs.

There were less grim subjects, like airplanes, camping, and sports, but even the last category provided training in such skills as target practice with a military gun, driving a military truck in combat, and fighting off paratroop landings. The future communist was taught that all Hungarian strength came from its friendship with the Soviet Union. One handbook described the aims of the youth organization as: "The education of the coming generation and of all working people in the principles of socialist patriotism, of devotion and love toward the Hungarian communist party, and of boundless loyalty toward the great Soviet Union in the spirit of militant revolutionary vigilance and battle preparedness." A young man who did not rely upon the Soviet Union altogether was held to be a dangerous youth who would bear watching by the AVO.

But it was in school that the pressure of communist propaganda became intense. In every class a boy's teachers were required to indoctrinate him in communism. They gave lectures about the glory of Russia and instruction in the communist history of Hungary. They took their students to march in communist parades, to see propaganda movies and to protest against American imperialism. The teachers praised what communism said should be praised and damned its supposed enemies. From the first grade through the last, no child could escape this pressure.

It was not applied by all teachers, for many were to prove themselves extraordinary heroes in the revolution, but rather by a few fanatics who were planted in each school by the AVO and who reported upon every fellow teacher to the secret police. Thus a teacher who might in his heart hate communism was nevertheless required by fear of these perpetual spies to indoctrinate his pupils with hatred of Britain and America and an unreasoning trust in Russia.

One thing absolutely required of each teacher was that he keep prominently posted in his classroom three huge portraits of communist leaders. Marx, Lenin and Stalin were most popular, but some nationalist-minded teachers would use Lenin, Stalin and Rakosi. School children universally called these portraits, "The Holy Trinity," and there was confusion throughout the schools when Stalin's huge portrait had to be hurriedly taken down, to be followed briefly by round-faced Malenkov and then by pudgy Khrushchev. Maps were skillfully drawn so as to magnify the glories of communism and emphasize the weaknesses of democracy.

It was in textbooks, however, that the communists showed their greatest ingenuity. A geography book would accord Russia seventy-five per cent of its pages, and compress the decadent nations into the remaining twenty-five per cent. One atlas, reviewing World War II, summarizes the military contributions of England and America under the heading, "Breaches by the Anglo-Americans of Their Obligations as Allies." Another heading reads, "Advances by the Anglo-American Armies in Second-Rate and Unimportant Theaters of War." And in explaining how Japan was defeated, the only American achievements shown are minor victories at Midway and the Solomons in the early stages of the war. The final crushing of Japan was brought about, of course, by Russian armies.

One of the most significant changes took place in the attitudes of students toward each other. "You must report any actions that might be harmful to the communist state," students were constantly warned. As a result, no student was safe from the revenge of his fellows, for although most Hungarian students refused to spy upon their mates, there were always one or two who had been corrupted or dragooned by the AVO and sometimes their identity was not known, so that one had to be careful of everyone.

Most dreadful were the occasional cases in which a son would gain approval by informing upon his parents' love for religion or persistence in old-fashioned ideas. AVO teachers held this to be the apex of good communist behavior.

Under AVO scrutiny, the school became a potential trap for every household. Teachers would ask their students, "Does your father keep a picture of Comrade Stalin in your home?" "What radio station does your mother like best?" "Does your father think that Comrade Rakosi is always right?" "Does your mother ever take you to religious meetings at night?"

Religious instruction was a very touchy problem. In some schools it was available, but only if parents requested it for their children in writing. The child was then allowed to receive highly colored official interpretations of religion, while the parents' letters were forwarded both to employers and to the AVO, who would order that any man in a sensitive position who insisted upon religious instruction for his children be fired immediately and placed in the labor corps. In fact, in the cities retaliation was apt to be so severe that cautious parents quickly learned to ignore the school's sanctimonious announcement: "If any parents want their children to have religious instruction, all they have to do is write a letter stating that fact."

Therefore, any Hungarian youth who had reached the age of twenty had spent the first half of his life in war, starvation and insecurity, and the next half in the bosom of communism, coddled and tempted. Quickly he learned that for any preferment in life, he had to be a good communist. Did he like games? Only communist groups could have teams. Did he want to attend a summer camp? He could do so only if he was a communist. If he wished to go on to the university, he had to have an exemplary communist record. In all of Hungary there was no conceivable escape from this crushing burden of propaganda which bore down upon him to remake his personality. If the human soul could be transformed, communism proposed to transform it.

Any young man or woman who had experienced ten years of such relentless pressure should have become a living testament to the boast of Joseph Stalin, who once growled, "Education? It's just a weapon whose effect depends upon who controls it and whom he wishes to strike with it." Hungarian boys and girls had been trained by Stalin as intensively as human beings could be to strike the enemies of communism. They were bound morally and spiritually and economically to the two pillars of Hungarian education: love Russia and defend communism.

Yet when the test came, almost a hundred per cent of Hungarian youth hated Russia and tried to destroy communism.

This fact is so striking, and has so many ramifications for world history, that we must try to discover why the Russian plan went wrong. Why did these young people behave exactly contrary to expectations? And how were they able to resist the poison with which they were daily inoculated? To find one answer we must study the nature of the Hungarians themselves and the role they have played in history. For another answer we shall pick up one typical family as it struggles through the Hungarian marshes, on its way to the bridge at Andau and freedom. From this inspection we may comprehend what the Russians were up against.

It was an American diplomat, exhausted from days of work during the crisis, who best described the Hungarian. Limply he cried, "When this pressure lets up, I want just one thing. A transfusion of Hungarian blood. I want to feel like a man again." It was the consensus of observers that the Hungarians were some of the toughest individual human beings of recent years.

In those days much was written that both inflated Hungarian pride and ignored history. It is true that the Hungarians have always been brave, but they have also been an extraordinarily cantankerous people. Their neighbors have usually found it almost impossible to get along with them. At one time or another, and often within recent years, Hungary has either fought or quarreled with each nation that touches her borders.

To the east the enmity with Rumania has been historic and undying. It centers on conflicting claims to the province of Transylvania, and given a chance, it would surely flare up afresh tomorrow. Much of Hungary's curious predilection for alliances with Germany has sprung from her desire to be revenged on Rumania.

To the south Hungary has experienced quite bad relations with her Serbian neighbors, so that the history of this border is one of war and retaliation, the most serious flare-up having occurred in 1942, when Hungarians were charged with the massacre of at least ten thousand Serbs. Less than four months after signing a treaty of perpetual friendship with Yugoslavia, Hungary invaded that country in an act so flagrantly in violation of international morality that the Hungarian prime minister, Count Paul Teleki, committed suicide in protest.

Hungary's relations with Croatia on the southeast and with Slovakia on the north were little better, while Austrians held that one of the main reasons for the collapse of the Austro-Hungarian empire that used to bind Central Europe together was Hungary's intransigence in empire affairs and her unwillingness to accord her own minorities fair treatment. Few nations, for example, have a worse record of antisemitism, or a longer one.

A long-time student of Balkan affairs has remarked, "Hungary has customarily had only one staunch friend in this area, Bulgaria. That's because there is no Hungarian-Bulgarian border." Since most histories of this part of the world have been written by scholars with Serbian or

Rumanian sympathies, it is easy to guess what nation is usually cast in the role of villain. However, even an unbiased American scholar like Carlton J. H. Hayes* can summarize Hungarian behavior in this manner:

". . . the Magyar aristocracy made no pretense of sharing the management of Hungary with the masses of their own people, to say nothing of sharing it with any subject nationality. They preserved their hold on large landed estates throughout the realm. They forced the use of their own language in the public schools of the whole kingdom. They did their best to Magyarize the Slovak peasantry in their northern provinces and the Serb population of the south. They abolished all traces of local autonomy in the large Rumanian-speaking province of Transylvania, in the east. In the west, they put more and more restrictions on the partial autonomy which they had granted in 1868 to Croatia. They kept the Hungarian parliament and the ministry at Budapest under their own domination. They persistently refused to extend the suffrage for parliamentary elections; and so high were the property qualifications for its exercise and so intricate were the electoral laws that in 1910, out of a total population of over twenty million in the Hungarian kingdom, fewer than one million were voters, and, though the total population was about evenly divided between Magyars and non-Magyars, almost all the seats in the parliament were occupied by Magyars.

"The subject nationalities in Hungary were thus even more discontented than those in Austria, although their wholesale exclusion from the Hungarian parliament at Budapest deprived them of a central place, such as the parliament at Vienna provided for dissident Austrian nationalists, where they might collaborate against the existing regime and advertise to the world their grievances and demands.

"The poorer classes of Magyars as well as the subject peoples suffered from the aristocratic character of the Hungarian government. Though much was done by the

* A Political and Cultural History of Modern Europe, Volume 2. Copyright, 1939, by Carlton J. H. Hayes. New York: The Macmillan Company. Used by permission of the publishers.

Hungarian parliament to foster popular education, and though some of the worst grievances of the peasants against their landlords were redressed, the remarkable agricultural development which Hungary experienced between 1867 and 1914 redounded chiefly to the financial advantage of the great landowners and governmental oligarchy. This fact was evidenced by a startling emigration from the country, amounting to over a million for the years from 1896 to 1910, and by a widespread popular agitation for electoral reform, an agitation which in the first decade of the twentieth century brought the kingdom to the verge of civil war."

I must point out, however, that there is a Hungarian explanation of such ugly evidence, but since Hungary has produced few persuasive historians, her side of any quarrel has not been well presented to the public. My own introduction to this fiery nation is a case in point. For some months in the early 1930s when I was first a student in Europe I roomed with a Transylvanian, whose native land had often been switched back and forth between Hungary and Rumania. At this time, most of Transylvania was under Rumanian rule, it having been so ordered by the victorious Allies at the conclusion of World War I, but his particular village still remained in Hungarian hands. My stubborn friend was a revolutionist who dreamed constantly of correcting that fault, and he fed me such a constant torrent of abuse against Hungary that in self-defense I began to study Hungary's interpretation of events, and although these accounts were poorly written and lacking in subtle persuasiveness, I found myself developing a marked partiality for this small nation. In later life my Transylvanian revolutionist must have suffered several cyclonic reactions, for under Hitler all Transylvania went to Hungary, while under Soviet Russia it was returned to Rumania, where it now rests. At any rate, in me his intemperate denunciations produced a pro-Hungarian.

I found the Hungarians to be a sensible and a unique people. Their history even prior to the 1956 uprising against communism was a long testament both to their courage and to their determination to exist as a nation.

If communism had had the intelligence to ingratiate itself with these strong people it could have erected in Hungary a powerful barrier against the west. For according to the facts of their history, they were a people who could find a logical home either with the Western European nations, with whom they shared a religion (Catholicism) and a cultural history, or with an Asian-European block, with whom they shared a linguistic kinship and a common ancestry.

It was some time toward the beginning of the ninth century that a group of about twenty thousand nomads from Central Asia were living on the western slopes of the Ural Mountains, looking down into what was to become Europe. In a series of daring westward thrusts these relatively few Ugrian-Turkic tribesmen moved successively across four great rivers: the Volga, the Don, the Dnieper and the Dniester. This brought them close to the mouth of the Danube, but after scouting parties found those areas occupied, the nomads appear to have decided on a brave trek into less contested lands.

By the middle of the ninth century the Asiatic tribesmen had begun to cut boldly right across the Carpathian Mountains and by the year 892 had reached the glorious plains of Central Europe rimmed by protective mountains. To the east lay the forbidding East Carpathians, to the north the West Carpathians, to the south the Dinaric Alps and to the west the towering Alps themselves. It was a noble plateau, cut approximately in half by the lovely Danube, which here took its dramatic ninety-degree swing to the south.

The vast, rich plain was scarcely inhabited. The dying Roman empire had maintained small settlements at Vienna and at the village of Buda, each on the right bank of the Danube, but there was little else, and the Ugrian-Turkic tribesmen swept in and soon controlled the plains. Their German neighbors on the other side of the Danube nicknamed them "The Hungry People" (hungrig), and the name lasted. They, of course, always referred to themselves by their correct name, the Magyars.

Thus by an accident of history, and because of the

bravery of the first Hungarians, an Asiatic people was thrust down into the middle of Europe. Slavs surrounded them to the north and south, Germans to the west, and a mixture of Germans and Romans to the east. They retained many of their Asiatic ways and their speech—among the European languages Hungarian is related only to Finnish, the Finns probably having started from the same section of Asia and having reached Finland by some alternative route—and they proved a tough, rugged people, loyal to the death and committed always to the idea of a free Hungary.

Europe is deeply indebted to Hungary, which made many sacrifices to protect the safety of the west. For centuries this small group of herdsmen, only recently from Asia themselves, fought off subsequent waves of invading Mongols, who otherwise would have ransacked Paris and Rome. Later it was the Hungarians who bore the brunt of Europe's fight against the Muslims of Turkey, refusing to relinquish either the Christian religion, which they had adopted around the year 1000, or their European way of life.

But if the Hungarians prevented other Asiatic invaders from reaching Western Europe, they saw no reason why they should not go there themselves, and in a series of wars they swept into German, Italian and Slavic lands until the west united and said in effect: "The Hungarian plain is yours. Stay there!" After this understanding was reached, an uneasy equilibrium was maintained whereby Hungary, of Asiatic ancestry, served as a buffer state fending Turkey off from German areas, and keeping the northern Slavs of Russia from establishing a common border with the southern Slavs of Yugoslavia. Now completely Europeanized, Hungary's historic role has been to keep Asia out of Europe, whether the threat of invasion has come via Russia or Asiatic Turkey. Hungary could well be called the cornerstone that holds Western and Eastern Europe together.

The Hungarians developed into a remarkably attractive people. Small, wiry, quick to anger, they have finely chiseled faces and bodies admirably adapted to games. They love music and hunting, show great affection for folk arts, old national costumes and bright color harmonies. After a thousand years in Europe they have lost most of their Asiatic charactertistics, though one sometimes finds a Hungarian with high cheekbones and the skin pulled tightly back from the eyes. And although they were violent in their reactions to their neighboring lands, they lived in peace among themselves. Their family life was extremely close-knit, and their loyalty to the family group made feudalism an attractive system, under which they produced some of the most powerful noblemen in Europe and some of the most stubborn. The changes that could have made Hungary a modern nation were fanatically resisted by these noblemen, so that in the peace treaties following World War I, Hungary was savagely stripped of its border lands by her neighbors. No nation suffered more national humiliation in 1918 than Hungary.

Even then the noble families, who retained control, refused to accept modern concepts of government, and a gallant land was kept in a state of strife, bickering and dictatorship. At the end of World War II, after pathetic switches in policy in a vain attempt to regain lost border provinces, Hungary stumbled and fumbled her way into communism.

It was this people, contrary and brave, that Russia decided to mold into an ideal communist satellite, and everything was in Russia's favor. The Hungarian plain, under the careful attention of peasants who were naturally good farmers, produced more food than it needed. Mineral resources were to prove of great value, and the people of the plain were surprisingly well suited to a technological society, for Hungarian boys liked machines and the men made excellent engineers. Finally, the nation had proved over a thousand years that if its loyalty could be enlisted in a reasonable cause, one could find no better men in Europe to have on one's side than these unique, rugged descendants of the tribesmen from the Ural Mountains.

On the other hand, Hungary's neighbors had uncovered ample proof that any nation which insulted Hungary's sense of honor would find it a land most difficult to deal with. Hungarians were by nature contrary, by conviction patriotic and by training heroic. Their friends called them "The Irish of the East"; their enemies termed them "The Prussians of the Balkans." To understand how these characteristics combined to motivate an individual Hungarian family, let us journey to the bridge at Andau, where in mid-November a group of Hungarians were struggling across the last few miles of Hungarian soil.

It was a bitterly cold day as Janos Hadjok and his wife Iren led their two children, a boy of nine and a girl of thirteen, through the last Hungarian swamp and onto the rickety bridge. They could have moved faster except for Mrs. Hadjok's brother, Gyorgy Lufczin, who seemed about to collapse. Twice he stumbled and was unable to get up, and his ashen face, made doubly grotesque by two days of beard, showed that he might be near death.

"You've got to come," Janos Hadjok argued with his brother-in-law.

"Leave me here and go on," the sick man pleaded.

"We'll never leave you," the Hadjoks replied. Then they helped the poor man to his feet and dragged him across the bridge to freedom, but then his nerves totally collapsed, and he seemed about to die. "Leave me and go on," he begged.

"No, Gyorgy, we'll get you to a hospital," his brother-in-law assured him, and with the help of Austrian rescuers, the little family got the sick man to a restaurant in Andau, where they propped him up in a corner.

There one of the Austrians had the good luck to meet Mrs. Lillie Brown, dynamic wife of Irving Brown, the AFL-CIO representative in Europe. She happened to be of Hungarian ancestry, her father having emigrated to the United States in the early years of this century. Mrs. Brown spoke to the sick man in his native tongue and found that he had been wounded in the stomach and then hastily patched together. On the long hike to freedom his insides had literally been falling out. Now his face was ghastly to see, and it seemed that within a few hours he must be dead.

"I'll rush you to the hospital in Eisenstadt," she offered.

"The family too?" he asked weakly.

"No, we can't take the family," she explained carefully. "They have to go to another place."

"Then I won't go," he said simply.

Mrs. Brown is both energetic and forthright. "You are dying," she snapped in Hungarian, "and you're worrying about people who are well. Are you crazy?"

"If they had not stayed with me," he argued, "I would have died. I won't go."

Mrs. Brown lost patience and cried to a guard, "Throw this man in a car and rush him to the hospital."

"I won't go!" he protested.

Finally Mrs. Brown asked, "Well, where is your family?"

"Over there."

And then Mrs. Brown could understand why a man in pain of death would insist upon keeping with his own clan. Mr. Hadjok was a handsome, well-built man in his early thirties and Mrs. Hadjok was a solid Hungarian housewife of the same age, with a marvelous smile. But it was the children who were special. Dressed in her brown winter suit, Vera was a scintillating beauty with a tiny mole on her upper lip which made her look like Greta Garbo, while young Johan was a dashing blond terror of nine. They were two of the most appealing children to cross the bridge of Andau, and on the long bouncing trip over the rough roads to the hospital at Eisenstadt, Mrs. Brown had an opportunity to get better acquainted with this typical Hungarian family.

She found that in spite of hardships that would have crushed a lesser breed, the Hadjoks had kept together, had protected one another, and had demonstrated a depth of family unity that would amaze a casual onlooker who had never known the rich experience of being one of a closely knit group. At the hospital Mrs. Brown didn't even try to argue with the officials, whose strict rule it was not to allow families to accompany operation cases.

"Look, nurse," she said, "I know your rules and I know they're right. But this family has got to stay together." The nurse started to argue, but the sick man refused to enter the hospital unless the four Hadjoks trailed along, so the rules were broken.

When the brother-in-law had been sewed up again and had recovered sufficiently, Mrs. Brown moved the entire family, at her own expense, into a Vienna hotel, and one day in a nearby restaurant some interrogators who were interested in how a family withstands the pressures of communism gathered to talk with the Hadjoks.

Janos Hadjok, the father, said bluntly, "Our whole family despised communism from the moment it reached Hungary. Three times we tried to escape. In 1948, when little Johan was a baby, we tried to sneak into Yugoslavia, but we were caught. In 1949, when he could walk, we tried again, but again we were caught and punished by the AVO. On the day the revolution broke we said to one another, 'Now maybe we can have a decent nation,' but when the Russians stormed back we agreed, 'We will leave this cursed business.' And we walked most of the way to Andau."

"Did your children feel the same way?" an interrogator asked.

The question made beautiful Vera quite angry. Tossing her lovely head she said in clipped accents, "In school we were taught the Russian language and Russian history and how great the Russian communist state was. But we all sat there very still and bitter inside. We despised the teachers who told us such lies."

Perhaps such sentiments from a thirteen-year-old girl made some of the questioners think that the interpreter was polishing them up and that they were not Vera's own words; so they asked for another interpreter, but to him the girl spoke even more forcefully. "Neither Russia nor the communists in Hungary could ever make us believe the lies they told us."

"How did you know they were lies?"

Mrs. Hadjok answered briefly. "At night after we had put out the lights upstairs we would gather in the cellar, and I would teach the children the true history of Hungary. We would discuss morality and the Catholic religion and the lessons of Cardinal Mindszenty. We never allowed the children to go to sleep until we had washed away the evil things they might have heard that day."

There was a moment of silence in the restaurant and finally someone asked, "Did all families do this?"

Mr. Hadjok spoke. "I don't know. You see, we never knew who the AVO were in our community, and it would have been a great risk to tell even your best friend. But I think most families did it, in secret."

"How did you know enough history to teach the children?"

Mrs. Hadjok replied, "Books which told the truth about the great revolution of 1848 were circulated mysteriously and I had one. I made my children memorize it, especially the parts about Louis Kossuth, who was our greatest patriot. They considered this book almost sacred, since it was the only place in their world where they could find the truth."

"Besides," Mr. Hadjok interrupted proudly, "my father knew personally the son of Louis Kossuth, and if we had allowed that tradition to die, it would have been shameful."

An interrogator pointed his finger at beautiful little Vera, who in a kindlier world would have been playing with dolls, and asked, "Do you know who Kossuth was?"

Instantly Vera leaped to her feet, stood calmly beside her mother and delivered an oration which rang out fearlessly in the restaurant. "Louis Kossuth was Hungary's greatest hero, for he endeavored to bring freedom to a nation and hope to its people." She spoke for about ten minutes, a golden flow of emotion learned in a cellar.

When she had finished, one interrogator shot questions at her. "Did Kossuth succeed in his revolution?"

"No, he failed."

"What reforms did he specially want?"

"Freedom, a separate legislature, good judges, breaking up of big landholdings."

"If he failed, what did he accomplish?"

"He showed us the way, for later on."

"How long ago did he live?"

"One hundred years."

The most pressing questions were shot at Vera, and she answered them all. When she sat down, her father said proudly, "And if you questioned her in religion or ethics, she would answer as well. My wife is a proud teacher." Then he added, "She is brave, too."

On the fifteenth of March, which, before Russia took over, all Hungarians celebrated as their day of national independence, it had long been customary for children to appear on the streets in national dress. Adults would wear little rosettes of the national colors—red, white, green—in their buttonholes, and children would sometimes flash big bright arm bands. But under communism this became unpopular, since there were more important holidays to be celebrated, like Red Army Day and May Day. On the fifteenth of March, in 1953, Mrs. Hadjok surprised her family by dressing her six-year-old son in full national costume with an arm band so big it could be spotted a block away.

"The AVO will see it," friends warned.

"Today he's six," she argued, "and I want him always to remember that on his sixth birthday he was a Hungarian."

Proudly she sent him into the streets, and the first man he met burst into tears. The second was the policeman, who stopped the child and asked, "Where are you going?"

"Today is our national day," Johan replied. "Where are your colors?"

"I wear them in my heart," the policeman answered, and he brought the boy home for fear he might get into trouble.

From that day on, Johan was a Hungarian. In the cellar his parents taught him the fiery old poetry of Hungary and it became his chief joy to declaim it, but they warned him that he must not speak it in public, for the AVO might hear about it. But at the age of eight he entered a speaking contest for boys and girls of ten, and in the big school he dramatically recited an intensely patriotic poem. The effect on the teachers was astonishing and several wept silently. At the conclusion of his recitation one older instructor openly applauded. Apparently spies reported this teacher to the AVO, for later on he was taken away.

"School was not easy for our children," Mrs. Hadjok said. "We dared to apply for religious instruction, but Vera was flatly told that if she attended such classes she would not be promoted. The leader of the school went so far as to forbid her ever to come into the school again if she studied religion. But later on, when the teacher who had applauded Johan's recitation came back from the AVO, he bravely established secret classes for religious training, even though he knew that if he were caught again he would probably be beaten to death. He was an excellent man."

The battle between school and parents never relaxed an instant. "The communists had everything on their side," Hadjok explained. "Candy, fruit, games, terror. We had only one thing, the lessons at night."

Mrs. Hadjok said, "We taught them above everything else to trust in God. But almost as strongly we told them to hold together as a family."

Hadjok explained, "The more the communists tried to destroy our family life, the more we taught family loyalty. It was like their pressing us down all day, in every way you could think of, but at night we grew up strongly again."

"Take Vera," the brother-in-law said. "At six she disliked the Russians. At nine she hated them. At ten she understood the evil of communism. At thirteen she is a holy patriot. She knows and understands more than I do."

"When communist teachers lectured to such children," Mrs. Hadjok said, "the boys and girls knew what lies they were being told before the teacher stopped speaking."

"Weren't you afraid the children would betray you . . . by accident, I mean?" an interrogator asked.

There was a long pause in which the five members of the Hadjok family contemplated the studied chances they had taken in preserving their religious and intellectual life under communism. Each member knew exactly what exquisite judgments had been made, what fundamental risks had to be taken, and above all, what complete faith had to be invested in the children. The Hadjoks were unable to speak of these delicate judgments, for to do so would have been to lay bare the very soul of a family, but the interpreter suddenly said with intense emotion, "Perhaps I can explain what a Hungarian family went through. I'll speak in English and they won't be embarrassed."

The interpreter said, "When we watched our children growing up there were moments of unbearable anxiety. We would see our sons come home from school wearing bright red ties and repeating communist lies. When we asked them who they loved they would say, 'Mama and Papa and Brother Stalin.' They would bring us pictures of Stalin to put in our living rooms. And we would know that their teachers were asking them each day, 'Do your parents love Comrade Stalin?' and we would have to make believe that we did. And almost every night when we went to bed, we husbands and wives who had young children would whisper, 'Do you think they are old enough yet to know?' And usually the husband would say, 'Not yet.'

"But the time always came when the mother would cry, 'I won't see my child perverted any longer. Tonight we will tell him the truth.' And the father would protest, 'Not yet! The boy is only eight.' And then mother and father would begin to inspect their child with an intensity that no other parents could possibly know. 'He's a good, honest boy,' the mother would reason. 'He's strong and honorable,' the father would agree. Then there would be more whispering at night and always the mother would be the one who pleaded for the family to take a bold chance and save this child.

"Now the family would look about Budapest, trying to find some other family it could trust. Hints would be dropped, always with the intention of discovering at what age a child could be trusted with the entire security of his family. A man would say to a life-long friend, 'Can a child of eight—' He wouldn't finish the sentence but the friend would reply, 'I talked to my boy at nine.' That was all. But the mother would have quietly found some other woman who had talked to her children at eight. Or another wife would grow pale and say, 'Not before ten . . .'

"You see, this family had to judge the exact moment at which a boy could be saved from communism and yet not too soon for fear the child might inadvertently blurt out the truth and destroy the whole family. Because if the AVO suspected, they simply came around some night and took the father away. Sometimes he was never seen again.

"More whispering, more consultations. I myself have been asked by at least six of my friends, and three times I have participated in the first family meeting. It was almost always at night, and the parents would bring the children together and they would ask casually, 'What did you learn in school today?' and the child would explain how Russia and Stalin were the only things Hungary could trust in, and the father would say simply, 'That's all a lie, son.'

"It was a terrifying moment. You could feel death in the room, and then usually I would speak and I would say, 'Istvan, do you know what death is?' and regardless of what Istvan replied, I would say, 'If you ever tell anyone about tonight, your father will die.'

"Always the children understood, and they would begin to ask questions, and pretty soon the mother would say, 'We want you to keep in your heart certain things that will help you.' And usually it would be a part of the Bible or a poem of Petofi's.

"But the moment always came when such a father had to discipline such a son. Then the father would take down the strap with the certain knowledge that if the boy wanted revenge on his family, he could have it. Nevertheless, the father had to trust his earlier judgment. I remember when I had to discipline my son. When I was through he stood looking at me, and he knew that I was afraid, but he also knew that since I was afraid I would never have whipped him if he had not needed it . . . that more than my own life I wanted to see him grow up to be a good man. Out of such moments our family life was built."

The interpreter paused a moment, then put his hand on little Johan Hadjok's tousled blond head. "This family knew," he said, "that when they started teaching this little fellow the truth he could have destroyed them."

The Hadjoks had been able to follow the English fairly well, and while the group looked at little Johan, Mrs. Hadjok said, "That was a chance we had to take."

It was therefore a tightly knit group that faced the outbreak of the revolution. "Without our saying a word," Mrs. Hadjok said, "Vera and Johan, at the first news, solemnly burned their Russian books. 'We'll never study them again,' the children swore. In many other families the same thing happened."

"But what gave me the biggest thrill of the revolution," Hadjok said, "was when Johan, without prompting, began to recite aloud, as if he was no longer afraid of anything, a poem of Petofi's."

"Who was Petofi?" an interrogator asked.

Johan quickly replied, "Sandor Petofi was the glorious poet of the 1848 revolution, and a brave fighter and a good man."

"That sounds like a recitation," the interrogator replied. "Tell me in your own words who he was."

The restaurant was filled with Hungarians and they grew silent as this fair-haired child of nine looked at the stranger and said in a clear voice, "Petofi was a young actor who never made much money. In the revolution he did fight some, but what he did that was best was to write poetry. From street corners he would recite his poetry, and all over Budapest other people would recite it, too. The poem I like best is this."

In a childish voice, but with tremendous emotion that rang throughout the restaurant, Johan Hadjok declaimed the beautiful and flaming words of Hungarian independence:

"Arise, Hungarians, the Fatherland calls you!
The time is now! Now or never!
Live oppressed—or live in freedom.
That is the question to be decided!
By the God of all Hungarians, we swear, we swear
That we will nevermore be under the yoke!"

When he stopped, the restaurant was silent. Mrs. Hadjok, remembering the years of patient instruction, wept. Mr. Hadjok blew his nose and looked proudly at his son. Some of the interrogators bit their lips, and at adjoining tables Hungarians who had been nurtured on Petofi were silent.

To break the tension one of the interrogators whispered, "Pay no attention. A Hungarian is never happy unless he's weeping."

After the group had laughed at this partly true comment, there was to be a moment even more electric, for Mr. Hadjok said, "Against such children, what could communism do? Does this explain why in all of Budapest you could not find one child who fought with the Russians?"

An interrogator asked, "But didn't some of the students from the Marx-Lenin Institute march against the freedom fighters?"

Hadjok looked up in blank astonishment. "They did?"

"Yes."

"Many?"

"Only a few."

"Those poor, poor souls," the Hungarian said. "How could they have done it?" He pondered this question for a moment, then reflected, "Probably because their parents never taught them Petofi's great poem to his baby son."

"What was it?" a stranger asked.

"Vera," Mr. Hadjok said, "you recite it."

In the once more noisy restaurant Vera Hadjok, more beautiful than a dance of childhood, rose, held her hands to her side and said softly at first, then in almost terrifying tones, the words Petofi had once written as he looked down upon his baby son. The translator kept pace with her in whispers, and again the restaurant grew silent. This time the poem was not a battle cry, no call to fury against the enemy. It was the poem of a man longing for a new Hungary, a man trying to look into the future of a nation he deeply loved. "He pleads with his son to be a good man," the translator whispered. "He wants him to be a good man all his life. He says this boy will be a better man than Petofi has been. He will know a better Hungary than Petofi has known."

When Vera finished no one in the restaurant could look at another. There was only the ache of exile, and the silence. Then, in the agonizing pause Vera volunteered an astonishing bit of information. "We had to leave Hungary, you know. We wanted to leave, but after what Johan did, we had to leave."

"What did he do?" a stranger asked.

In some embarrassment Mr. Hadjok explained, "At

school a big Russian boy—he was the son of an official—insulted Hungary and Johan tried to cut off his ear."

Again there was nothing to say, but after a while an interrogator asked Vera, "How did Petofi die?"

"There are two theories," she said in precise Hungarian. "Nobody really knows, but when the Russians invaded Hungary to crush our revolution of 1848, it is thought that Petofi died resisting some Russian lancers. They ran him through the heart. But others claim that the Russians wounded him and then, because he insulted them without stopping, they buried him alive. In either case, he died at the age of twenty-six."

It is obvious that the elder Hadjoks were determined that their children should not grow up to be communists, and although they acted both in secrecy and in isolation from their neighbors, we can judge from what the interpreter said of his own experiences that many other Hungarian families were similarly determined. These facts, if taken alone, would justify the Soviets in claiming that the major thesis of this chapter is false.

I have contended that communism failed to win the young people of Hungary in spite of unprecedented pressures brought to bear on youth. I have claimed that Stalin's boast that he could accomplish anything with the pliable minds of children was proved false.

But communism could counterclaim, with some justification, I fear, that Hungary proved nothing of the sort. It merely proved, communists could claim, that reactionary, capitalists, priest-ridden, fascist parents were determined to keep their children's enslaved minds and that against such fiends honest communism had little chance. For by communist definition, Janos Hadjok and his wife were fiends.

Taking only the evidence I have given in this report, it would be obvious to a communist that the Hadjoks were reactionaries (they taught their children history); they were capitalists (they had once owned a small enterprise of their own); they were priest-ridden (they believed in

God); and they were murderous fascists (didn't their son try to cut off the ear of a decent communist?).

However, the most damning part of the story of Hungary's youth is still to come. The Hadjok children were counterindoctrinated, that is certain, so it is not surprising that they fought communism. But the number of children whose parents were less brave than the Hadjoks, and whose families did not re-educate them at night, was far greater. These children also fought communism.

There were hundreds of thousands of children whose parents were either dedicated communists or at least on the surface subservient to the Soviets, yet these children also fought the evil system. There were some well-established cases in which the children of AVO men turned their backs on communism and fought with the independent fighters. And there were even some sons of highly placed officials, like young Imre Horvath, who took arms against their fathers' government.

These facts seem to prove one thing: In all of Hungary there were only a few young people—some of the students at the Marx-Lenin Institute—who remained faithful to the system into which they had been lured and imprisoned; all the rest, regardless of their parents' opinion, rejected communism in its moment of crisis.

9 The Bridge at Andau

There was a bridge at Andau, and if a Hungarian could reach that bridge, he was nearly free.

It wasn't much, as bridges go: not wide enough for a car nor sturdy enough to bear a motorcycle: It was a footbridge made of rickety boards with a handrailing which little children could not quite reach.

It wasn't actually in Andau, nor even near it, yet it was known throughout Hungary as "the bridge of Andau," and many thousands of refugees, coming from all parts of Hungary, headed for it. Fleeing the Russians, with only a paper bag, or with nothing, they headed for this insignificant bridge and for freedom.

Andau, of course, is not in Hungary. It is a village in Austria, but since it was the nearest settlement to the bridge, the name was shared, and the tiny village, which showed surprising capacity for accepting refugees, gained fame from a bridge which in no way belonged to it.

Nor did the bridge cross a river of importance. It did not even cross a rivulet, nor a sizable gully. It merely crossed the muddy Einser (First) Canal, which had been dug generations ago to drain the nearby swamps. Now it formed part of the boundary between Austria and Hungary.

No roads led up to the bridge, no railroad. It had been erected years ago as a convenience for local hay farmers who reaped the rich grasses that luxuriated on the swamplands around the canal and who, for most of their history, had never bothered much about the separation of Austria and Hungary. Actually, since the bridge was entirely inside Hungary, when a man did cross it, he still had a few hundred yards to go before he reached Austria.

You can see that this bridge at Andau was about the most inconsequential bridge in Europe, and if it had been left to its placid farmers and their hay fields it might have lasted for several more generations, until its timbers finally rotted and fell into the canal. It would have vanished unremembered.

But by an accident of history it became, for a few flaming weeks, one of the most important bridges in the world, for across its unsteady planks fled the soul of a nation. Across the bridge at Andau fled more than twenty thousand people who had known communism and who had rejected it. They had seen this new way of life at close hand, and they had learned in sorrow that it was merely ancient terrorism in horrible new dress, for it not only robbed and cheated a man of the material things to which he was entitled; it deprived his mind of every challenge, every breath of new life and all hope. It was at Andau that the refugees from Russian terror finally told their story. It was here that the world learned, in unmistakable accents and dreadful clarity, how bankrupt communism had become as a system of government.

The far-off men who had originally built the little wooden bridge at Andau could not possibly have foreseen what a story was ultimately to be carried across their structure. Nor could they have foretold that across their bridge would flee the flower of Hungarian manhood, abandoning the homeland for which they and their fathers had continuously fought. With great reluctance and with grief the brave people of Hungary finally decided that they must abandon their wild and lovely country and go into exile.

To understand the drama of Andau, it is necessary to visualize the border area, for it is unique. This corner of Austria resembles a low-lying football field, in the middle of which an Austrian guard stood with me one night and said, "To the south is Hungary, but over there to the east is Hungary, too. We're a tiny corner of freedom, with Hungary all around us."

To the south, along the long side of the football field, ran a high canal bank, entirely in Hungary. South of that the bank dropped sharply into the sluggish Einser Canal, too wide to jump, in most places too deep to wade. Still farther south lay the Hungarian swamps, completely covered with reeds and rushes and cattails. It took determination to escape through this border of Hungary.

Along the shorter side of the Austrian football field, the eastern, things were different. Here Austria ended in a drainage ditch which could be waded if a refugee was willing to wade up to his armpits in the deepest spots, or only up to his knees if he were lucky. But in order to get to this ditch the refugee had to penetrate a formidable Hungarian swamp choked with reeds head high.

At the point where the ditch to the east emptied into the canal to the south—the corner of the Austrian field— stood two Hungarian border guards, and about half a mile beyond them rose a tall, gloomy machine-gun tower manned by AVO men. A few hundred yards beyond the foot of this tower stood the Andau bridge.

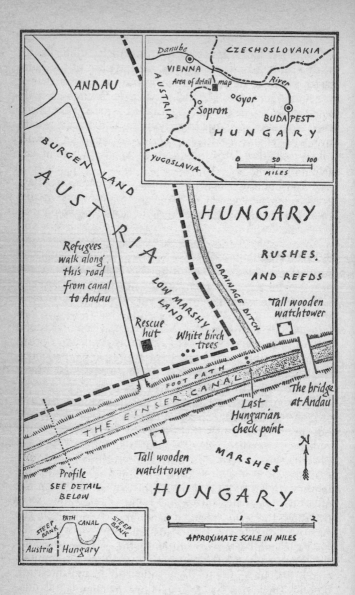

ANDAU

CZECHOSLOVAKIA

Danube

VIENNA

AUSTRIA

River

Area of detail map

o Gyor

Sopron

BUDA PEST

HUNGARY

YUGOSLAVIA

0   50   100

MILES

BURGEN LAND

AUSTRIA

Refugees
walk along
this road
from canal
to Andau

HUNGARY

RUSHES.

AND REEDS

DRAINAGE DITCH

LOW MARSHY LAND

Rescue
hut

White birch
trees

Tall wooden
watchtower

FOOT PATH

THE EINSER CANAL

Last
Hungarian
check point

The bridge
at Andau

Profile
SEE DETAIL
BELOW

Tall wooden
watchtower

MARSHES

HUNGARY

STEEP
BANK

PATH

CANAL

STEEP
BANK

Austria | Hungary

0   1   2

APPROXIMATE SCALE IN MILES

One other factor made escape into Austria difficult, for when a refugee finally had pulled his feet clear of the Hungarian swamps, he found upon arrival in Austria that it was swampland, too. He had to struggle through an additional mile of marsh until he reached a road. Here Swiss and German Red Cross trucks waited at a rescue hut to carry women and children to safety, but men had to walk a final five miles into the village of Andau, where at last they were free.

In spite of these obstacles, there were occasional days at Andau bridge when escape was like a lovely picnic! Then the AVO guards were, for some unfathomable reason, absent from their towers, the bridge was open, and the marshes were frozen over. Russian snipers were not operating and refugees were free to walk boldly down the broad canal bank. On one such day, for example, thousands of singing people came down that joyous path, and it was here, in the extreme corner of Austria, that I began to have one of the most amazing experiences of my life.

In my day I have observed many emigrations—pathetic Indians struggling out of Pakistan, half-dead Korean women dragging down from communist-held North Korea, and Pacific Island natives fleeing the Japanese—but I have never witnessed anything like the Hungarian emigration. First, there was the unprecedented youth of the emigrés. In the other evacuations the refugees had been mainly old people. But while I was at Andau, it was the finest young people of the nation who were leaving; their average age was only twenty-three. Second was their spirit. They were not dejected or beaten or maimed or halt. In considerable joy they were turning their back contemptuously upon the Russians and their communist fraud. Third, they were young people with a purpose. They wanted to tell the world of the betrayal of their nation. Any watcher at the border heard them say a dozen times, "I wish the communists of France and Italy could live under communism . . . for just six months." Then somebody would interrupt, "No, let's not wish that on anybody." Fourth, it was difficult to find among these people any reactionaries, any sad, defeated human beings looking toward the past. World communists are trying to convince themselves that only fascists, capitalists, American spies, Catholic priests and reactionaries fled Hungary. I wish they would ask any one of us who greeted these refugees what kind of people fled their evil system. They were the best people in the nation, the most liberal.

But if the people were as I describe them, why should we watchers at the border who welcomed them into freedom feel universally a sense of tragedy? I met no westerner who failed to have this sensation of great tragedy in the Greek sense, and I have seen some of the toughest newsmen, refugee teams, disaster officials and photographers in the world stand at this happy border and have tears well into their eyes.

I think they were overcome by the tragedy, not of these refugees, but of Hungary. What terrible fate had befallen a nation when such young people had grown to despise it and had fled? Consider, for example, eleven groups that had left their homeland, and imagine the loss they represented to a nation.

One, at the university in Sopron five hundred students, thirty-two professors and their entire families simply gave up all hope of a decent life under communism and came across the border. I am sorry that no American university was able to accept them as a unit; we were all glad when Canada's University of British Columbia did so. What a vital impulse Vancouver is going to get.

Two, the finest ballerina of the Budapest Opera walked out with several of her assistants.

Three, enough football players fled Hungary to make several teams of world-champion caliber.

Four, the three finest Gypsy orchestras of Hungary came out in a body and have begun to play around the restaurants of Europe.

Five, some of the top mechanics in the factories at Csepel left and were eagerly grabbed up by firms in Germany, Switzerland and Sweden.

Six, a staggering number of trained engineers and scientists in almost all phases of industry and research fled, some carrying slide rules and tables applicable to their specialization, others with nothing. I myself have met accidentally at least fifty engineers under the age of thirty. A careful census would probably reveal more than five thousand. Their loss will hurt Hungary dreadfully.

Seven, a majority of both the Budapest symphony orchestras came out and plan to give concerts in the west. Several of the best conductors came with them.

Eight, many of Hungary's best artists crossed the border.

Nine, and many of her notable writers.

Ten, several members of the Hungarian Olympic team decided to stay in Australia, others defected along the way home and still others refused to take the final plunge back into communism. This was a major propaganda defeat.

Eleven, and most impressive of all, were the young couples with babies. No group came across the bridge at Andau without its quota of young married couples. At a point fifteen miles inside Hungary, doctors of amazing courage passed among the would-be refugees and gave each mother some sedative pills for her children, so that they would be asleep during the critical attempt to pass the Soviet guards, lest an unexpected wailing betray the whole convoy. Then, in Austria, other doctors would have to revive the children lest they sleep too long.

For an American to understand what this great exodus meant, this comparison might be meaningful. When the final count is in, it will probably be found that about two per cent of the total population of the nation has fled. If this happened in America, about 3,400,000 would leave the country, or the population of Philadelphia, Boston, Providence and Fort Worth combined. If that happened, it would be obvious that something was wrong with the United States.

But even this comparison misses the essential truth, for it was not the total population of a city like Boston—the young and the old—that left Hungary. It was mainly the young, often the elite of the nation.

Here is a better analogy. Suppose things got so bad in America that the following types of people felt they had to abandon a rotten system: the University of Southern

California en masse, the Notre Dame football team and the Yankees, Benny Goodman's orchestra, the authors of the ten current best sellers, the actors in six Broadway plays, Henry Ford III and Walter Reuther, the Chicago Symphony Orchestra, all the recent graduates of the Massachusetts Institute of Technology, the five hundred top practical mechanics on the General Motors assembly line, the secretaries of the eighteen toughest unions, and a million young married couples with their children.

Now suppose that the average age of these Americans fleeing their homeland was twenty-three, that they were the kinds of people who might normally be expected to have brilliant futures before them, that there were no aged or sick or mentally defeated among them . . . only the best. Would you not say that something terribly wrong had overtaken America if such people rejected it? That's what happened in Hungary.

The drama at Andau never ended. Robert Martin Gray, the hard-working operations officer of the Intergovernmental Committee for European Migration, guided into camp a nine-year-old boy and his mother. The boy's story was so ridiculous that Gray checked his age several times. The child said, "When we ran out of gasoline we used water in our bombs. They worked just as good, because when we threw them into a tank, the Russians would get scared and try to get out and older boys would shoot them."

The child's mother said, "On the first two mornings after he had stayed out all night I gave him spankings. A nine-year-old boy out on the streets all night. He said, 'But Mother, I've been blowing up tanks.' How can you spank a child who has been blowing up tanks?"

Each story was more bizarre than the last. Through the dusk one evening came a tall, very handsome young man who said in perfect English, "See if you can do anything for the men back there. We were fired on. Of a hundred and ten who tried to get through, only twenty-nine made it."

When we asked his name, he said boldy, "I'm Josef Kormany, a citizen of Canada. My home is at 82 Emerald

Street in North Hamilton, Ontario." His story was so pathetic, and his manner of telling it so free from bitterness, that we were amazed both that he could have lived through it and that he could have retained such an appealing simplicity.

"I had a good job with General Motors of Canada, and I was a high official in United Auto Workers Local 199 of the CIO. All my life I had been a good union man, and on the side I served as program manager for Hungarian-language programs over Station CKTB.

"Why did I got to Hungary? It was my homeland and I wanted to see what was happening under communism. I found out. The AVO took away my passport, told me I was now a citizen not of Canada but of Hungary. So I tried to escape and they shouted at me, 'Who sent you in to spy, Tito or Truman?' I would rather not tell you what they did to me.

"They finished by beating me senseless and sending me to the coal mines as a slave laborer. I had some really awful experiences, but do you know what infuriated me most? I could still strangle that guard. . . .

"This is what that monster did. We weren't slaves; we were worse than slaves down in this awful mine. We worked twelve hours a day, but to make things look good, they paid us a regular wage. Of course they took it all away from us for food and lodging and renting our prison uniforms and paying for the guards. But if we worked long hours overtime we got just enough cash to buy a few cigarettes and some jam. You'd be astonished at how men would cry when they could get one piece of bread with a little jam on it.

"So on the day after we bought our cigarettes and jam, while we were down in the pits where you wouldn't be able to get a free man even to visit, let alone work, this guard, may God damn him perpetually, would go through our prison cells and crumple up our cigarettes and mix them with the jam and then smear it over the dirty floor."

Nobody said anything, and after a moment Josef Kormany, who wanted me to use his real name, swore, "In Canada there used to be two Hungarian-language newspapers that were communist. I now have only one job in life. I'm going back to Canada and fight those newspapers. I used to think that they told lies. I used to wonder about some of their promises. I don't have to wonder any more.

"From 1951 to 1956 Hungarian communists kept me bottled up in prisons so bad I can't describe them. Why? Because they guessed that I had seen through the lies by which communists govern. I'll tell you one thing, I never forgot, no matter how bad they treated me, that I was a Canadian citizen. I knew I'd get out some day. But God help the Hungarian I meet in Canada who tries to peddle communism now."

His name was Josef Kormany, of North Hamilton, Ontario, and he was vitally important to me for a special reason. Some time earlier I had heard the athlete narrate his hair-raising story about Major Meat Ball, the sadistic woman jailer. I wanted very much to report this story but I held back because I was tormented by a fear that I had been told either a lie or a vast embroidery worked onto a thin fabric of truth. So I had asked dozens of refugees, "You ever hear of Major Meat Ball?" and no one had. So I decided not to use the story. Then along came Josef Kormany.

"Know her? You bet I know her! She worked out of 60 Stalin Street. About thirty-five, pockmarked, thick lips, red hair. Anybody like me who was taken to 60 Stalin Street knew the Meat Ball."

"Would you say that she was a sadist?" I asked casually.

"I wouldn't tell even you what she used to do."

So if anyone doubts my reports on Major Meat Ball, he can write to Josef Kormany, North Hamilton, Ontario, and he will find that I have told only a selected part of the horror. Kormany can provide the details.

Through the darkness the refugees came, men who had walked the hundred and ten miles from Budapest, and often they carried with them some single document that would testify to their honorable participation in the fight for freedom. Under some flickering light they would produce a torn and sweaty piece of paper, which they had carried in a shoe, stating, "Lajos Bartok fought at the

Kilian Barracks for three days. The Revolutionary Committee. He has a brother in Los Angeles, 81 Queen Street."

It was in such a wavering light that a rugged workman with gray eyes and brown hair one night drew his family of three sons and a tired wife about him and produced his document: "Letter of Commendation. Csepel, November 3, 1956. The Revolutionary Committee of Csepel has asked Gyorgy Szabo to carry a gun and to ride in a car if necessary while doing his work in defense of the revolution. Ivanitch Istvan, President of the National Committee." There was a stamp on the document, and it is Szabo's story that I have told in my account of the men from Csepel. After his wife had broken down on that last night in Csepel, the family had walked over a hundred miles to freedom, the parents carrying two of the children most of the way in their arms.

Others came out more dramatically. Imre Geiger, the tough kid with the useless rifle and dangling cigarette, walked miraculously straight down the open railway track to Nickelsdorf, the most dangerous single escape route in Hungary, since it was patrolled by Russians. On came the cocky young fighter, lugging his rifle right toward an Austrian outpost, which under the rules of war would have had to arrest him, disarm him and send him back to Hungary.

Another refugee already safe inside Austria ran down the railway track to scream at Geiger, "Throw away the gun!"

"Never!" the wiry dead-end kid shouted back.

"They'll send you back to Hungary!"

Young Imre Geiger stopped dead in the middle of the Nickelsdorf tracks. Why he was not shot down I will never know. "They'll send me back?" he shouted, a standing target for the Russians.

"Run, run!" His adviser scrambled back to safety and watched in horror as young Geiger remained outlined against the barren sky, just standing there looking at his rifle. Finally, as if surrendering an arm or a mother, he tossed it aside and continued his stroll down the tracks. No refugee came out of Hungary with greater bravado, and it is perplexing to think that while he came right through the Russians, lugging his rifle, more cautious groups, tracing their way through swamps in secrecy and silence, were being caught.

Each night contained its miracles. For me the most haunting came when Barrett McGurn of the New York *Herald Tribune* and I stood watch toward four o'clock one morning. There had been crowds of refugees, singing and kissing each other and some even with bottles so they could toast freedom the moment they touched Austrian soil. Never were they alone, for they traveled in groups to sustain their courage on the last long hike through the swamps.

It had been a night of almost unbearable tension, watching these souls from the grave well up out of the dark canal and then burst into song. But toward dawn, when the cold was tearing at your ability to stay by the canal another minute, there loomed out of the darkness a solitary figure whom neither McGurn nor I will ever be able to forget as long as we live.

It was a woman, all alone in the bitter night. She was a tall woman with gray hair and a handsome face. She wore a coat that would have been suitable for an evening at the opera. It had a bit of fur about it but no warmth. Her dress was thin and her scarf was quite inadequate.

She loomed out of the darkness like a demented queen from some Shakespearean play. Why she was alone we never knew. When she saw us she hesitated, and if we had been Russian soldiers, I am sure she would have jumped into the canal and tried to escape, but when she heard us speaking English she came up to us through the icy air and spoke rapidly in French. "I have been walking three days," she said. "Before that the Russians caught some of us and held us in a bunker for forty-eight hours. Some of us were shot. I escaped. How far must I go now?"

"Only one more kilometer to the hut," McGurn lied to encourage her.

"I can make that. If I have survived the last three years, I can survive the last kilometer."

Then she went into the cold mists. Who was she? We never knew. What torments was she fleeing? We could only guess. But as she went down the silent canal, a great gaunt figure of triumphant tragedy, fighting against the darkness totally alone, I saw something that haunts me still. She wore high-heeled shoes and had worn them through the long miles, the Russian prison and the swamps.

I missed the most gallant incident at Andau, but Dan Karasik, the red-headed announcer for CBS, not only saw this beau geste but photographed portions of it. On a rainy day, when the swamp to the south had become impassable, large numbers of Hungarians, including many families, tried to penetrate the marshes to the east, and here, in the tall rushes, they became hopelessly lost. The AVO, discovering this, moved in under Russian direction, and started to pick up the would-be escapees and haul them off to prison camps.

At this point Karasik saw, coming through the head-high rushes to the east, a young Hungarian man of perhaps twenty. He wore no cap, no overcoat. He was a husky chap, and when he reached the shallow drainage canal that separated the eastern rush fields from Austria, he plunged heartily in, splashed his way across and asked one question: "Austria?"

"Yes," Karasik said.

"Good," the young man grunted in German. He then turned, splashed back through the icy water and in about ten minutes led to safety some fifteen Hungarians, blue with cold.

"Austria," the young man said, but before the refugees could thank him, he had disappeared into the rushes, and for a while Karasik heard him thrashing around; then he dramatically appeared with another convoy, muttering only the magic word, "Austria."

He made three more trips, but on his next the lookout in the tower spotted him and by means of signals and gunshots directed a team consisting of two border guards and an AVO man into the very rushes where the young scout had gone for his sixth group. There were shots, a scuffle and then, to the horror of the watching Americans inside

Austria, the three patolmen appeared with the young bareheaded Hungarian as their captive.

They led him down the canal path to the tower, but before they got him there he broke away and dived into the rushes alongside the canal. There was a mad scramble, and after many tense minutes the young guide broke once more through the rushes and splashed to safety. Karasik says, "A cheer went up. You couldn't help it."

But many brave men faced equal perils. What set this particular young man apart was his next action. Says Karasik, "After the guards had gone disconsolately back to their tower the young man sat down, took off his soggy shoes, and disclosed the fact that he had no socks. His feet must have frozen. But from around his neck he took another pair of spare dry shoes and put them on. We thought he intended to use them for the hike to the trucks and some dry clothes.

"Instead he stood on the Austrian side of the canal and listened. Over in the rushes he heard a noise and he started back into Hungary. We pleaded with him not to take such a risk, but he said, '*Ungarn!*' (Hungarian!) which meant, 'There are still some Hungarians lost in there.' And while we watched in silent wonder, he made three more trips through the bitter-cold waters of the swamp and brought out all his countrymen."

But if I missed this remarkable performance, I did see one that became a legend along the frontier. When Russians guarded the bridge, and when the thermometer dropped to a paralyzing nine degrees above zero, we prayed that the deep canal which cut off the marshes to the south would freeze, thus providing another escape route. But stubbornly it refused to do so; only a thin film of razor-sharp ice formed on the surface. To this semi-frozen canal came a young married man, his exhausted wife and two children. There was no way for them to cross to safety, and AVO men with dogs could be expected along at any moment.

So this father took off all his clothes, then lifted his little girl in his arms and plunged into the deep canal.

Breaking the ice with his chest and one free arm, he waded across, climbed up through the marshy slopes and deposited his child in Austria.

Then he returned to Hungary, rolled his clothes in a ball and handed them to his son, whom he lifted high in the air for his second trip through the freezing waters of the canal. Again he stumbled up the steep and marshy bank and delivered his child to freedom.

Once more he sloshed his way back through the deep canal to lift his weary wife in his arms and bring her to safety. Not one of his family got even so much as a foot wet, and if this man lives today—it seemed doubtful when I last saw his totally blue body—he is a walking monument to the meaning of the word love.

Out of the reeds and out of the rushes, out of the mud and the muck, through the swamps and across the canal, over the rickety bridge they came—the finest people in Hungary. A Norwegian Red Cross woman once caught my arm as she saw them and cried, "How can a nation let such people go?"

How arrogantly they came, with honor stamped on their faces. Once I met forty-four of the most handsome, brave and cocky young people I have ever seen. They had come from all parts of Hungary. No one had led them, no one had driven them, but from every type of home they had converged on the bridge at Andau, and as they passed me on their way to exile I counted the things they had brought with them: these forty-four refugees had among them two girls' handbags, two brief cases and one paper bag of bread. That was how they left, in the clothes they wore.

I asked one of them, "Why did you bring so little?"

And he said, "Whatever the communists let us have, they can keep."

They came only with their honor.

The overpowering drama of this great exodus gripped me as previous evacuations had failed to do, and I went back night after night to help bring in the fugitives. Most of the stories told in this book were acquired initially at Andau. Many of the Hungarians I speak of here I first met in the night watches at Andau.

Boys like young Josef Toth, who fell wounded at the attack on the radio station, were helped here by their friends and limped to freedom. Married couples like Zoltan and Eva Pal walked to the border and escaped after their brief taste of peace. Csoki, the Little Chocolate Drop, strutted his way across the bridge, and so did Istvan Balogh, the university student—Peter Szigeti, the communist intellectual, had come out by another route. The most memorable family, of course, were the Janos Hadjoks and their crippled brother-in-law, but there were others whose stark drama shocked all who came into contact with them.

It was nearly four o'clock one wintry night when out of the mists came a man of middle size, his attractive, trim young wife and their two children. I greeted them at the edge of the bridge and said that Austria was just a few hundred yards away. To my surprise the husband said in excellent English, "That's good news." And his excited wife cried happily, "Now my two children are safe." Then the quartet passed on to freedom with perhaps the most significant story of the evacuation, although I did not know it at the time.

For the traveler was John Santo, and soon his story was flashed around the world as indicative of what was happening in Hungary. Santo had once been secretary-treasurer of the Transport Workers of America (CIO) in New York and had been deported in 1949 on charges of being a communist. With a great flourish, Hungary had given him and his Brooklyn-born wife political asylum and then a top political position: dictator of the meat industry for all of Hungary.

His story was inevitable. He had become disillusioned with communism in practice and was now fleeing the country to seek new asylum in America, as a penitent communist who was willing to help unravel strands of the conspiracy in America. "Communism," he said, "is a dictatorship against the proletariat, against the farmers, against the former factory owners, against the aristocracy, against everyone." He had suffered the economic tyranny of the system as long as possible and had then walked out.

There were many curious aspects to this great migration. No one ever understood why the Russians allowed so many Hungarians to escape. On good days more than eight thousand walked across the border unmolested. They had been brought to points only a few miles away in trains and trucks which the Soviets could easily have intercepted, and the rumor became current: "The Russians are sending a hundred thousand spies into Austria." Certainly the bulk of the refugees moved with Russian knowledge, if not with their full approval. A likely theory developed that "the Reds have had so much trouble with Hungarians that they don't care if they all leave the country." Indeed, if the rate of exodus of the first two months had been projected into the future, Hungary would have been totally depopulated in less than eight years.

But on other days, and one never knew when this would happen, the Russians clamped down with machine guns, police dogs, phosphorous flares, road blocks, land mines and special patrols. Then either escape from Budapest or penetration of the border defenses became most difficult, and many would-be refugees either stumbled into AVO hands or were betrayed by their guides, and were sent, the survivors feared, to Siberia.

Thus one man might make the trip from Budapest in the manner of a gay excursion, whereas the next went through mud and hell to gain freedom. It was truly said of the refugees, "Each man who crosses the border is a novel; any ten men comprise an epic."

We often suspected that the Hungarian guards along the border were fed up with the evil system of which they had to be a part. One day while I was standing at the check point directing refugees where to go as they came down the canal from the bridge, a father appeared with two sons, the older a strong lad of about thirteen, the younger a boy of nine. The father was a sober-faced man in a fur shako, and after all the other refugees had been allowed to pass down the canal footpath and into Austria, the two Hungarian guards at the check point made him remain in Hungary with his two sons.

Those of us who were watching assumed that the guards

had refused permission for this man to pass, and there was a visible mood of tragedy upon us all, but finally one of the Hungarian guards, slinging his sub-machine gun over his back, came to speak in German to Claiborne Pell, an officer of the International Rescue Committee who was observing the border.

To Pell's astonishment, the guard said, "The little boy is afraid to leave Hungary until his mother gets here, too. She may never get here. Won't you see if you can get the boy to join you. It would be better if he left Hungary."

I was given the job of talking with the boy, although I knew no Hungarian, but since I had on a good overcoat the child assumed that I must be a communist official, and when I bent down to talk with him he bravely opened his shirt and raised his hands to show me that he had no weapons or official documents hidden on his person.

I knelt on the frozen ground and put my arm about the whimpering boy. "You better come on over on this side of the line," I said. The fact that I did not strike him, that I was apparently not an official, was too much for the boy and he collapsed in my arms weeping. I said to the father, "Tell him his mother may get out later."

The father and the older boy stepped into Austria and the Hungarian guard turned his face while I carried the weeping boy to join them. I had gone only a few steps when there was a shattering explosion of machine-gun fire, and I turned back panic-stricken. Claiborne Pell was laughing. He explained, "The guard wanted the other guards back in the tower to think he was on the job. So he fired a volley into the air."

When Pell and the shakoed father had left the frontier with the two boys, the communist guard and I looked at each other for some time, and after a while he took me by the arm and led me well into Hungary, right past the observation tower with its machine guns and across the bridge. There was a woman with two children, and one of the girls was unable to walk any further. The Russians might come along at any moment, and it would be wise if the family hurried on.

So the guard hoisted the little girl and put her on my

shoulder. Then he hustled the woman and the other child over the bridge and led us all back into Austria. At the border he fired another blast to let his AVO bosses know that he was on the alert, and I carried the sick little girl to freedom.

And there was one freedom fighter with no legs, and no wooden legs to replace them. This man caught a bus ride from Budapest to a point about fifteen miles from the border. These last fifteen miles he covered by pulling himself along on his hands. When we got to him the stumps of his legs were almost rubbed raw, and his hands were cut and bleeding from the frozen soil. Nobody said much about this man, for there was nothing that words could add.

One night at Andau an extremely handsome young blond giant of twenty-four came swinging down the path, as if he had not a care in the world nor any bad memories to forget. I got to know him and found that he bore one of Hungary's noblest names—something like Festetich or Tisza or Andrassy or Karolyi or Esterhazy. These are names which hold no charm for me, personally, because it was partly due to the reactionary principles of such nobles that Hungary was prevented from taking the necessary steps that might have forestalled communism.

But I was impressed by this young man, let's call him Esterhazy. He was able, quick-witted, good-humored and not at all disposed to feel sorry for himself. He said, "My branch of the family dates back well before the sixteenth century. We wound up with fifty peasants and four thousand holds of land near Budapest. I was only fourteen when our land was expropriated, but I understood why that had to be done. Yet when my family of six was moved into a two-room peasant cottage I found that the peasants were very good to us, even though it involved some risk. They brought us food and clothing and sat around with my father as if he were an equal friend.

"It was when I started to grow up that I appreciated what had really happened. I started college, but when they found out I was an Esterhazy, I was kicked out. I had to live surreptitiously with friends, but when anyone on the street discovered that I was an Esterhazy, I had to move.

My friends were willing to take the risk, but I wasn't willing to subject them to it.

"I tried to go to the university but was told, 'There is no place in Hungary for people like you.'

"I asked, 'Then can I leave Hungary and get a job in America?'

"They said, 'No. In America you would tell lies about the new Hungary.'

"When I asked, 'Then what can I do?' they gave no answer."

But because he had dared to ask about leaving Hungary —a fearful crime in a land where the leaders say everyone is happy—the AVO began to torment him and he was thrown into a forced-labor gang to work in the sugar-beet fields. I don't know whether this next statement is true, it sounds so unbelievable, but young Esterhazy said, "We were hauled out of bed at three o'clock in the morning and we worked with only one decent meal till midnight. Three hours later we were hauled back to work. This went on for three months until the AVO felt that we had been properly indoctrinated. Then we were set free.

"But we still could take no job, find no place in society. I asked in despair how I was to spend my life and they said, 'In the labor battalion.'

"My life in this army was one of long persecution. Officers would see my name and call out, 'All right, Esterhazy! You clean out the sewer.' Day after day they found joy in assigning me to such jobs, but I found that my fellow workers in the labor battalion took no part in the persecution. Their attitude seemed to be, 'So he's an Esterhazy. But that's no reason why he shouldn't live.' "

Yet in the revolution against the Soviets these same labor battalion men, who were among the most furious fighters, would not permit Esterhazy to aid them. "We don't want anyone to say that former noblemen helped us," the fighters told him. "Wait until we have won, then things will be better for everybody."

I hesitated a long time before including the story of the young nobleman. I reasoned, "If I even mention an Esterhazy the Russians will say, 'See, he wants the old regime back.' " But then I thought, "My former students in Colorado, who remember how I argued in 1938 that if the nobles of Hungary did not distribute their lands there would have to be revolution, will know that I never had much sympathy for the Festetichs and Esterhazys." I was glad to find that young Esterhazy did not have too much sympathy for them, either.

For the important aspect of this story was that the young man I met at Andau was a marvelous human being. He could have made a fine engineer, or a good professor, or an excellent manager of a freight office. He had an affinity for machines, taught himself German and French, seemed to be promising in mathematics. No one I know in Hungary wants to put young Count Esterhazy back in control of his 1938 peasants, or even to restore to him his four thousand holds of land near Budapest. Those days are gone, and he knew it better than I.

But for a society conscientiously to degrade human beings because of their accidental birth is disgraceful. For any nation to deprive itself of the capacities of any man is really a sin against the entire society. And if a system not only refuses to use native capacities but establishes a regime for stunting or destroying those capacities, then such a regime is doomed.

Young Esterhazy played no part in organizing or operating the revolution. That was done by others who were disgusted with the way their nation in all its aspects was being criminally abused. When I last saw Esterhazy he was on his way to Great Britain. "Maybe plastics or automotive engineering or electronics," he said. "Anything that's useful to the world."

No matter how long one stayed at the border, he was constantly surprised. One night a Hungarian man of thirty who spoke English helped me with translations and I sought to repay his kindness.

"Do you need any money?" I asked him as dawn came over the frozen marshes.

"Not money," he replied. "But I have always wanted to see the Vienna opera."

"You shall, tonight."

Like everyone else, he had come out with one suit, but somehow that first day he got it pressed, and as we entered the bright new building of the Vienna opera he said, "I've heard about this new production of Carmen. In Budapest we were hungry for any news of European art."

"What new production?" I asked.

"Vienna has hired a brilliant young Russian, Georges Wakhewitsch, to design a completely new Carmen. It's supposed to be glorious."

When the curtain rose, Wakhewitsch's Carmen hit me right in the eye. It was dazzling. First, the designer had built on the stage several complete houses with roof-top patios, and large plazas hung midway between the village street and the roofs, so that action took place on three levels. Next he had dressed literally hundreds of extras and chorus members in brilliant costumes, so that as the action swirled about the stage, there was a constantly changing kaleidoscope of color harmonies. Finally he had arranged the opera so that there was a great ebb and flow of human beings, more than I had ever dreamed Carmen could accommodate.

Wakhewitsch's Carmen was not a Spanish opera, but it was grand opera. Micaela was a winsome little German girl down from the Alps in a dirndl. The big blond chorus girls were German girls come to Seville from Munich. And the pace of the opera was heavily deliberate, with the best notes hung onto by both orchestra and singers until the spirit of the action was lost.

"I don't mind the words being sung in German," my Hungarian whispered. "Gives a kind of Spanish effect." I agreed with him. They sounded more Iberian than the customary French words.

And I thought that Wakhewitsch had been downright brilliant in his staging of the toreador's song, during which the top tier of the stage was filled with Spanish dandies dressed all in black and lighting the song with dozens of candles. My refugee thought the third act was best, when no footlights of any kind were used, only traveling spots which followed the principal figures from above and made Carmen's song of fate and death immensely powerful.

In the intermission following this gloomy act my Hungarian said quietly, "You cannot know what it means to come back into the full world of art. A modern production of *Carmen*. How we used to long for communication with the rest of Europe." He sat literally bathed in the joy of hearing Bizet, and toward the end of the intermission he said, "And to see as my first opera one in which a new artist is trying to accomplish something new. This is very exciting."

But neither of us was prepared for the last act of this bright new *Carmen*. From Bizet's *Fair Maid of Perth* the music for an extensive ballet had been lifted, and now as the curtains parted we were thrust into the middle of Seville. The entire depth of the stage was used, several house fronts having been built, and the rim of a complete bull ring. To the left a chorus of many Spaniards stood vocalizing the borrowed music, while from the distant rear of the immense stage at least sixty ballerinas approached from so far away that they looked like children. After them came sixteen separate groups of bullfighters, followed by officials, townspeople, hangers-on and finally Escamillo and Carmen. And from the rafters that crossed his stage, Wakhewitsch had hung some two dozen great chunks of cloth in brilliant colors, draped like bullfighters' capes. It was an overpowering scene and prepared one for the magnitude of the final tragedy.

If the reader is surprised that I have interrupted my account of the revolution so long to speak of *Carmen*, I would say only this. Those of us who met the refugees at the border or in Vienna were unprepared for the spiritual hunger with which these people wanted to talk about art and ideas, about politics and the nature of man's experience. One of the most promising aspects of the Hungarian revolution was that it was initiated by men who wanted the human spirit to be inquiring and free. They wanted the simple rights of talk, and honest newspapers, and respect for differing opinions.

The aspect of the revolution which surprised me most was the profound longing with which Hungarian intellectuals wanted to return to the community of European nations. Many spoke of this with fervor. "Of all that Russia robbed us of," my chance interpreter said that night, "the most precious was communication with our fellow citizens of Europe." Shortly before the revolution broke out, a Hungarian poet, Tamas Aczel, expressed this longing in his "Ode to Europe," passages of which have been translated as follows:

> Europe, our common mother, we return to thee.
> Set an example, show us how,
> As you have done for centuries . . .
>
> Be with us, Europe,
> Common fate, love, work, future.
> Oh, beating heart, pure truth
> To plow, to sow, to harvest, to die and rise again
> 　　a thousand times.

After the opera my companion observed, "The intellectuals inspired the students and the students inspired the workingmen from Csepel. But do you know why the students felt they had to revolt? Because whenever they wanted to read one of the world's important books they were forbidden. But they were free to read some communist's critique of the book. I know what communism thinks is wrong with Schopenhauer. But I don't know Schopenhauer. Only what some third-rate communist thought about him.

"For example, Georges Wakhewitsch is a White Russian. I'm sure that in Budapest I could have read everything that was wrong with his version of Carmen. It would have been a corrupt capitalist work that offended the great soul of the workingman. I like things better the way you do them in Vienna. You don't lecture me about what's wrong with Carmen. You let me see for myself.

"Does all my talk about Carmen bore you?" the refugee asked finally. "You don't know how wonderful it is to be able to sit here with a glass of beer and talk. And if discussing Carmen leads you to get mad at Eisenhower or Bulganin, you can say so, and nobody arrests you. How delightful it is to let talk lead on to new ideas. In Budapest if you talked about Carmen you always stopped with the music, and even then you had to be careful to say what was accepted at that moment."

If Americans forget that Hungary rebelled against communism primarily because the young people of the nation wanted intellectual freedom, we would miss one of the focal truths of this revolution. We must remember that there are men in this world who are willing to fight for the right to read newspapers and to argue about what has been said. There were young men in Budapest who laid down their lives because they wanted to return to a system in which a man could sit with friends over a glass of beer and let the wild flow of ideas lead where it would.

At one camp near Andau, a Catholic priest visited a group of refugee students and asked, "Now that you are free, would you like me to conduct religious services here next Sunday?"

The boys were embarrassed, but finally one said, "Father, we thought we'd just sit around and talk."

The priest understood and laughed: "Yes . . . after so much silence."

The climax at Andau came on Wednesday, November 21, when the maximum number of refugees came into Austria across the Einser Canal. It was a cold, crystal day of memorable beauty, and thousands of Hungarians sought refuge. They resembled the procession of prisoners who march into daylight from the dungeon in Beethoven's *Fidelio*.

Then, as dusk fell, there was an ominous halt to the procession. Figures already on the canal bank passed us . . . but no more came. A whispered rumor flashed down the canal: "The AVO have arrived." There was a silent half hour as cold winds from the marshes moaned through the bare branches of the white birches that lined the canal, and those of us who were watching tried to penetrate the faltering light to see what was happening at the bridge.

Suddenly there was a dull, distant garrrummmph! We peered into the darkness and saw nothing, but a refugee who had been waiting for a chance to escape came rushing down the canal bank shouting, "They dynamited the bridge!"

In order to find out how much damage had been done, two daring spies wormed their way along the canal and well into Hungary. By the dim light of flares which the guards in the watchtower were using they saw that the bridge at Andau had indeed been destroyed. The two rude pillars on either bank were standing, and part of the bridge itself, the southern span, if so inconsequential a bridge could be thought of as having spans, had been blown apart. Gloomily the spies confirmed the bad news. "The bridge can't be used."

Night now enveloped us, and we thought of the thousands of refugees who were huddling in chilled groups throughout the Hungarian swamps. They were only a few feet from freedom, seeking desperately some way to cross that final barrier of the canal and the steep banks they must negotiate before reaching Austria. But the bridge was useless, and unless some alternative was discovered quickly, these refugees would be stranded in sight of freedom but powerless to attain it.

The moon rose over the silent canal. Frost grew mysteriously on the frozen marshes and reeds crackled when a man walked through them. We were about to experience one of the fabled white nights of Central Europe, when the birches and the shimmering icy swamp and the pale, powdery moon combined to make one of the most beautiful sights I have ever seen in nature. This was not only my opinion; five different war-toughened reporters from countries around the world reported the same fact. The silence of this magnificent night, following the joyful chatter of the day, created an atmosphere of almost unbearable emotional intensity.

For several hours we listened in real agony as the escape route remained empty . . . the great flood of humanity finally cut off. I cannot explain the pain we felt that strange night, for in contrast to the empty footpaths, the heavens were a thing of crowded glory. There was a shining harvest moon, a wealth of stars, a white glaze over the world. The night was bitter cold and had therefore pre-cipitated a hoarfrost that covered both the rushes to the south and the Austrian swamps to the north. But most memorable of all was the tragic silence, for where there had been the laughter and uncontrolled joy of people finding safety from communism, now there was only silence.

Toward midnight a brave team of three Austrian college students decided that something must be done, and they lugged logs into Hungary and repaired the dynamited bridge—not well, but enough for a precarious foothold—and by this means they saved more than two thousand people that night alone.

They were just college kids with earmuffs and no caps, but they had abundant courage, for after their wet clothes had frozen on them, they crossed their own improvised bridge and combed the Hungarian swamps, dodging com-munist guards and Russian outposts. They led many refugees to their bridge, and we marveled at their daring.

Then came the flood! Hundreds upon hundreds of refugees came across that frail footbridge. They would come down the canal bank in an excess of joy, having found rescue when all seemed lost. They would hear the Austrian students cry, "This is Austria!" and they would literally collapse with gladness.

But as they walked along the canal bank, another more cautious student would warn them, "Don't walk on the bank. It's still Hungary, Russians have been shooting at the silhouetes." And the refugees would climb down the bank and fan out across the frozen, snow-white marshes of Austria. One aspect of their flight had given them a weird, ethereal being: they had come so many miles through the crisp night air that hoarfrost had formed on their backs, and they looked like bent-over snow men from a fairy tale. Mists rose from the bitter cold ground and enveloped them, but still they moved on under the silvery November moon, like ghost figures from another world, walking neither in time nor in space but in freedom.

I have never seen anything more beautiful. Not only was nature dressed in cold perfection, but the emotion of that starry night was beyond the capacity of a man to absorb. Once a woman nearly fainting from hunger and exhaustion came down the trail and I thought she was going to collapse, but when she heard the word "Austria!" she summoned up her last energy and rushed across the line. There, as if by some supremely appropriate accident, she ran into Barrett McGurn, who had done so much to explain Hungary's plight to the world. In his arms she collapsed, kissing him a dozen times on the forehead and cheeks and lips.

"Oh, God! I reached Austria!" she cried.

McGurn, who had been on the border for hours, handed her on to an Austrian student, who carried her to safety. "I can't take any more," McGurn said, and he trailed off through the mists, through the frozen marshes of Austria.

It was at this time that I met a brave and daring photographer whose pictures helped tell the story of Hungary's mass flight to freedom. He would go anywhere, and for the next several nights we patrolled the border together, bringing in hundreds of Hungarians. Sometimes we went well into Hungary, occasionally up to the bridge and always with an ear cocked for that sweetest of night sounds, the soft, tentative calls of men and women seeking freedom.

One very cold night we were on the watch when toward dawn we heard curious sounds coming from the temporary bridge. We crept up as close as we dared and saw a revolting sight. The communist guards, well liquored up, were chopping down the bridge and burning it to keep their feet warm. Then, as we crouched there observing them, we witnessed a tragedy that neither of us will ever forget.

A band of some thirty refugees, led by a man in a fur cap, appeared mysteriously out of the Hungarian swamps and walked directly toward the drunken guards. These unlucky people had no way of knowing that the bridge was no longer a route to freedom, and we were powerless to stop them. Quickly the guards grabbed their rifles and dogs, and the last refugees to reach the bridge at Andau were rounded up and carted off to prison. They had walked no one knew how far and had come to within fifty feet of freedom. Heartsick, the photographer and I crept back with the sound of communist axes in our ears, and by the time we reached the corner of Austria the bridge at Andau had forever vanished.

But there was to be one final miracle. Long after the bridge had burned and when AVO policemen and Russians with trained dogs patrolled the routes, a night came when freezing rains had made the swamps totally impassable and even the teams of Austrian students gave up hope. But a beautiful young English newspaperwoman, Shelley Rohde of the *Daily Express*, went out for one last midnight look.

She walked along the dike, past the rush fields and the swamps and into Hungary to where the bridge of freedom had once stood. It was a cold, quiet night, broken only by the chatter of a machine gun somewhere back in the swamps or lighted for a moment by star shells of flaming phosphorous which the Russians used for trapping escapees unexpectedly. Miss Rohde had taken a few mental notes describing this desolate land of swamps and had started back toward Andau when she heard off in the distance the crying of a baby.

She was alone, but the crying was so insistent that she went, at rather great peril to herself, in pursuit of the wailing night sounds. By great good luck the baby's mother could not silence it, and before long Miss Rohde came upon a group of twenty-two starving, water-soaked, freezing refugees. They had tried to penetrate the Hungarian swamps without a guide, and when this Englishwoman found them, they had been wallowing for two days in a great circle. They had been in Austria once, but had not known it, and were now heading directly back into a Russian encampment.

They were in such condition that they no longer cared whether the baby betrayed them or not. They only wanted to escape the swamp. Whether escape led to freedom in Austria or to prison in Hungary they did not care, for they had spent two days floundering in mud up to their waists and some of them had begun to freeze to death. It was then that the baby had begun its final, before-death wailing, and it was then that an English newspaperwoman decided to take one last look.

The nearly two hundred thousand refugees who reached Austria—it is significant that less than five hundred fled to communist Yugoslavia, which also borders on Hungary—arrived in three clearly defined waves. My experience at Andau, as I have indicated, was almost exclusively with the middle wave—mostly young people, carrying nothing, but containing a surprisingly high percentage of engineers and well-trained technicians. They were, as I have said, the elite of the nation and of the revolution. Already their loss is being felt in the Hungarian economy, and as the years pass, the loss in leadership which they might have exercised will also be detectable. This second group was as fine a body of people as I have ever seen.

The first wave, which I did not see, had a much different construction. A Hungarian sociologist, who left Budapest after the fall of Csepel and later returned surreptitiously, defined this small but very lively first group as follows: "There were a good many prostitutes, who throughout the world seem to have a fine sense of when to move where. The rest of us were fooled by the days of peace, but not these girls. They saw a chance to get out of a doomed city, and they left. Then there were the young adventurers, boys and girls of unstable homes who had always heard of the bright lands to the west. They left us like children in a fairy story going off in search of adventure. Finally, in those first days, there were many cowards who could not face up to the requirements of a free Hungary. Few of us who stayed in Budapest to fight the returning Russians felt any sense of loss at all when those first people left us. But we did feel resentment, and we continue to feel it. It was Hungary's misfortune that her first representatives abroad were such people. I think the countries which took in these particular Hungarian refugees are going to have a lot of trouble with them, and I feel sorry that they accepted such ambassadors. The good name of all of us will suffer."

Fortunately, the first wave was not large and its members will probably do less harm than Hungarian patriots fear. I came into no direct contact with this group, but I did often hear bitter complaints against them. Said one later refugee with a good battle record, "What can you say for a man who fled Hungary before the Russians returned? One word. Coward." In having my written words checked and corrected by Hungarian experts, I encountered the depth of feeling these first refugees had aroused. I had described a young man who had left Budapest at the height of the temporary victory, and one critic said, "Please, sir, change this. No decent Hungarian left when we had a chance to win." I checked my notes and insisted, "It says so right here. I remember what he said." My critic studied for a moment and drew a line through the passage. "If he behaved in that way, it's better we don't even mention him."

It was the third wave that brought in the most refugees and the most problems. In considering this particular group it would be well to keep in mind the unofficial estimates of certain Austrian immigration officials. "Counting all refugees, including those who slipped in without registering, we will probably wind up with around two hundred thousand. Of these, the first wave of adventurous young people numbered not more than three thousand, and they quickly found homes abroad. They're gone and forgotten. The second wave of real refugees, like the ones you saw at Andau, totaled about twenty-five thousand. But remember, even of this select group not more than two thousand had played any vital role in the revolution. That leaves around one hundred and seventy thousand who came out in the third wave, and practically none of them ever fired upon a Russian or committed himself in any way during the revolution. You've seen them. They're fine, clean, healthy, middle-class people who hated communism and saw a good chance to escape. No doubt many of them had wanted to get out ten years ago. This was their chance."

I imagine that the Austrian's figures were correct: about two hundred thousand refugees ultimately, of whom about one per cent participated actively in the revolution. This points up the difference between the second wave of refugees like those I had met at Andau and the third. Members of the former were apt to have had some connection with the revolution (although even among this group the percentage of actual fighters could not have been higher than two thousand among twenty-five thousand) and many fled Hungary because to have remained behind would have been to invite execution or deportation to slave labor camps in Russia. Members of the third wave neither participated in the revolution nor had any reprisals to fear therefrom.

A second difference is more important, even though it grows logically out of the first. True revolutionaries from the second wave who can prove fighting records against the Russians may one day be welcomed back into a free Hungary and might even participate in the government of the country. But members of the third wave who left primarily because they felt they could better themselves abroad will probably never be welcomed back into their homeland. Moreover, if they persist in returning, they could play no part in any foreseeable future government of Hungary.

It was of these later escapees that Representative Omar Burleson of Texas complained when he said, "America is heaping honors befitting a hero upon Hungarians who are deserting those who are willing to remain behind to carry on their fight for independence from the Soviet Union. We know little or nothing about these people who are being admitted. It would be interesting to know how many of those leaving Hungary were really 'revolutionaries' in the first place."

I do not share Representative Burleson's fears, for although it is true, as I have explained above, that only one per cent were fighters in the revolution (two thousand out of about two hundred thousand), nevertheless, many of the remaining ninety-nine per cent were honest seekers after freedom who supported the actual fighters spiritually, and they merit the attention and the sanctuary the world has given them.

However, the friends of Hungary must not underestimate the bitterness felt by those who stayed and fought toward those who fled, particularly against those who scuttled out for personal economic reasons during the third wave. This resentment could be of importance in subsequent political decisions regarding Hungary, and refugees themselves were quick to realize this. Even those unquestioned patriots of the second wave, men who had fought valiantly and who had fled to save their lives, were aware of the dangerous step they had taken. Often they told me, "We left Hungary in its hour of crisis. We will never be welcomed back. Those braver ones who stayed behind will inherit the new Hungary."

Later these refugees tried to rationalize away their first reactions. "Maybe those of us who can prove we fought will be welcomed back," they reasoned. I rather think their their first fears were correct. Hungarians who remained in Budapest and who bore the full brunt of Russian fury will be the eventual rulers of their country, and although it is possible that under extenuating circumstances they might accept participation from their brothers who fled, for them to accept guidance from the refugees who will sit out the great storms of the future in some haven like France or America is unthinkable.

One refugee with a very good record in the 1956 revolution lamented, "The only way for me to work my way back into Hungarian life is with a sub-machine gun as a volunteer patriot when the next revolution occurs. That's the only way I can establish my credentials. I'll never do it by talking. Especially if I do my taking from safety in France or America."

Americans must understand this, for we are prone to uncover refugees whom we like—especially if they had titles or ran big businesses—and to assume that the citizens of other lands are ungrateful if they don't like them too. We set up our self-chosen governments-in-exile, and condemn as radicals those who remain behind and won't accept them. Refugee Hungarians in New York and Chicago, no matter how attractive they may be at cocktail parties, are not going to run the new Hungary when it evolves.

We really ought to stop this nonsense. Hungary will not

be governed by refugees of our choosing; it will be governed by those hard-headed young men who stayed in the universities and in Csepel and who matured with the events of their own national society. What happened in the case of Ferenc Nagy should be a warning to well-intioned Americans.

For several years Ferenc Nagy, a former Hungarian official, has lived in the United States as a kind of unofficial spokesman for his fatherland. He has done a great deal of good in reminding America of Hungarian problems, and has been an able defender of the Hungarian point of view. He became "the Hungarian whom Americans could trust."

When the revolution broke out, Ferenc Nagy was flown posthaste to Vienna, where he started issuing statements and instructions. The reaction from the revolutionary leaders in Budapest was explosive. One message said simply, "If Nagy doesn't get out of Austria within twenty-four hours, we'll shoot him." The Austrian government, which itself had been plagued by several would-be governments-in-exile, many contaminated with former Nazi collaborators, was glad for this excuse to get Ferenc Nagy off its soil, and gave him twenty-four hours to leave. As one Hungarian patriot said, "We weren't mad at Nagy Ferenc. We just didn't want him meddling in our government."

I know that my warning on this delicate point is useless. I suppose that right now governments-in-exile are being established in Paris and in New York. All members of the former speak French and all the latter English, and they are unquestionably fine people. Frenchmen and Americans like them very much, but not the people of Budapest. We must be careful not to ruin our chances in Hungary by trying to foist such a government upon a liberated Hungarian people. This strategy never works, and maybe in another two or three hundred years we'll learn to avoid it.

It is possible that some of the legitimate freedom fighters with impeccable records might be invited back to full participation in some future Hungarian government, but not if freedom is too long delayed. It is tragic how quickly an exile loses touch with the vital currents of his homeland and how outmoded he becomes. However, I do think that in prudent self-interest any future Hungarian government, from extreme left to extreme right, would welcome back in full forgiveness the young scientists who fled, for the loss here was critical. But world industry is so hungry for scientists that within a year those fugitive experts will be dug into fine jobs in Birmingham or Sydney or Detroit. I doubt if Hungary will get many of them back. As for the children, the communist government of Hungary is already demanding that all youths under the age of eighteen be returned, claiming that these infants were kidnaped away from the blessings of communism without their consent and against their wishes, forgetting that a large percentage of Russian tanks were destroyed by just such young people, who certainly knew what their wishes were at that point. But the pull of homeland is a tremendous force, and possibly some of these young people will return to Hungary and find there a satisfactory place for themselves.

For the most part, however, each human being who walked out of Hungary in late 1956 represented a personal tragedy, as well as a momentary triumph. He was walking into freedom, true, but he was also walking away from his homeland and its future, and that is a pathetic thing for a patriot to have to do.

The guides played a strange role. First they were local farmers who, out of the goodness of their hearts, led fellow Hungarians across the last dangerous miles to the border. By one of the coincidences of history, only three months before this enormous migration took place, some communist official in Budapest had ordered all land mines along the Austrian border lifted and destroyed. This single decision probably saved ten thousand lives, for had the entire border been peppered with mines, the loss of life would have been shocking. Who ordered the removal we do not know, but one refugee said of him, "I'll bet he's looking for a new job now."

"No," said another. "He's looking for a new head."

But even without mines, a guide through the swamps and up to the likely crossing spots was a necessity, and after the refugee flood had settled down into a steady flow, these guides charged up to fifty dollars a head to perform their dangerous work. Women and children with no money were ferried to freedom without charge, and many who refused to pay the fee nevertheless found their way into Austria, but there were gloomy tales of groups who tried to save money and did, at the expense of wandering back and forth in Hungary without being able to strike the border.

After the first refugees were settled in Vienna, a deadly game developed. Two or three daring young men would approach likely strangers and ask, "You have anybody in Budapest you want brought out? We'll do it for a thousand American dollars."

These fearless groups would then sneak back into Hungary, repenetrate the border defenses, infiltrate the Budapest check points and appear at an apartment house in the city with the startling news, "Your brother in Vienna asked us to rescue you." Then the three guides and their customer—or sometimes several customers—would retrace the risky journey and fulfill their contracts. Few people who paid the thousand dollars were gypped; all agreed that the young men had well earned their fee.

There was, however, a contemptible racket that grew up around this practice, for some Russian officials learned of the escape route and decided, "If the Hungarians are going to escape anyway, we might as well get some of the money," and they insisted upon part of the rescue fee. This developed into a weird system whereby certain refugees rode from Budapest to a spot about two miles from the border in Russian staff cars, driven by Russian officers. This was escape in the grand manner.

Most hilarious, however, was the experience of one superdaring Hungarian college student who volunteered to rescue an aged man from Budapest for a thousand dollars. He was an honorable young man and he said, "I won't take a penny unless I can bring the old man out. If I succeed, I'll call you from the border and you bring a car to get him. Then I'll take the money." With that he plunged back into Hungary.

Eight anxious days later the man in Vienna who had offered the thousand dollars was vastly relieved to get a phone call from the Hungarian student, who sounded a bit wan. "I have the old man, but don't bring a car. Bring a bus." For when word of escape had trickled through the old man's apartment house, everyone living there had decided to join the trek to freedom. For one fee, the college student had brought out a full bus load of refugees: twenty-seven Hungarians ranging in age from seventy-one years to eight months!

Not all the refugees were heroes. Some men demanded that women leave babies behind lest their cries alarm the guards. Thus, there were numerous cases in which mothers came through the swamps alone, in order to save their children, but the risks taken by one young wife near Andau were beyond the average.

"When my wife left Budapest," her husband relates, "she was already eight months pregnant. We didn't want her to make the trip, but she said she wouldn't live under communism another day. And she didn't want her baby to be born there, either.

"Our trip was a hard one and we had to walk a great deal. All the members of our party tried to help her, but the time came when she couldn't walk any more, so one by one the party had to forge ahead. I was left with my wife in a little woods not far from Andau and we knew her time had come. She said, 'You walk to some farmhouse and see if you can get a woman to help me.'

"I didn't want to leave her alone in the woods, but she kissed me good-by and I tried to find a farmhouse. It took me a long time, and when I brought the farmer back with me we found that my wife had given birth all by herself and had fainted. But before she fainted she had wrapped the baby under her dress. We waited till night and carried her and the baby back to the farmhouse. The farmer's wife kept us hidden for four days, and on the fifth day the farmer led my wife and me and the baby into Austria."

By common consent, the popular hero of the evacuation was a railroad engineer who pulled a stunt which had all Central Europe laughing for weeks. Mihai Kovacs, in the first days of Russia's reoccupation of Budapest, was called to his station in Pest and ordered to drive a long train of sealed boxcars into Russia. He could guess what the cars contained. After he reached Russia he was certain that he was carrying many hundreds of Hungary's finest rebels to concentration camps in either Siberia or Central Asia.

So he used his head. He got one of his crew to fix him up a real big sign in bold black letters. He turned his train around at a little-used siding and came steaming back down the tracks, out of Russia and into Hungary. Through Budapest and Gyor he kept his train going, for the sign encouraged Soviet guards to step aside and let Mihai Kovacs steam ahead.

He took his sealed boxcars right to the Austrian border, where he jammed on the brakes, flung open all the doors and shouted, "Over here is Austria. I'll lead the way." He and his deportees all made it so safety, but he left behind his train and its dazzling big sign: FOOD FOR HUNGARY FROM SOVIET RUSSIA.

At no time did Austria close her borders to such refugees. Instead she welcomed them with a warmth that surprised Europe, for there were many reasons why it would have been prudent for Austria to reject Hungarians who were attempting to flee from communism. For one thing, Austria herself had only recently been freed of Russian occupation and there remained a real danger that the Soviets, on any flimsy excuse, might come storming back. Therefore, Austria's bold offer of sanctuary to the revolutionists was a most gallant action. For America to accept Hungarians was mere charity; for Austria to do so could have been suicide.

For many years there had been a gool deal of friction between Austria and Hungary, the last war between the two nations having ended only recently, and tempers were customarily so touchy that Austria could have been forgiven for any lack of generosity. Instead, she accepted her Hungarian cousins as if she truly loved them.

Finally, Austria is a small nation, with only seven million people and no great resources to share. Had Austrians been niggardly, they could understandably have refused charity to the revolutionists on the grounds that they had few spare goods to share. Instead, they shared them in abundance. For Austria to have accepted, clothed, fed and housed two hundred thousand refugees would be like the United States accepting about five million unexpected guests. We are a rich country, but five million strangers would tax our energies. Austria was not a rich country, yet somehow she made do.

The impact of this torrent of refugees was felt most strongly in the ancient province of Burgenland (Land of Castles), where little Andau huddles near the eastern border. The farmers of Burgenland are not wealthy and the villages are not spacious. Yet it seemed as if every citizen of Burgenland opened both his heart and his resources to the refugees. Farmers with tractors trailed up and down the border roads, hauling women to safety. Farm wives reported to soup kitchens at midnight and worked till dawn. One night I stumbled accidentally into the tiny village of Pamhagen, southwest of Andau, where Burgenlanders were working like pack animals to process an unusually heavy flood of arrivals. At three o'clock in the morning the mayor of Pamhagen arrived in neat uniform, to greet each Hungarian. "We are glad to offer you our homes," he said simply. The women of Pamhagen that night were taking off the muddy shoes and washing the feet of each new Hungarian.

There were villages in Burgenland which had more refugees than citizens. There were schools which literally had sleeping Hungarian children stacked one upon the other. There were farmhouses in Burgenland which held twenty Hungarians to a room. Many communities across the world rise to unexpected and noble performances in times of emergency, but I have never seen anything to surpass the 1956 performance of Burgenland.

To many foreign observers, the most extraordinary behavior was that of the Austrian university students. For sixty nights in a row these daring teen-agers combed the border bringing refugees to freedom. I myself could count from my own experience a dozen lives they saved, and I saw but little. Some formed patrols and probed deep into the swamps. Others tended night fires, and still others watched the canal for drowning Hungarians. Their performance was in the greatest tradition.

The charitable spirit that motivated Austrian behavior was well illustrated one bitterly cold morning when a friend and I were watching a swampy section of the border. An Austrian soldier was with us when we three spotted a large group of Hungarians who were apparently lost and trying to find Austria.

Instinctively the three of us started running forward to aid them, and just as instinctively this young Austrian soldier stopped, pushed me in front of him and said, "Please, hide me. It's better they don't see for their first sight of Austria a gun."

It would require another book to describe in detail Austria's contribution to freedom. I can express it briefly only in this way: If I am ever required to be a refugee, I hope I make it to Austria.

I cannot guess by what twists of history Hungary will regain her freedom. I cannot yet see clearly by what means the Russian yoke will be lifted from the necks of the Hungarian people, but I am convinced that in that happy day Hungarians from their new homes all over the world will send in their money—their francs, their dollars, their pounds Australian, and their pesos—to erect at Andau a memorial bridge.

It need not be much, as bridges go: not wide enough for a car nor sturdy enough to bear a motorcycle. It need only be firm enough to recall the love with which Austrians helped so many Hungarians across the old bridge to freedom, only wide enough to permit the soul of a free nation to pass.

10   The Russian Defeat

The Hungarian revolution of 1956 was a turning point in
world history. Of this there can be no doubt. Unfortunately, we cannot yet predict in which direction the road
of communism will now turn, but it simply cannot continue in its old course. Perhaps Russian troops will have
to occupy Hungary outright in an undisguised iron dictatorship, turning the land into a moral and economic
desert. But on the other hand the Russians may find this
policy too costly in men and money and may have to
modify their grip on the land and permit some kind of
autonomy and freedom to the Hungarian people. But
whatever the new course, it is absolutely clear that Russia
has lost a propaganda battle of critical proportions, and
the extent of the loss cannot even now be estimated.

There is a way, however, to understand how grievously
Russia has been hurt. Imagine the total Soviet position as
a lake over which a green scum of lies, propaganda, window
dressing and deceit has been allowed to grow. This seem-
ingly placid lake has for some years been held up to the
world as the serene portrait of life under communism. Not
only happy Russian peasants, but also happy Hungarians
and Mongols and East Germans and Poles are supposed
to have lived harmoniously under the deadly green scum.

Before Budapest it was possible for Indians and Indo-
nesians, Italians and Frenchmen to believe the fable that
life in the Soviet lake was as idyllic as painted, for the surface was kept perpetually calm. Hungary, however, was a
gigantic stone thrown into the middle of that lying lake,
and waves of truth have set out from the point of impact.
Now, as they move far outward toward the remotest
shores of the lake, we can begin to see what life was truly

like under the green scum. Here is what the great Hungarian splash revealed.

First there was the shuddering effect upon Russia itself. The Soviets can no longer trust any satellite armies stationed along their borders. Not only will Rumanian and Bulgarian armies refuse to protect Russia. They will pretty obviously join the enemy. This probably also applies to the subsidiary armies in Central Asia. This is not only disheartening to the Russian leaders. It is positively frightening.

Russia can no longer trust any of the satellite intellectuals whom she enlisted to build the outposts of her empire. In Hungary they not only failed to oppose the uprising; they led it. Intellectuals in all the other satellites are waiting to do the same.

Russia has lost her fight for the souls of young people. In perhaps no other nation along the frontier will youth give quite so astonishing an account of itself as it did in Hungary, but Russia had better be prepared to defend herself against young Latvians and Poles and Turkomens and Mongols.

Russia's most crushing defeat, of course, came at the hands of workers in heavy industries. Here everything held most dear by communist theoreticians was proved to be one hundred per cent wrong. One cannot even imagine additional insults which the workers of Csepel could have heaped upon the Soviets. Here the Russian defeat will have incalculable results.

Russia retained no support at all among women. It had preached oily and sanctimonious sermons about how only communism was concerned with the welfare of women—while at the same time it tormented and starved them—but apparently the women of Hungary were not fooled by such lies. When the test came they were also one hundred per cent against communism. Here the Soviets lost another major propaganda battle.

Russia found little support among the peasants, who, along with the workers in heavy industry, were supposed to be the darlings of the new regime. In one area after another throughout Hungary peasants took immediate steps to dissolve their collective farms. A large majority apparently wished to revert to old-style systems in which a man owned his own land, while holding onto certain new-style innovations like the collective use of expensive machinery. And when the general strike was threatened, peasants agreed to produce no extra food which might find its way into Russian hands. This Russian defeat by the peasants must have choked the Kremlin.

Russia found that it could not trust the ordinary police of a satellite nation, for well over three-fourths of Budapest's police turned their weapons and frequently themselves over to the revolutionists. Only the AVO remained true to their Soviet masters, and that no doubt through a certain knowledge that their only alternative was death. They knew they had so corrupted the nation that the freedom fighters would refuse any compromise.

Finally, Russia discovered in the Budapest defeat that her own troops, if stationed too long in an area of superior culture and enviable standard of living, will defect. Probably the military leaders of the Kremlin had suspected this before, since some of their procedures indicated such a fear, but now they know. Henceforth, every unit commander will have to suspect what his troops might ultimately do if forced to fight enemies whose guilt is not clearly agreed upon by all Russia and her satellites.

These are stupendous defeats, but they apply only to Russia itself. Grave as they are, it is the second wave of effects, spreading out from the Hungarian disturbance and reaching all of the satellites, that could have the gravest consequencies. Of the Soviet tactics for controlling satellites, every device except one has proved bankrupt. Cajolery, threats, purges and promises have proved equally futile. Only force can hold a satellite.

As to promises, events in Hungary have proved how ineffective they are. Russia had a potentially rich ally which she governed ruthlessly. If she had been able gradually to relax her control and to provide real benefits, she ought to have been able to establish communism here. But the Hungarians grew so tired of windy promises of material goods and political freedoms which never came that revolution became inevitable. Now the other satellites must expect the Soviets to abandon the use of vague promises and to rely upon force, openly used for the rest of the world to witness.

If the promises failed, so did the terror. Horrible as the AVO seems, it was probably no worse than the similar terrors in the other satellites, and probably less than the terror that operates in Russia itself. But if such terror failed to build good communists in Hungary, the other terrors have probably also failed, and we should expect to find in nations like Poland and East Germany not only a body of noncommunists, but also ardent enemies of communism whose determination has been strengthened by the events in Hungary. This also applies to Red China, a fact of enormous significance.

Any potential nationalist leader in any satellite nation who studies the accounts of what happened in Hungary can probably conclude that the national army and the police in his country, too, will fight on the side of nationalists as opposed to their Soviet masters. This could be of great importance in helping potential revolutionists —if the world climate ever encourages them—to take the first steps against the Russians.

It is difficult to see how any of the satellite peoples can ever again take very seriously Russia's propaganda about the better life, the brotherhood of communist nations, and the gentle protective friendship of the Soviet Union. A much more realistic approach will be required. This also applies to the education of youth, the propagandizing of labor, and the nonsense handed out to national soldiers. Now Russia must stand forth to the satellites as the monster she is.

The satellites will also begin to make cold, honest calculations as to what has happened to their resources under communism. One of the most important aspects of the Hungarian revolution was the open cry, "Russia has stolen our uranium from us." Prior to the revolution a man would have been shot for such a charge, although it was often whispered within the bosom of the family. Now it is common knowledge, and in all satellites similar charges are going to be made, for Russia has been systematically and callously plundering her neighbors.

Of great importance will be the satellites' new attitude toward purges. Since 1945 the Soviet rulers of Hungary had decreed a really astonishing sequence of purges, which the Hungarian communists were forced to make believe they had themselves thought up. First the Trotskyites were assassinated, then the Titoists and national communists, then the Stalinists (at which time the already murdered Titoists were exhumed and told, "You were honest communists after all! We're sorry we shot you. It was all a mistake."). And finally anyone who could be termed a deviationist. All these purges accomplished exactly nothing, and it is doubtful that the satellites will continue to sponsor them. From now on, the Russians will have to do their own murdering.

From this we can see that the basic structure of satellite society will be under fire and will continue to be from now on. Russia will be faced with terrible decisions in regard to each of the satellite nations, and every decision will be either a defeat on the military-economic front (if she surrenders to satellite demands) or a defeat on the peace-propaganda front (if she moves in with her army to crush the satellites completely). Either way, Russia must lose.

It is in the third wave riding out from the central splash, however, that Russia's losses will be most severe. This wave reaches countries that might conceivably have gone communist, like Italy and France in Europe, India and Indonesia in Asia, and parts of Central Africa. It also reaches lands where there are vocal communist parties, such as Uruguay, Australia and Japan. And here the result of the Hungarian revolution is not a wave at all. It is a hurricane, and this is what its great storms disclose.

If France were to vote a communist government into power, accompanying that government would be an apparatus of terror that would mutilate the country, corrupt every aspect of life, and humiliate the spirit of all Frenchmen, even those who had called it into being.

It Italy were to choose a communist government, the

economic life of Italy would steadily deteriorate, and the people who would suffer most would be the workers in big cities.

And if either France or Italy were to choose communism, at the first moment when some leading party henchman felt his power slipping, he could call in Russian aid, and if Soviet tanks could get into the country, they would happily blow either Paris or Rome to rubble. That is the big lesson of Budapest. Russian tanks are willing to annihilate any city where there is protest. And if the tanks run into trouble, as they did in Budapest, we can expect that next time the heavy bombers will be called in.

Russia's greatest loss in countries where there was once a chance for a communist victory lies in the matter of popular support. Die-hard communists who hope to keep the reins of power for themselves will not be affected by the destruction of Budapest, which probably did not surprise them. But those wavering voters who might possibly have one day voted the red ticket will see clearly what a tragic price they would have to pay for their folly. The Soviet losses among such groups are already staggering.

Communist parties in these nations are already beginning to lose many card-carrying members who cannot accept the mass murder of civilians. These once-faithful communists are stating that after what happened to Budapest they would be unwilling to have some ruthless local red leader impetuously call in the Russian tanks merely to preserve his own position. Already the defections of prominent leaders who can foresee the destruction of cities like Paris and Rome have hurt communism, and the list will probably grow when the full story of Budapest is known.

Of special importance in Asia is the fact that in Budapest, Soviet communism finally disclosed itself as much more barbarous than the colonialism against which Asia understandably protests. Up to now Russian propaganda has been extraordinarily successful in portraying itself in Asia as the smiling big brother to a host of European satellites who lived with it in harmony and who loved its gentle friendship. Asia was constantly being asked by implication, "Why don't you join our happy brother-hood?" Now the nature of such a relationship has been made clear.

It is difficult to see how Russia can fool foreign nations any longer, or how it can enlist the support of sensible local patriots. It must now rely almost entirely upon those committed communists who are determined to take their nations into communism; the rest of the country will now combat such betrayal, for they have seen what it will mean. Russia has suffered a staggering defeat in the world battle for men's minds.

One of the reasons why Russia will be unable to peddle her poisonous propaganda in the future as successfully as it has been doing in the past is that the nearly two hundred thousand Hungarian refugees who have scattered over the face of the earth go determined to tell the world the story of what communism is like. I would hate to be a Soviet apologist in Detroit if some of the refugees from Csepel are in the audience. The effect of these two hundred thousand reporters will be tremendous, and as their stories are relayed from one American or Canadian or Australian village to the next, even such communist propaganda as has begun to take root will find it difficult to grow.

This brings us to the fourth, and outer, wave disturbing the once-placid lake of world communism, and it is this wave that washes the American shore. It touches all nations—Great Britain, Brazil, New Zealand, Ceylon—and its effect throughout the world is great. But America is most deeply affected by this wave.

When the patriots in Budapest struck, we were unprepared. We neither knew what to do, nor had the will to do it. We stood before the world in very shabby moral clothes, and should this happen again we might have to surrender our position of world leadership. For if the Russians lost severely in Budapest, we also lost. Any American who served at Andau experienced a psychological shock which hit him in four predictable impacts.

First, he was deeply shaken by the courage of the people he saw streaming toward him. Many Americans stepped aside in silent deference when Hungarians came out of the swamps and passed them. During the days when refugees had to crawl through deep mud or swim the canal, Americans would study them with awe as they came forth resilient and laughing, ready for their next test. To be in the presence of raw courage is apt to be a humbling experience.

Second, after this initial shock, the sensitive American had to ask himself, "Why was my country unable to help these brave people?" This question, of course, permitted several reasonably acceptable answers. Americans could argue, "Everyone knows we are a peace-loving nation which abhors war. We have told everyone that." But then came the gnawing doubt that although we loved peace for ourselves, we had perhaps encouraged the Hungarians to abandon that peace for themselves, and that somehow we had profited illegally from their action. And that is about as ugly a doubt as a man can entertain. So one next reasoned, "The Hungarians had only themselves to blame. Why did they ever start their revolution in the midst of a presidential election? They should have known we would be hamstrung." But then came the other gnawing doubt which reminded us that for years we had been hoping for just such an uprising, and regardless of elections, we should have been prepared for this one. Finally, the American could point to the map of Europe and say, "You can see our position. Hungary has no seaport through which we could have poured supplies. And our airplanes could not have flown over the sovereign states of Austria and Yugoslavia. There was really no way we could have helped, even if we had wanted to." The confusion of this argument was always self-apparent, for Americans usually offered it with rising voices, ending in the rhetorical question, "See?" And so this second portion of the chain reaction ended in embarrassment.

Third, the Hungarians, sensing American confusion, were surprisingly studious about putting American friends at ease. "We know you couldn't have helped us," the refugees would say consolingly, as if it were the Americans who needed reassurance. Sometimes an especially sensitive Hungarian would reason, "We know you would have helped us if you could have found a way. On the radio you were always so powerful in your words of encouragement. We are sorry our revolution was so poorly timed, but we are proud if we were able to help you." Americans at Andau, like those who happened to be in Budapest during the revolt, can all cite Hungarian friends who said without sarcasm, "Don't worry about it. We understand why you're powerless to help us. But we're glad to fight for your cause." In time, Americans took refuge in these statements and some of the embarrassment of shock two dissolved, being replaced by a feeling of great warmth toward the Hungarians who had lost so much, so gracefully. Reviewing this unreal third wave of shock, I can only say that I shared the reactions of an American who observed, "One of the most startling aspects of the revolution was that the Hungarians, deserted by the world, ended by being mad at nobody."

But if Hungarians were not lamenting in public, they were privately circulating among themselves sharp observations on what had happened, and occasionally an American was brought face to face with harsh and agonizing facts. I first heard these underground Hungarian comments from a twenty-six-year-old refugee named Ferenc Kobol. Originally he swore me to secrecy, for he did not want me to portray Hungarians as crybabies, but I was so impressed by his comments that I not only persuaded him to absolve me of my pledge but also to write down in his own words a summary of what he said, for I wanted to quote him exactly.

He said, "Of course Hungarians are bitter about the lack of interest you Americans showed in our struggle for freedom. For years now, as part of your battle with communism for the possession of men's minds, you have been giving us hope and assurance. You have been saying to us, 'You are not forgotten. America's ultimate aim is to help you win your freedom. To achieve this we will support you to the best of our ability.'

"America spent millions of dollars and every known psychological trick to bring this message to us behind the iron curtain. Your Voice of America broadcast fifty hours a day of freedom programs. You used seventy frequencies and sometimes I would hear you from Tangiers or Munich or Salonika. I can remember the thrill we got when we heard that you were outfitting one of your Coast Guard cutters, the Courier, to dodge jamming stations. You said the Courier 'would punch deeper holes in the Iron Curtain.'

"Then you set up Radio Free Europe in 1950 and you got right down to the business of freedom. You had eleven separate stations which broadcast one thousand hours of encouragement a week from Frankfort, Munich and Lisbon. RFE told us many times, 'Our purpose is to keep opposition to communism alive among the people of the slave states behind the iron curtain. We want to help such people gradually to make themselves strong enough to throw off the Soviet yoke.'

"How did you help us to grow strong? You constantly reassured us that we were not forgotten by the west. You said that the fact that so many American citizens supported RFE proved that your nation was with us. We believed you.

"Next, to make your message even more clear, you began to launch balloons to fly over our country bearing leaflets and aluminum medals. I got one with a Liberty Bell on it and the legend 'Hungarians for Freedom—All the Free World for Hungarians.'

"These balloons were very important to our phychological reactions. I remember thinking at the time, 'At last something tangible. Something other than words. If America could reach us with these aluminum medals, why couldn't they reach us with parachute supplies if a revolution started. Obviously, America intends to help us.'

"In 1952 all of your radio stations broadcast over and over the promises made in your election campaign. We were told that America was going to roll back the iron curtain. You would stimulate a desire for freedom among the eight hundred million people under communist domination. We were assured many times that your President would find ways to make the Russians want peace. The speeches of your leaders were quoted to us day after day.

"Then young Hungarians who had been abroad began mysteriously to appear among us and they promised, 'If trouble starts, don't worry. America will be on hand to give you support. But yon don't have to wait for the other side to begin. Do something yourself. After all, you've got to show the world what you are worth. You've got to prove that Hungary deserves the freedom you claim for her.'

"We were told that in 1953 America was putting aside one hundred million dollars to support activities against communist regimes in the satellite countries. We thought that this meant you were actively on our side.

"Then what happened? When Germans in East Berlin rioted against the Russians, your stations told us each detail. This year when the Poles rioted against the Russians in Poznan, we were again fed the full propaganda of freedom. Should we be blamed for believing what we heard? You must put yourself in our place. We had no honest newspapers, no honest radio stations of our own. We could rely only upon what you told us, and you told us to love freedom.

"Do you know why Hungarians like me are so bitter against the United States? For six years you fed us this propaganda. For six years the Russians trampled us in the mud. But when we rose in rebellion for the very things you told us to fight for, how many Americans stepped forth to help us? Not one. Who did join our side? Russian troops. How many American tanks helped us? Not one. What tanks did join us in our fight for freedom? Russian tanks. This is a terrible indictment.

"But what drove us almost to desperation was not your failure to support us with matériel. It was your failure to speak up boldly on our behalf. My nation died in silence. Could not one clear voice in America have spoken forth in late October? Mr. Bulganin spoke out about Suez, and England and France retreated. There was a ten-day pause in our revolution when one daring American voice might have made Bulganin retreat. It never came. There was silence along the Danube, and in the United Nations. Days later, when only the dead could hear, America finally spoke. It was a message of condolence."

Ferenc Kobol was by no means a wild-eyed young revolutionist. He was a thoughtful young man with few illusions and a nice ability to calculate what could and could not be attained. He understood America and said, "Hungarians are disappointed in America, but you hear no one say, 'We should never again follow American leadership.' We know we can be free only through your agency. I don't know how you are going to accomplish this, but I do appreciate that in an age of the hydrogen bomb, to start a world war merely to salvage Hungary would be unthinkable. We have got to rely upon the United States, and we trust that your President will find a way to accomplish all of our freedoms—Hungary's, Poland's, Germany's. But I think your people must study two problems very carefully." And he proceeded to make two points that are frightening in their clarity and ominous in their portent.

First he said, "No Hungarian is angry at Radio Free Europe. We wanted to have our hopes kept alive. Probably we believed too deeply what was not intended by the broadcasters to be taken seriously. The wrong was not with Radio Free Europe. It was partly our fault for trusting in words. It was partly America's fault for thinking that words can be used loosely. Words like 'freedom,' 'struggle for national honor,' 'rollback,' and 'liberation' have meanings. They stand for something. Believe me when I say that you cannot tell Hungarians or Bulgarians or Poles every day for six years to love liberty and then sit back philosophically and say, 'But the Hungarians and Bulgarians and Poles mustn't do anything about liberty. They must remember that we're only using words.' Such words, to a man in chains, are not merely words. They are the weapons whereby he can break his chains."

Ferenc Kobol took an honorable part in the freedom movement within his country. He risked his life to attain freedom, and he said, "I was motivated primarily by words." He added, "If America wants to flood Eastern and Central Europe with these words, it must acknowledge an ultimate responsibility for them. Otherwise you are inciting nations to commit suicide."

Americans, challenged by critics like Kobol, tended to be angry at Radio Free Europe for having broadcast to the world what had merely been intended as campaign oratory for home consumption; whereas Hungarians tended to be angry, not at Radio Free Europe for having told them what leading Americans were announcing as national policy, but at Americans in the United States for never having intended to support what was, after all, mere oratory.

Kobol's second warning to America warrants even more careful attention. "In the case of Hungary you had several good excuses for not acting. There was a political campaign, you had no access to Hungary and you hadn't realized that nations were taking your words seriously. But when trouble starts in East Germany or Poland you will no longer have those excuses, for there you will have immediate access, you will not be involved in an election, and you will have been warned that men do take words seriously. You had better be thinking, 'What will we do if Germans and Poles start a revolution?' Because the kind of words you have been sending forth, the words America has always stood for, are the kind that men want to believe.'"

The initial American performance in relation to the Hungarian revolution was not good. I have explained why Hungarians and Americans alike could excuse our failure to act, and even our failure to speak, but it is difficult to explain away some of our later behavior regarding refugees. We dangled before some of the most dedicated fighters for freedom the world has seen since the days of George Washington the possibility of entrance into the United States as if this were a privilege one step more sanctified than entry into heaven. We turned the job of selecting the refugees we would accept over to voluntary religious groups who stipulated the most extraordinary requirements and made themselves the laughingstock of Vienna by sending out notices that no divorced persons could enter the United States, since such people had obviously broken with religious teaching, and America wanted no one who was not openly devout. The countries of Europe, by contrast, backed steam-heated trains up to camps and said, "England or France or Switzerland will take every man, woman or child who can find a seat on this train."

When our ridiculous policies had caused much bitterness in Austria, an official of our government held a press conference in which he pointed out, "We may have been tardy in accepting refugees, but we have given every Hungarian who crossed the border a warm blanket." This so outraged one listener that he asked, "How many refugees have there been so far?"

"Ninety-six thousand."

"How many has America taken?"

"Five hundred."

"How many has Switzerland taken?"

"Four thousand."

There were no more questions, but soon the American gates were opened, and those of us along the border could at least hold our heads up. But even then the American reaction to Hungary couldn't seem to get straightened out. We rushed our Hungarians to Camp Kilmer and processed them under such chaotic conditions that the *New York Times* (November 28, 1956) had to protest: "The reception and housing of the Hungarian refugees —at least in the New York area—is a disgrace to the country. If ever there has been a case of bungling and bad judgment in handling this relatively small group of people, whose courage has fired the hearts of freedom-loving people everywhere, Camp Kilmer takes the prize.

"Everybody has gotten into the act. It is an Army operation from the moment the planes touch down, so that the very first taste of American life for the refugees is uniforms and regimentation all over again. The refugees are taken by Army buses to the barren, desolate acres of barracks at Kilmer, then cordoned off by military police. Their living quarters are as primitive as many a D. P. camp of Europe—numbered barracks. Though the great private and religious agencies, with their years of experience of handling refugees, have representatives at the camps, they have to work desperately against Army and bureaucratic red tape to find the families in their barracks, to welcome them, to give them some feeling of civilian America, even to interview them in order to find sponsors, homes and jobs for them.

"Why couldn't New Yorkers have found a more humane way to welcome the refugees? . . . What happened to New York's good intentions on the way? Why was this turned into a show for the Army and bureaucracy, instead of its being the great, voluntary, civic operation it should have been—and can still become?"

One story of the Camp Kilmer debacle caused much amusement in Europe. We were told that when the first refugees arrived, some of them after having fought Russian tanks for ten days, having walked over a hundred miles, and having crept through the swamps and swum the canal, an official stepped before them at the camp and said, in resounding tones, "Now I want to tell you a few things about freedom."

A Hungarian in one of the depots asked, "Did he speak from a balcony?"

In the first awed days after the revolution a Polish newspaperman reviewed what had happened. He was ashamed that his country had been able to do so little to help the Hungarians, and he was embittered that neighboring Czechoslovakia had actually tried to hamper the Hungarians and help the Russians. He wrote, "Sadly we must admit that the Hungarians acted like Poles. The Poles acted like Czechs. And the Czechs acted like swine." An observer added, "But the Americans didn't act at all."

At this point the American who had been following his nation's performance was bewildered, but he was saved by a fourth psychological shift: the recovery of national self-respect. For the United States government finally came forth with a program both vigorous and generous. Legal restrictions which had hitherto impeded the flow of refugees into America were suspended or ignored. Our embassy in Vienna speeded up the flow of paper work required for emigration. Emergency relief organizations—Catholic, Jewish, Protestant and lay—reached a truce among themselves and worked literally twenty-four hours each day reuniting families and insuring them entry into the United States. Aid societies in America sent into Austria a torrent of blankets, money, medicines and food. Our educational foundations provided both scholarships in American colleges and badly needed cash grants to overloaded Austrian institutions which had offered haven to Hungarian scholars.

Then, when it seemed as if the United States had done all it could, there occurred the Christmas visit of Vice-President Nixon, who cut additional red tape, reassured the Austrians of our continued support of their efforts, and spurred our own government to further generosity in accepting refugees. A massive air lift was organized; Camp Kilmer was transformed into a warm-hearted reception center, and across America thousands of families who had never seen a Hungarian before suddenly opened their doors and welcomed strangers to whom they could not speak a single word. When the United States finally got organized, it behaved rather well, and by mid-March, 1957, had accepted over thirty thousand Hungarian refugees.

So the emotional cycle was complete: initial shock, embarrassment, reassurance, and finally a modest pride in traditional American generosity.

But the fact that America finally accepted its responsibilities in a time of great crisis must not obscure the more important fact that originally we were befuddled. We have got to rethink our attitudes in the cold war. A careful study of all messages broadcast by Radio Free Europe to Hungary fails to disclose any that incited revolution, but this radio did broadcast messages of freedom and is presumably still doing so. Are we now prepared to assume direct responsibility for these messages? How long can we broadcast such messages without assuming direct responsibility for our words? Why should officials of the United States government abdicate their appointed responsibility for the selection of immigrants and turn that job over to accidental groups who are then free to set up quotas reflecting their private beliefs and to apply moral and religious tests of their own devising? When a man has given proof in blood that he loves freedom, how many further tests must he pass before he is deemed worthy of entry into America? And how much of the rare quality contemporary American life is due to the contributions of the great revolutionists of 1848—many of them from Hungary—who brought to our rather tired Anglo-Saxon heritage a burst of fresh, bold blood and a tradition of gallantry? Maybe we do need another transfusion of Hungarian blood.

In one respect the United States has already begun to rethink its attitude in the cold war, and for this clarification of our national policy we must thank the Hungarian crisis. The Eisenhower Doctrine puts the Soviet world on notice that communists cannot operate among the nations of the Middle East as they operated in Hungary. We still lack an announced policy covering similar contingencies in Poland, Czechoslovakia, Rumania or Bulgaria, but no doubt one is evolving, and for this we must again thank Hungary, for the shock waves riding out from Budapest have affected America profoundly.

The hurricane that I spoke of as striking Asia could have far-reaching consequences. One of the main reasons why many Americans grew to feel, between 1948 and 1956, that any further effort on our part to co-operate with Asia was futile, was the way in which Asian leaders refused to accept facts. Common words were redefined out of their ordinary meanings, and intercourse became difficult, since no matter what the nature of a fact, it was always used to prove that Americans were scoundrels whereas Russians were the protectors of the weak and peace-loving nations of the world. The energy required even to keep up with such reasoning is immense, while the work required to combat it is herculean.

For example, recently an Asian student argued with me in impassioned words: "You must admit that America holds its empire together only by means of the imperialist hydrogen bomb, whereas Russia had united under her leadership a large group of friendly and peace-loving nations whose bond of union is not fear of the hydrogen bomb, but justice for working people. What a difference!"

"What American empire are you speaking of?" I asked.

"Japan," he replied. "Formosa, the Philippines, England."

"You're convinced that we tell Japan and Britain what they must do?"

"Or course."

"And you're equally convinced that the iron-curtain countries are happy under Russian domination?"

"I won't answer that," he said. "You speak of iron-curtain countries. That implies that countries like Hungary and Rumania don't want to remain with Russia, whereas obviously they do. You speak of Russian domination as if it were a fact. Russia doesn't dominate any of its allies."

The Hungarian revolution not yet having occurred, I was rather short of ammunition, but I asked, "Wasn't the Russian occupation of Lithuania especially brutal?"

"That's a capitalist warmongering lie!" he cried. "Apparently you haven't read Stalin's statement on Russia's relations with its neighbors."

"What did it say?" I asked.

"Stalin said"—and here he read from a booklet published in Moscow—"'If you think that the people of the Soviet Union have any desire to alter the face of the surrounding States, and to do so by force, you are badly mistaken. I fail to see what danger the countries surrounding us can see in the ideas of the Soviet people, if these States are really firmly established.' And that's how Russia has behaved toward her neighbors. How has America behaved toward hers? Hydrogen bombs raining atomic dust on Japan."

"I thought that dust came from Russian bombs," I argued. "Don't you think that Russia is exploding such bombs, too?"

"Yes, but she explodes hers only for peace."

"Don't you think that Russia uses her bombs to keep her subject peoples enslaved?"

At this my Asian disputant laughed. "You capitalist

warmongers always use words like enslaved. Russia enslaves no one. In election after election, through all her friendly nations, the people have said they wanted communism and friendship with Russia by votes of about ninety-five to five."

"And you believe those figures?" I asked.

"Of course," he replied, and after many such discussions I found that every item of data used by the Asian communists about Rumania or Poland or Hungary came from Moscow.

In time, I found myself exhausted by this frustrating business of trying to argue against skillful propaganda without any hard-core facts that I could make my adversaries accept. Always they had Russian-imagined statistics and I had only logic and common sense.

I remember saying once in real anger, after a baffling session with some young Chinese who were trying to drag Singapore into communism, "I wish I could take those kids to some communist heaven like Poland or Lithuania. I'd like to have them ask Poles and Lithuanians what they thought of Russian communism."

It is now possible to ask Hungarians. For Hungary exposes to the world's eyes and to the world's intelligence the way in which a total population rejected Soviet domination. The Hungarian evidence goes far beyond prejudice or clever deduction or wishful logic. It even transcends the reporting of individual witnesses. The Hungarian revolution says simply, "Nineteen out of every twenty Hungarians were nauseated by communism."

This fact is incontrovertible, and if it could be reported to the people of Asia it could have a profound effect upon the history of that continent. For Asians pride themselves on their adherence to logic. They have penetrating minds and know how to handle facts when they are made available. An overwhelming majority of Asians wish their homelands well, for they are patriots, and it was largely due to this intense patriotism that Russia had an easy job planting, nurturing and reaping a propaganda harvest against the United States. Russia argued, "You Asians saw British colonialism in India, French colonialism in

Indo-China and Dutch colonialism in Indonesia. Well, America is twice as large as those three nations put together, and her colonialism is twice as bad." How great the Russian propaganda victory was, only those who had to combat it year after year can know. The intelligent people of Asia, having little other data to go by, often accepted the Russian logic.

Now there is a superior logic, the logic of Hungary, and it is imperative that the facts of Hungary reach Asia and penetrate to the farthest bazaar. And the facts that we must hammer are these: it was the intellectuals who led the revolution, because they had been defrauded by communism; and it was the workers from Csepel who supported it, because under communism they not only made no gains, they lost what they had previously enjoyed; and it was Russian tanks, crudely interferring in the government of a neighboring nation, that destroyed the city of Budapest. These facts, if known in Asia, could make a difference.

But unfortunately, the effect of the Hungarian revolution in Asia cannot be determined, for just when it seemed as if Russian propaganda about her friendly relations with neighboring nations was punctured, Asia was looking elsewhere and the lessons of Hungary did not penetrate even to the capital cities, let alone the remote bazaars. For it was at this untimely moment that the democracies invaded Egypt.

Of course this action nullified any moral values the Hungarian revolution might have enjoyed in Asia. In the first flush of the Budapest revolt I wrote to several of my Asian friends and said, "I hope you have been reading what Hungarians honestly think about communism. Now do you see what I meant?"

But before my letters could reach their targets, Egypt was invaded and in their replies my friends never even mentioned Hungary. Something much bigger was on their horizon and they asked, "Now do you see what we meant by imperialism?"

When the history of the Egyptian adventure is finally written, the apportionment of blame will surely be much different from what we now see it to be. But surely, assessors of that extraordinary act will have to point out that the Egyptian crisis involved two unforeseen losses to the democracies. First, Egypt diverted the world's spotlight from Hungary and condemned that brave nation to expire both in darkness and in silence. The moral precepts which could have been deduced from her heroic action were largely lost, and lost to those who could have profited most. Second, the repetition of classic imperialist invasion completely blinded Asia to the suddenly revealed characteristics of a greater imperialism to the north.

That these great losses should have been the consequence of a gesture that failed is bitingly ironic. I remember the summary of America's role in this dual crisis made by a friend who was saddened by the moral collapse of his world. "When our secrets agents can't discover what our enemy Russia is going to do in Hungary," he grieved, "it's regrettable. But when our diplomats can't discover what our allies have already done in Egypt, that's appalling."

It is possible that out of this catastrophe America may evolve a sounder foreign policy, and although the automatic values that should have accrued to us in Asia as a result of Hungary's bold action were dissipated, we can nevertheless start patiently to talk with our Asian friends about the lessons of Hungary. We can say, with honest humility, I hope, that whereas we had to learn the hard way, we trust they will do the same. And we must never allow the main object lesson to be obscured: after eleven years, most Hungarians abhorred communism; but the Soviets, refusing to accept this judgment, sent in their tanks and destroyed a country.

There was another fact about the Hungarian revolution which applies to Asia, but it is of such staggering implication that I wish merely to mention it without according it the detailed discussion which it merits. I suppose that all nations concerned in any way with Asia are asking themselves these momentous questions.

If ninety-five per cent of Hungarians hated their brand of communism, what per cent of Red Chinese hate their brand? If Hungarian troops deserted communism almost to a man, what percentage of Chinese soldiers would remain loyal? If communism could be maintained in Hungary only by the exercise of brute force, is not a similar force required in Red China, and must not the people hate it? And, to extend the scope of the question somewhat, if one of the most striking facts about the Hungarian revolution was the number of North Korean visiting students who volunteered to fight the Soviets, how secure is communism in North Korea?

For the present these remain rhetorical questions, but we do not know when they may explode into real situations requiring national answers. For in such matters the entire world is interrelated and the answers we apply in Europe will commit us in Asia.

I am convinced of this interrelationship by the observations of a wise Hungarian who pointed out, "Some people argue that our revolution started in 1848 with Kossuth and Petofi and that it is destined to continue forever. Others reason that it began on October 6, 1956. That was the day when two hundred patriots marched past the grave of Laszlo Rajk. He was the nationalist-communist who was executed as a traitor by Stalin. His memory was cleansed by Khrushchev and his honor restored. But how? His widow was taken, on October 3, to a mass grave that had been filled in years before. The communist leaders said, 'We are going to restore your husband's good name. Pick out a set of bones that we can call his.' It was these make-believe bones that we marched past, muttering in our hearts.

"It's possible," he continued, "that the emotionalism of the Rajk purification rites might have deteriorated into civil riots, but it seems more likely that our revolution started in 1953 when the East German uprisings showed us what a civilian population could accomplish against an iron dictatorship. Then our determination grew when the Poles at Poznan proved the same facts. You see what I'm driving at? The East Germans who threw stones at tanks died without any reasonable hope of success, but they inspired the Poles, who did achieve success. I'm sure the Poles acted only as Poles, but their greatest effect was on us Hungarians. Now who can say where the lesson that we gave the world will end? We can't foresee in what land our seed of revolution will mature, but it will grow somewhere. Even Russia is now liable to explosion. For we Hungarians, acting upon what the Poles taught us, who based their knowledge on what the Germans proved . . . we have shown the way."

As we Americans contemplate our future responsibilities, we could well remember the women of Budapest. It was a cold sunny day in the ruined city. For six agonizing weeks the revolt had been under way, and still boys on the street and workers in Csepel defied the Russians. Budapest was known as "the suicide city," since it seemed that the entire population was determined to resist communism to the death. The world marveled at such courage.

Then, on December 4, a full month after the overpowering return of the Russian tanks, the women of Budapest, dressed in black, marched to the tomb of the unknown Hungarian soldier to place flowers at his grave. Russians with machine guns and tanks tried to stop them, but they came on, waving small bunches of flowers and crying, "You have guns, we have only flowers. Why are you afraid?"

A Russian soldier panicked and shot one of the women through the leg. It had no effect on the women in black; they continued their solemn march. Another Russian soldier started shouting at the women to stop. When they ignored him, he grabbed one of the women by the arm. She pulled herself loose, stared at him in contempt, then spat in his face.

11   Could These Things Be True?

In two respects I was, perhaps, an appropriate writer to deal with this story. I am cautious in my evaluation of contemporary problems, and I have learned to be suspicious of anyone who tells me a good story about himself.

I am cautious because of my education. In 1925 I entered a small liberal Quaker college whose faculty was deeply chagrined that one of their graduates, A. Mitchell Palmer, had gained some notoriety as Woodrow Wilson's wartime attorney general. Mr. Palmer, a good Quaker, had believed all he heard during the war and had allowed himself to be stampeded into certain unwise postwar actions which the government and the people of the United States later regretted. I have never forgotten the caustic reassessment that his legal moves suffered, not the least critical being the comments of his own former professors.

While in college I made a personal study of the servile work done by the George Creel committee on wartime propaganda, and again I was shown the perils into which a writer can fall if he accepts without using his own cooler judgment all that is told him in wartime. I followed this with an analysis of the Belgian horror stories and became one of the first American undergraduates to undertake a study of the revisionist theories of the historians who were beginning to cast honest doubt on some of the things we were told during World War I.

It was with this background that I approached the Hungarian story. If I have accepted lies, if I have unknowingly repeated them, and if I have been played for a fool by clever propagandists, I have only myself to blame. Both in knowledge of history and in awareness of precedents I have been forewarned, and if some superior critic should later prove that I was duped, I ought to be severely reprimanded if not publicly disgraced.

As to my suspicious nature where personal stories are concerned, I have found that most people are dubious sources when they speak of themselves. A favorite expression of mine, acquired from having checked a lot of likely stories is this: "I wouldn't believe him if he told me what day it was." The translators who worked with me can testify with what patience we went over and over the same ground, not only with one Hungarian but with dozens. Four or five of us would sit around a big table in Josef Smutny's restaurant near the opera house in Vienna and we would pursue only one problem for about four hours at a time. Then we would get another four refugees, and another, and we would endlessly go over the same material.

When I perceived what a staggering fact the Hungarian revolt was, I asked that a highly trained research expert, who spoke five languages, be sent to help me, and he without ever duplicating any of the Hungarians with whom I had talked, reviewed the same ground in a similar way with refugees whom he picked at random from the camps. Wherever my final account differed from his, we assembled four or five new Hungarians and put the difrences before them. Each point was argued out to a final conclusion, and in almost every instance we wound up with specific photographs or documents proving that a given individual had been where he said he was, or corroboration from a third party. The most dramatic example of this came in my two-week search for proof of the incredible Major Meat Ball story. The most reassuring was to find, after a seven-week delay, verification of Mrs. Marothy's extraordinary claim that Imre Horvath's son had decided to escape with her.

When my final version of each incident was finished, it was reviewed by two fresh teams of Hungarian experts, working independently and checking each word written. Each such critic had been in Budapest during the time the events here described were taking place and in several instances was able to identify to the day and the hour both the occurrences and the people about whom I was writing.

Let me explain my personal estimates of the validity of each of these stories. Young Josef Toth represents the combined experiences of three eighteen-year-old freedom fighters whom I met at the Andau border. They had fled Budapest at the request of their mothers or fathers, and each boy was not only deeply implicated in the revolution, but each left behind him brothers and sisters who could be picked up by the AVO. These three boys made up the name Josef Toth in honor of two boys their own age killed in the revolution. I have described only small parts of their amazing adventures in Budapest, but those parts were checked endlessly. The boys knew that I would have preferred to use only one boy, only one real name, but they were afraid of retaliation, so this was their compromise.

Istvan Balogh and Peter Szigeti were individuals of great courage. Each name is completely masked; in the case of Szigeti even incidents had to be changed lest he implicate others. Each story was corroborated by other intellectuals, who supplied some of the masking materials.

Csoki, Little Chocolate Drop, was a very brave young man, and he said, "Sure, put my real name in the book! I want them to know what I did to their rotten system!" When after hours of discussion I learned that he had a mother and brothers remaining in Budapest, I prevailed upon him to change his mind; but he insisted on inserting one telltale incident, "which," he said, "will let the gang know I got out all right, and they'll tell my mother." I think most of what Csoki told me was true, and I used only the Kilian Barracks part of his wild days. But the facts of that attack, and General Maleter's part in it, have been substantiated by four other soldiers who were there and by one of the critics. I was glad when Csoki told me he thought he would go to America. He'll fit into a Boston jitterbug hall or a chili parlor in Dallas without any difficulty, and ten years from now he'll own a garage and vote Republican.

Zoltan and Eva Pal were composites made up by three

attractive young couples, two of whom I had met at Andau. Each of the six young people was terrified lest he be identified in Budapest and cause the torture of his parents. I spent many hours with these couples and feel sure that all of what they said was true, but the most poignant story they told me I did not use. At the end of one long interview with two of the couples I happened to notice that neither of the young wives was wearing a wedding ring, so with no embarrassment, because one suspects such tricks, I said, "You really aren't married, are you? You just came out together and made up these stories, didn't you?"

All four looked at me in amazement and said, "We . . . we can't prove that we're married. But we are." Then one of the wives said to her husband, "Oh, yes! You have that paper." And he produced an official paper of some kind which at least referred to him and his wife as a married couple.

"Why did you ask such a question?" he inquired.

"Because I notice that neither of you girls has a wedding ring," I said.

"In communism," the girls explained, "young couples like us can't afford wedding rings."

But later I saw that the third couple, which I used for another part of the story, had a wedding ring, and the wife said, "Well, a couple could manage to buy a ring if they were very religious . . . and gave up other things." So some couples have rings.

Imre Geiger, the dead-end kid with the cigarette and the rifle, I picked up just after he had crossed the border at Nickelsdorf. I saw him come swinging down the middle of the railroad tracks, and why he was not shot I do not know. He was a delightful boy to talk to, and he wanted me to use his real name, but he too had parents and friends who could be hurt, and since he was so deeply implicated in the latter days of the fighting, we both agreed that maybe he should remain anonymous.

Gyorgy Szabo, the man from Csepel, is one of the finest human beings I have ever met. He had documents to prove most of his story and a stamp of authenticity on his face that humbled all of us who talked with him. Others corroborated his story in all details, except the conditions of his leaving, but many of those details have been altered purposely in my account.

The Hadjok family, of course, were a tremendous family of that name. I met them at the bridge, then at the restaurant where Mrs. Lillie Brown rescued them. I saw them later in Vienna and was so suspicious of any children nine and thirteen who knew as much as they did that I questioned them in private. There can be no question of the authenticity of this story.

Mrs. Maria Marothy is also a real name, at her request. The coal miner, whose story of his American suit appalled everyone who heard it, dared not use his name for family reasons, but he had satisfactory credentials and his story was corroborated by others.

That leaves the tragic characters who appear in the account of the AVO man. Ferenc Gabor was so terrified by the retaliations he had witnessed in Recsk that we avoided his real name even in our notes. His particular story of Recsk could have been an invention; Recsk itself was not. It existed and in the form that I relate. The story of the world-champion athlete was to me particularly doleful because it was delivered so simply. I insisted upon a documentation of his athletic record, upon seeing the bullet wounds, checking his story of slave labor, and further evidence on his report of Major Meat Ball. Unfortunately for him, it was all true. Tibor Donath, the AVO man, is, as I stated earlier, a reconstruction for which I am solely responsible. He is founded upon a great deal of research, some confidential papers, and the question that I asked every Hungarian who mentioned the AVO: "You tell me the young people of Hungary were so patriotic and brave. But here are pictures of fifteen AVO men. They're all young. And they're all Hungarians. What about them?"

Patiently we would then build up a portrait of the AVO men that this Hungarian himself had known—the AVO man at the corner police box, the AVO man in the factory, the AVO man who checked residential blocks, the AVO man at Recsk, the AVO man who would beat and kick a coal miner for thirty-three days because he didn't like the man's suit, and the AVO man who would set out to break a woman's hand and knock her teeth out. I think I can visualize an AVO man.

I would point out one additional fact. Many of these people I personally helped lead out of Hungary. I met them on the wintry canal bank at Andau, I helped them across the bridge. There was no selection operating in my choice of the Hungarians with whom I talked. For example, I met my finest interpreter standing a hundred feet inside the border a few minutes after he reached freedom.

I found my stories by the operation of pure chance, and after I had talked with hundreds of Hungarians, after I had painstakingly discovered that their stories interlocked and substantiated one another, I came to two conclusions.

First, it is entirely possible that everyone I met told me nothing but lies, but there is a rule of probability which says that an investigator should accept a plausible theory if its rejection entails an obvious absurdity. If you want to say, as the Russians will, that all these stories were inventions, then you must also say that nearly two hundred thousand Hungarians who fled to Austria convened somewhere along the way and agreed upon a monstrous lie, which they all remembered in exact detail. And that is an absurdity.

Second, when I had studied the evidence, and when I had carefully reminded myself of A. Mitchell Palmer and the Creel committee, I decided that perhaps I was taking a risk, but that if I didn't—in view of the risks my Hungarian informants had taken—I would henceforth be ashamed to walk among free men.

Editor's Note

On page 200 of this book, Mr. Michener refers to a photographer as "he"; this was done deliberately in order to conceal the identity of his companion in the episode described, who was actually Mrs. Georgette Meyer Chapelle. As this book was about to go to press, Mrs. Chapelle was still in a Hungarian prison, having been arrested on December 4, 1956, by a border patrol while she was on a scouting trip that took her deep into Hungary; and her name was left out of the text so that this book could not be used as evidence against her by the communist authorities.

Mrs. Chapelle, known to her friends as "Dickie," is an expert photographer and a veteran of many refugee flights. Before her arrest, she and Mr. Michener were often on watch together at the Austrian-Hungarian border, frequently on the wrong side of it. After an imprisonment of fifty-five days in Hungary, Mrs. Chapelle was released and reached Austria and safety on January 27, 1957.

IN WORDS AND PICTURES

Bantam introduces three unique books dealing with important events and figures in America's history. Each book gains added dimension through the combination of important words from speeches, letters and news reports—together with fine illustrations via photographs, engravings, cartoons, paintings. Each book is a new and exciting reading experience.

•

THE CIVIL WAR AS THEY KNEW IT (SP134 • 75¢)   The Civil War comes to life through the combination of Abraham Lincoln's important words and Mathew Brady's striking photographs. This year-by-year account of the historic conflict includes Lincoln's notable comments, writings and speeches matched with on-the-spot war photographs by Brady, the first photographer to cover an entire war. Edited by Pierce G. Fredericks.

THE YANKS ARE COMING (SP136 • 75¢)   The total experience of World War I as detailed through brilliant eye-witness descriptions by outstanding writers and reporters of that era. The illustrations include famous photographs and maps tracing every battle from 1914 through 1918. Compiled and edited by Pierce G. Fredericks.

PRESIDENTS OF THE U.S.A.: PROFILES AND PICTURES (SP135 • 75¢)   In one up-to-date volume, here are illustrated biographies of the nation's chief executives from George Washington to Lyndon Johnson. There are important facts and statistics as well as anecdote-filled profiles of each president. These are matched with hundreds of rare prints, paintings, political cartoons and family snapshots to create a rounded portrait of each president. Edited by Cornel Adam Lengyel.

AVAILABLE AT NEWSSTANDS EVERYWHERE

Which of these Pathfinders have you missed?